Qualitative Choice Analysis

MIT Press Series in Transportation Studies

Marvin L. Manheim, editor

Qualitative Choice Analysis
Theory, Econometrics, and an Application to Automobile Demand

Kenneth Train

The MIT Press
Cambridge, Massachusetts
London, England

This book was set in Times New Roman by Asco Trade Typesetting Ltd., Hong Kong, and printed and bound by Halliday Lithograph in the United States of America.

Library of Congress Cataloging in Publication Data

Train, Kenneth.
  Qualitative choice analysis.

(MIT Press series in transportation studies; 10)
  Bibliography: p.
  Includes index.
  1. Automobiles—Purchasing—Mathematical models. I. Title. II. Series.
  HD9710.A2T73 1986   338.4′76292′0724   85-15142
  ISBN 0-262-20055-4

For Mandy

Contents

Series Foreword

Today, transportation is a well-established professional field, with numerous subspecialties and international journals, and with educational and research programs at many universities and other organizations around the world. It is a field in which the dominant philosophy is intermodal, multisectoral, and multidisciplinary. It is also a field in which researchers and practitioners can and do focus on specific facets, modes, sectors, disciplines, or methodologies, working in the context of this broad philosophy.

The approach of The MIT Press Series in Transportation Studies mirrors this philosophy. The series presents works across the broad spectrum of transportation concerns. Some volumes report significant new research, while others give analyses of specific policy, planning, management, or methodological issues. Still others show the close interaction between research and practical application in policy or management. Each individual work is intended to be an in-depth treatment from a particular viewpoint. Together, the works in the series present a broad perspective on the field of transportation as a whole.

This book, the tenth in the series, presents the methods of qualitative choice analysis and their application to the analysis of consumer demand for automobiles. Issues concerning the automobile industry and the forces influencing it are, and likely will continue to be, major questions of national policy. In this book, Dr. Train shows the depth of insight that can be gained into an important aspect of this problem—the characteristics of consumer demand for automobiles of various types—through the application of the powerful techniques of qualitative choice analysis. This book should be of interest to those concerned with understanding the forces influencing the automobile industry as well as those interested in qualitative choice methods and their application to modeling consumer behavior.

Marvin L. Manheim

List of Figures

List of Tables

Preface

This book serves two major functions. The original concern in writing the book was to introduce a new model of automobile demand. Unfortunately, this model, like most of the recent auto demand models, is based on methods that are not widely known, namely, qualitative choice models. A steadily growing group of researchers is applying these techniques in a variety of fields, including energy, housing, labor, telecommunications, and criminology, as well as transportation; but access to the methods is difficult. Important concepts in the field are scattered through numerous papers, many of which are not readily obtainable. The few reviews and texts that are available are advanced, written primarily for people who are already in the field. Consequently, in order to introduce the model of auto demand, it was felt necessary to provide a textbook on the theory and econometrics of qualitative choice models that, while being fully rigorous, assumes no previous knowledge of the topic. Since these methods have application in many fields other than auto demand, their dissemination is an important function of the book independent of the analysis of auto ownership and use.

The book can be viewed in either of two ways. To the reader who is interested in learning qualitative choice methods, the book is a thorough text, with many of the more advanced aspects of the methodology illustrated through an extensive application to automobile demand. For the student of auto demand, the book introduces a new auto demand model; as an aid to understanding the model, the qualitative choice methods on which the model is based are fully explained without assuming the reader is acquainted with numerous background articles.

The book is organized in the following way. Part I provides the text on qualitative choice models. This exposition is written at the level of upper-division undergraduates and graduates with training in econometrics or statistics. The first chapter introduces the general class of models. Successive chapters are devoted to each one of the major types of qualitative choice models, namely, logit, probit, and GEV ("nested logit"). The fifth chapter describes continuous/discrete models, by which qualitative choice methods are combined with standard regression techniques to analyze situations that cannot accurately be modeled by either method alone. The final chapter of part I describes how qualitative choice models are used in policy analysis for forecasting aggregate demand.

Part II introduces the new model of automobile demand. The first chapter in part II reviews the literature on auto demand, providing guidelines and setting the stage for the new model. The next chapter describes the model: its structure, detailed specification, and estimation. For the final chapter, a case study is presented in which the model is used for actual policy analysis for the California Energy Commission.

I THEORY AND ECONOMETRICS OF QUALITATIVE CHOICE MODELS

1 Qualitative Choice Models in General

1.1 Motivation

In recent years the emphasis in econometrics has shifted from aggregate models that describe markets as a whole to disaggregate models of the individual decisionmaking units that underlie market demand and supply. There are several reasons for this shift. First, economically relevant behavior is necessarily at the individual level: market supply and demand are simply the aggregate of many individuals' actions. Consequently, attempts to capture the structure, or causal relations, inherent in behavior are more naturally pursued at the individual level. Microeconomic theory provides a way of looking at the actions of individual decisionmaking units, as well as a rich set of hypotheses concerning these actions. This theory can be drawn upon in specifying and interpreting disaggregate econometric models to a degree that is not possible with aggregate models. Second, survey data on households and individual firms are becoming more and more available, making it possible to estimate disaggregate models in situations that would previously have been impossible to examine at the individual level. Furthermore, with these data on individual decision-making units, more precise estimation of underlying parameters is possible. Data on individual units necessarily contain greater variation in each factor, and usually less covariation among factors, than aggregate data, simply because the latter are sums or averages of the former. This fact is important in estimating econometric models since the precision with which each parameter in a model can be estimated generally increases with the variance of the variable entering the model and decreases with the covariance among variables. As a result, disaggregate models are often able to capture effects that cannot be incorporated accurately in aggregate models.

With the movement toward disaggregate modeling came a need for new methodologies. Standard econometric methods like regression were designed for analyzing variables that can assume any value within a range, that is, for continuous variables. These methods are usually appropriate for examining aggregate data. When the underlying behavior of the individual decisionmaking units is examined, however, it is often found that the outcome of the behavior is not continuous and standard regression procedures are inappropriate. Automobile demand is a case in point. The aggregate demand for a particular make and model of automobile, say, Honda Accord, can be considered a continuous variable that varies over time and geographic regions. But the demand for Honda Accord by any one household is not continuous; at any given set of prices and other factors, each household either buys a Honda Accord or not. Examining this demand with methods developed for continuous variables ignores the structure of the behavioral situation.

A variety of methods have been developed for examining the behavior of individuals when continuous methods are inappropriate. Qualitative choice analysis is among these. It is designed for describing decisionmakers' choices in certain types of situations. These situations arise in a variety of contexts in such areas as transportation, energy, telecommunications, housing, criminology, and labor, to name a few. However, just as regression is inappropriate in some contexts, qualitative choice analysis is applicable in only particular types of situations. Defining these situations is the topic of the next section.

1.2 Situations Described by Qualitative Choice Models

In any choice situation, the person making the choice has two or more different items, courses of action, or, more generally, "alternatives" among which to choose. A qualitative choice situation, which qualitative choice models are used to describe, is defined as one in which a decisionmaker faces a choice among a set of alternatives meeting the following criteria: (1) the number of alternatives in the set is **finite**; (2) the alternatives are **mutually exclusive**: that is, the person's choosing one alternative in the set necessarily implies that the person does not choose another alternative; and (3) the set of alternatives is **exhaustive**: that is, all possible alternatives are included, and so the person necessarily chooses one alternative from the set. Examples of choice situations fitting these criteria are a worker's choice of mode for travel to work (with the alternatives being auto, transit, walk, etc.); a household's choice of make and model of automobile (VW Rabbit, Olds Omega, etc.); a household's choice of type of convection oven (electric versus gas); and a businessperson's choice of long distance telecommunication service (Allnet, Sprint, AT&T, etc.). Examples of choice situations that do not fit these criteria, and hence are not qualitative choice situations, are a consumer's choice of how many pounds of beef to buy at the store (since the set of alternative weights is, at least theoretically, infinite: the person can buy 1 pound, 1.1 pounds, 1.11 pounds, 1.111 pounds, etc.); a businessperson's choice between two different life insurance policies being offered by a salesperson (since the set is not exhaustive: the person could choose a policy offered by another salesperson); and a worker's choice of mode of travel when there is the possibility of driving to the bus stop and then taking the bus (since the alternatives of auto, bus, walk, etc., are not mutually exclusive: the person could take both auto and bus).

These examples of situations that are not qualitative choice situations suggest an important point. When a choice situation cannot be described as "qualitative" because either its alternatives are not mutually exclusive or its set of alternatives is not exhaustive, it is usually possible to redefine the set of alternatives in such a way that the redefined set meets all three criteria. Consequently, situations that might at first appear not to meet the criteria, can qualify with a redefinition of alternatives. For example, the businessperson's choice between two life insurance policies offered by a particular salesperson does not seem applicable because the alternatives are not exhaustive; however, if a third alternative is added, namely, the possibility of choosing neither of the two policies, then the set of three alternatives (choosing either of the two policies or neither) is exhaustive, and the choice situation is a qualitative one. Similarly, the worker's alternative modes of auto, bus, walk, etc., are not mutually exclusive if it is possible that the worker drives to the bus stop and then takes the bus; however, if the set of alternative modes is redefined to be auto only, bus only, bus with auto access to bus, etc., then the alternatives are mutually exclusive and the worker is in a qualitative choice situation.

Since careful delineation of alternatives can usually assure that the second and third criteria are met, the only truly restrictive criterion is the first one, namely, that the number of alternatives be finite. A distinction established by this criterion is that between continuous and discrete variables. The set of alternatives available to the decisionmaker can be denoted by a variable; for example, the amount of beef a consumer chooses can be denoted by x, where x is any nonnegative number; the type of convection oven available to a household can be denoted as y, with y taking either of two values: either one for electric or two for gas. The variable x is obviously continuous in that, within any range, it can take an infinite number of values, whereas the variable y discrete. Any choice situation in which the set of alternatives can be denoted by a continuous variable is not a qualitative choice situation.

The term "discrete choice situation," which is often used to denote the same thing as "qualitative choice situation," arose from this distinction between continuous and discrete variables for denoting the set of alternatives. This distinction also gives meaning to the use of the term "qualitative": most choices that concern how many or how much of something (which are choice of quantity) have alternative sets that are denoted by continuous variables, whereas choices of which item (such as which type of oven) are nonquantitative, or qualitative, and have alternative sets that can be denoted by discrete variables.

Unfortunately, both of these terms can be misleading. "Qualitative choice situation" would seem to exclude choices regarding quantity. However, some choice situations are quantitative in that the choice is in regard to "how many" yet nevertheless qualify as qualitative choice situations. An example is the choice of how many autos to own; if it can be assumed that a household cannot own more than some N autos, then the set of alternatives is $0, 1, 2, \ldots, N$, which is clearly a finite, exhaustive set of mutually exclusive alternatives.

The difficulty with the term "discrete choice situation" is that, in practice, the distinction between discrete and continuous variables is not always meaningful and hence does not serve to guide the researcher in determining whether to use qualitative choice methods. Many continuous variables can be represented, without loss of accuracy and sometimes with an increase in accuracy, by discrete variables. For example, the amount of beef a consumer buys is a continuous variable, since weight is a continuous variable. However, in practice the variable can be treated as discrete, since a consumer never asks for, nor gets charged for, fractional quantities such as 1.111 pounds; the number is always rounded off to some convenient figure. Similarly, since it is not possible to pay fractions of cents, one's expenditures on any good, while often treated as continuous, are actually discrete, with the set of alternatives being every one-cent interval above zero. If there is some conceivable maximum for these discrete variables, then the number of alternatives is finite and the choice situations are qualitative.

Whether or not to utilize qualitative choice methods in situations such as these is a matter of taste, or, more precisely, a strategy decision by the researcher. Usually, choices of "how many" or "how much" are more fruitfully analyzed with qualitative choice methods if the number of alternatives is fairly small. When there are a large number of quantitative alternatives such that the discrete dependent variable is essentially indistinguishable from a continuous one, then standard econometric methods for continuous variables, such as regression, can be used adequately to present the choice. Thus, qualitative choice methods are appropriate for analyzing households' choices of how many cars to own, since only a small number of alternatives are involved, whereas regression techniques are probably more appropriate for examining households' expenditures on particular goods, since, even though the alternatives are truly discrete, there are enough quantitative alternatives to be adequately represented by a continuous variable.

In short, qualitative choice models are used to analyze situations in which a decisionmaker can be described as facing a choice among a finite and exhaustive set of mutually exclusive alternatives. Furthermore, if the choice is one of how many or how much and nevertheless meets these criteria, then qualitative choice models are used only if the number of alternatives is fairly small.

1.3   Specification

The general term "qualitative choice models" designates a class of models; specific qualitative choice models, such as logit and probit, are members of this class. This section presents the specification of the general class and the manner in which specific models within the class are distinguished.

All qualitative choice models calculate the probability that a decision-maker will choose a particular alternative from a set of alternatives, given data observed by the researcher. The models differ in the functional form that relates the observed data to the probability. These concepts are now elaborated.

Denote the decisionmaker in a qualitative choice situation by n and the set of alternatives he faces by J_n. This set, sometimes called the choice set, is subscripted by n to represent the fact that different decisionmakers might face different sets of alternatives in similar choice situations. For example, in workers' choices of mode of travel, a person who cannot drive does not have the alternative of taking an auto, which is available to most workers.

The alternatives that the decisionmaker faces differ in their characteristics (otherwise there would essentially be only one alternative and no choice). For example, the time and cost of travel by auto is different than by bus; purchase price, fuel efficiency, interior space, and so on vary across makes and models of cars; monthly and per minute charges vary over long distance telecommunication services. Some of these characteristics are observed by the researcher and some are not.

Label the **observed** characteristics of alternative i as faced by decisionmaker n as the vector z_{in}, for all i in J_n. Note that the characteristics of each alternative are subscripted by n to reflect the fact that different decision-makers can face alternatives with different characteristics. For example, the cost of travel to work by auto will vary across workers depending on the distance from their homes to work.

The decisionmaker's choice of alternative obviously depends on the characteristics of each of the available alternatives. Different decision-makers, however, can make different choices when facing the same alterna-tives because the relative value that they place on each characteristic is different. The differences in the valuation of each characteristic of the alternatives depend on the characteristics of the decisionmaker, both those observed by the researcher and those not observed. Label the **observed** characteristics of decisionmaker n as s_n. Usually elements of s_n are income, age, education level, and so on.

The probability that decisionmaker n chooses alternative i from set J_n (labeled P_{in}) depends on the observed characteristics of alternative i com-pared with all other alternatives (i.e., on z_{in} relative to all z_{jn} for j in $J_n, j \neq i$) and on the observed characteristics of the decisionmaker (s_n). Qualitative choice models specify this probability as a parametric function of the general form

$$P_{in} = f(z_{in}, z_{jn} \text{ for all } j \text{ in } J_n \text{ and } j \neq i, s_n, \beta), \qquad (1.1)$$

where f is the function that relates the observed data to the choice proba-bilities. This function is specified up to some vector of parameters, β. In specific contexts, these parameters will usually have a particular meaning. For example, in the choice of mode for the commute to work, the param-eters might represent the relative importance, or value, of travel cost and time in the workers' choices. These parameters are usually estimated by the researcher in the manner described in the chapters to follow, but can conceivably be determined on the basis of a priori information or expert judgment.

In some sense, the general description of qualitative choice models is completely contained in equation (1.1). All qualitative choice models have this general form. Specific qualitative choice models, such as logit or probit, are obtained by specifying f.

It is useful, however, to elaborate upon this general description with concepts from the standard microeconomic theory of utility maximization. Relating the general specification of qualitative choice models to utility theory offers three benefits. First, in the discussion thus far, the meaning of the choice probability P_{in} is not clear. Usually a probability is interpreted as the proportion of times a particular event would occur if a situation were repeated numerous times (or, more accurately, the fraction to which this proportion converges as the number of repetitions increases without bound). In the previous discussion, the source of repetitions is not delineated. A clear meaning of the choice probabilities emerges from the derivation of probabilities from utility theory. Second, since different qualitative choice models are obtained through different specifications of the function f, the motivation for different specifications and the manner in which they are obtained is critical information for a researcher. Utility theory provides a context for motivating and deriving various specifications of f. Third, and largely because of the first two reasons, the literature on qualitative choice models uses terms that only have meaning in the context of utility theory. Understanding this literature requires knowledge of the relation of qualitative choice models to utility maximization.

The derivation of qualitative choice models from utility theory is based on a precise distinction between the behavior of the decisionmaker and the analysis of the researcher. Consider first the decisionmaker. As stated, decisionmaker n has a choice among the alternatives in set J_n. The decisionmaker would obtain some relative happiness or "utility" from each alternative if he were to choose it. Designate the utility from alternative i in J_n as U_{in}, and similarly for each other alternative in J_n. This utility depends on various factors, including the characteristics of the alternative and the characteristics of the decisionmaker. For example, when a person chooses which automobile to buy, the utility of each alternative make and model depends on the price, fuel efficiency, seating capacity, and other characteristics of the vehicle as well as the income, number of dependents, and other characteristics of the decisionmaker. Label the vector of all relevant characteristics of alternative i as faced by person n as x_{in} and the vector of all relevant characteristics of person n as r_n. Since x_{in} and r_n include all relevant factors, we can write utility as a function of these factors,

$$U_{in} = U(x_{in}, r_n), \qquad \text{for all} \quad i \text{ in } J_n, \tag{1.2}$$

where U is a function.

The decisionmaker chooses, of course, the alternative from which he derives the greatest utility. That is, the decisionmaker chooses alternative i in J_n if and only if [1]

$U_{in} > U_{jn},$ for all j in J_n, $j \neq i$.

Substituting (1.2), we have

n chooses i in J_n iff $U(x_{in}, r_n) > U(x_{jn}, r_n),$

for all j in J_n, $j \neq i$.

(1.3)

This completes the specification of how the decisionmaker behaves. Note that the decisionmaker's choice is deterministic: he chooses the alternative that provides the highest utility. If one were to define at this point the probability that person n would choose alternative i, then the probability would necessarily be either one or zero depending on whether or not alternative i provided the greatest utility.

To specify the choice probabilities, we focus on the researcher. Suppose that a researcher is interested in predicting this decisionmaker's choice. If the researcher observed all the relevant factors, i.e., x_{in} for all i in J_n and r_n, and knew the decisionmaker's utility function U, then the researcher could use relation (1.3) perfectly to predict the decisionmaker's choice. However, the researcher does not observe all the relevant factors and does not know the utility function exactly.

Partition the elements of x_{in} into two subvectors: those characteristics of the alternative that are observed by the researcher, denoted by vector z_{in}, and those that are not (not labeled). Similarly, partition r_n into observed characteristics of the person, labeled s_n, and characteristics that are not observed by the researcher. Finally, decompose $U(x_{in}, r_n)$ for each i in J_n into two subfunctions, one that depends only on factors that the researcher observes and whose form is known by the researcher up to a vector of parameters, β, to be estimated, with this component labeled $V(z_{in}, s_n, \beta)$, and another that represents all factors and aspects of utility that are unknown by the researcher, which is labeled e_{in}. That is,

$U_{in} = U(x_{in}, r_n) = V(z_{in}, s_n, \beta) + e_{in}.$

(1.4)

Note that this equation holds exactly, since e_{in} is simply the difference between true utility $U(x_{in}, r_n)$ and the part of utility the researcher knows, $V(z_{in}, s_n, \beta)$.

Since the researcher does not know $U(x_{in}, r_n)$ entirely, he cannot perfectly predict the decisionmaker's choice. However, the researcher knows part of the decisionmaker's utility, namely, the part denoted by $V(z_{in}, s_n, \beta)$, and with this information is able to make educated guesses as to the decisionmaker's choice. In particular, the researcher can (with one additional piece of information to be described) state the probability that the decisionmaker will choose each alternative.

Let us now define the choice probabilities. Suppose a researcher observed a group of decisionmakers all of whom faced the same alternatives with the same values for the **observed** portion of utility for each alternative. The unobserved part of each decisionmaker's utility is, by definition, not known by the researcher and, in general, will vary across decisionmakers in the group. Therefore, even though the observed part of utility is the same for all decisionmakers in the group, different decisionmakers would choose different alternatives depending on the values of the unobserved components of their utility. For example, if e_{in} is much larger than e_{im} for two decisionmakers, n and m, then person n might choose alternative i while person m does not. Within any group, a certain proportion of the decisionmakers will choose alternative i. The probability of choosing i is the fraction to which this probability converges as the size of the group increases without bound.

The choice probabilities can now be defined precisely. The probability that person n chooses alternative i, denoted P_{in}, is the limit of the proportion of times, as the number of times increases without bound, that the researcher would observe a decisionmaker who faces the same alternatives as person n, and with the same values of observed utility for each alternative, to choose alternative i. Note that this probability is defined on the researcher, reflecting the researcher's lack of information regarding all factors affecting the decisionmaker's choice. It is not defined on the decisionmaker, whose choice is deterministic.[2]

Given the definition of the choice probabilities, the function f that relates observed data to the probabilities is derived as follows. P_{in} is the probability that relation (1.3) holds, that is, that the utility of alternative i is higher than that of any other alternative, given the observed components of utility for each alternative.

$$P_{in} = \text{Prob}(U_{in} > U_{jn}, \text{ for all } j \text{ in } J_n, j \neq i). \tag{1.5}$$

By substitution of (1.4) and letting V_{in} denote $V(z_{in}, s_n, b)$ for notational simplicity,

$$P_{in} = \text{Prob}(V_{in} + e_{in} > V_{jn} + e_{jn}, \text{ for all } j \text{ in } J_n, j \neq i).$$

Rearranging,

$$P_{in} = \text{Prob}(e_{jn} - e_{in} < V_{in} - V_{jn}, \text{ for all } j \text{ in } J_n, j \neq i). \tag{1.6}$$

Let us examine the right-hand side of this equation. The researcher observes V_{in} and V_{jn}, and so he can calculate their difference, $V_{in} - V_{jn}$. The researcher does not observe e_{jn} or e_{in}; as explained, these terms are random, varying across decisionmakers with the same observed components of utility. Since e_{jn} and e_{in} are random variables, their difference $e_{jn} - e_{in}$ is also a random variable. Consequently, the right-hand side of (1.6) is simply a cumulative distribution: the probability that the random variable $e_{jn} - e_{in}$ is below the known value $V_{in} - V_{jn}$. More precisely, it is a joint cumulative distribution, namely, the probability that each random variable $e_{jn} - e_{in}$ is below $V_{in} - V_{jn}$, respectively, for all j in $J_n, j \neq i$.

By knowing the distribution of the random e's (though not knowing their particular values), the researcher can derive the distribution of each difference $e_{jn} - e_{in}$ for all j in $J_n, j \neq i$, and by using equation (1.6) calculate the probability that the decisionmaker will choose alternative i as a function of $V_{in} - V_{jn}$ for all j in $J_n, j \neq i$. This function is f in equation (1.1).

All qualitative choice models are obtained by specifying some distribution for the unknown component of utility and deriving functions for the choice probabilities. Different qualitative choice models are obtained by specifying different distributions for the e's, giving rise to different functional forms for the choice probabilities.

The meaning of equation (1.6) can be visualized if we restrict ourselves to examples with only two alternatives. Suppose the decisionmaker has a choice between alternatives i and j and that the observed component of utility for alternative i is one unit greater than that for alternative j. (Say, $V_{in} = 4$ and $V_{jn} = 3$, so that $V_{in} - V_{jn} = 1$.) Alternative i will be chosen if total utility, both observed and unobserved, is higher for alternative i than for alternative j, that is, if $V_{in} + e_{in} > V_{jn} + e_{jn}$. The values that e_{in} and e_{jn} take determine whether this occurs. If e_{in} exceeds e_{jn}, then alternative i will obviously be chosen, since both the observed and unobserved parts of its utility are greater than those for alternative j. However, even if instead e_{jn} exceeds e_{in}, alternative i will still be chosen as long as e_{jn} is no more than one unit greater than e_{in}. Alternative i will **not** be chosen (and alternative j will be) only if e_{jn} is more than one unit larger than e_{in}.

Equation (1.6) states these facts succinctly:

$$P_{in} = \text{Prob}(e_{jn} - e_{in} < V_{in} - V_{jn}),$$

which in this case, since $V_{in} - V_{jn} = 1$, becomes

$$P_{in} = \text{Prob}(e_{jn} - e_{in} < 1).$$

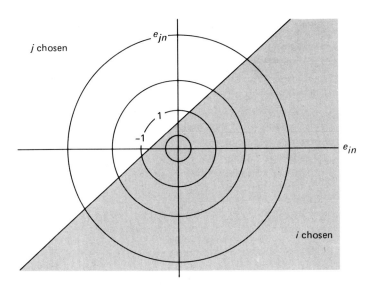

Figure 1.1
Probability that alternative i is chosen given that $V_{in} - V_{jn} = 1$.

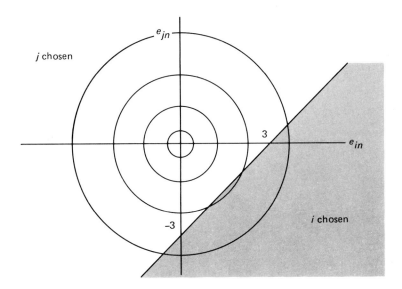

Figure 1.2
Probability that alternative i is chosen given that $V_{in} - V_{jn} = -3$.

This is, alternative i will be chosen as long as e_{jn} is no more than one unit larger than e_{in}.

Figure 1.1 depicts this probability. Each point in the two-dimensional graph represents a particular value of e_{in} and e_{jn}. The concentric circles represent the joint density of e_{in} and e_{jn}. The diagonal line connects those points for which e_{jn} is exactly one unit larger than e_{in}. For all points below this line, e_{jn} is less than one unit greater than e_{in} and so alternative i is chosen. For all points above the line, e_{jn} exceeds e_{in} by more than one unit and so alternative j is chosen. The probability that alternative i is chosen is the probability that e_{in} and e_{jn} fall below the line. That is, P_{in} is the volume under the shaded part of the joint density function. Different density functions for e_{in} and e_{jn} will obviously give rise to different probabilities.

The same type of analysis applies if the observed part of utility for alternative i is less than that for alternative j. For example, suppose $V_{in} = 2$ and $V_{jn} = 5$. Then alternative i will be chosen only if e_{in} is at least three units larger than e_{jn}. Stated conversely and in closer accordance with equation (1.6), alternative i will be chosen only if e_{jn} is no more than three units below e_{in}. The probability of this occurring is depicted in figure 1.2.

2 Logit

2.1 Function Form of Choice Probabilities

By far the most widely used qualitative choice model is logit. Its popularity is due to the fact that the formula for logit choice probabilities is readily interpretable, particularly compared with other qualitative choice models, and the parameters of logit models are relatively inexpensive to estimate.

Following the discussion of section 1.3, the logit probabilities are derived under a particular assumption regarding the distribution of the unobserved portion of utility. The basic notation of section 1.3 will be repeated for convenience, followed by the specification of the logit probabilities.

Suppose a decisionmaker, denoted n, faces a set of J_n alternatives. The utility that the decisionmaker obtains from alternative i in J_n, denoted U_{in}, is decomposed into (1) a part that is known by the researcher, labeled as V_{in}, and (2) an unknown part that is assumed to be a random variable, labeled e_{in}. This is expressed as $U_{in} = V_{in} + e_{in}$. Recall that the known part of utility V_{in} is a function that depends on the observed characteristics of the alternative as faced by the decisionmaker (labeled z_{in}), the observed characteristics of the decisionmaker (s_n), and a vector of parameters (β) that are either known a priori by the researcher or estimated: $V_{in} = V(z_{in}, s_n, \beta)$. For notational simplicity this functional dependence is suppressed; however, it is important to remember that V_{in} depends on observed data and known or estimated parameters.

Assume that each e_{in}, for all i in J_n, is distributed independently, identically in accordance with the extreme value distribution.[1] Given this distribution for the unobserved components of utility, the probability that the decisionmaker will choose alternative i is

$$P_{in} = \frac{e^{V_{in}}}{\sum_{j \in J_n} e^{V_{jn}}}, \qquad \text{for all} \quad i \text{ in } J_n. \tag{2.1}$$

The proof of this fact, while straightforward, is tedious and not particularly illuminating; for readers who are interested it is given, along with the formula for the extreme value distribution, at the end of this chapter (see section 2.9).

Since the unobserved component of utility is assumed, through the extreme value distribution, to have zero mean, the observed part of utility, V_{in}, is often called representative, expected, or average utility. It should be clear in using these terms, however, that the expectation or average is over all possible values of factors unobserved by the researcher rather than by the decisionmaker.

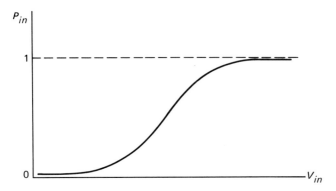

Figure 2.1
Graph of logit curve.

Three properties of the choice probabilities are important to note. First, each of the choice probabilities is necessarily between zero and one. If alternative i were as unpleasant as possible in the eyes of the decisionmaker, and hence its representative utility approached negative infinity, then P_{in} would approach zero. On the other hand, if alternative i were as wonderful as possible in the eyes of the decisionmaker, and hence its representative utility approached infinity, then P_{in} would approach one (given finite values for the representative utilities of the other alternatives).

Second, the choice probabilities necessarily sum to one:

$$\sum_{i \in J_n} P_{in} = \sum_{i \in J_n} \left(\frac{e^{V_{in}}}{\sum_{j \in J_n} e^{V_{jn}}} \right) = 1.$$

This follows from the fact that the choice set in a qualitative choice situation is exhaustive, so that the decisionmaker must choose one of the alternatives, and the alternatives are mutually exclusive, so that the decisionmaker cannot choose more than one alternative.

Third, the relation of the choice probability for an alternative to the representative utility of that alternative, holding the representative utilities of the other alternatives fixed, is sigmoid, or S-shaped (figure 2.1).

If the representative utility of one alternative is very low, compared with other alternatives, a small increase in the utility of this alternative will not much affect the probability of its being chosen; the other alternatives will still be generally preferred. Similarly, if one alternative is far superior to the others, so that its representative utility is very high, an additional increase in its utility will not much affect the probability of its being chosen; it will usually be chosen even without the extra utility. The point at which an increase in the representative utility of an alternative has the greatest effect on its probability of being chosen is when its representative utility is very similar to that of other alternatives. In this case, a small increase in the utility of one alternative could, in a way, "tip the balance," and thereby induce a large increase in the probability of the alternative being chosen.

Examples Consider first a binary choice situation: a household's choice between a gas or electric oven. Suppose that the utility the household obtains from each type of oven depends only on the oven's purchase price, operating cost, and the household's view of the relative accuracy or ease of cooking with the oven. The first two of these factors are observed by the researcher, but the researcher cannot observe the third factor. If the researcher considers the observed part of utility to be a linear function of the observed factors, then the utility of each type of oven can be written as $U_g = \beta_1 PP_g + \beta_2 OC_g + e_g$ and $U_r = \beta_1 PP_r + \beta_2 OC_r + e_r$, where the subscript g denotes gas and r denotes electric; PP and OC are the purchase price and operating cost, respectively, of the oven type denoted by the subscript; β_1 and β_2 are scalar parameters; and the subscript n denoting household is suppressed for convenience. The utility of a household is higher the less it has to pay for an oven, in either purchasing or operating it, since the household can purchaser other goods with the money saved. Therefore, β_1 and β_2 are negative.

The unobserved component of utility for each alternative, e_g and e_r, varies over household with respect to households' differing views of the accuracy and ease of cooking by each type of oven. If this component has an extreme value distribution, then the probability that the household will choose a gas oven is

$$P_g = \frac{e^{\beta_1 PP_g + \beta_2 OC_g}}{e^{\beta_1 PP_g + \beta_2 OC_g} + e^{\beta_1 PP_r + \beta_2 OC_r}}, \tag{2.2}$$

and the probability that it will choose an electric one is expressed analogously. Note that, since β_1 and β_2 are negative, the probability of choosing a gas oven decreases as the cost of purchasing or operating it increases (if the costs of an electric oven are constant). Furthermore, the probability of choosing a gas oven increases as the purchase price or operating cost of an electric oven increases.

A multinomial case is a simple extension of the binary case. Consider, for example, that the household could choose a microwave oven instead of either a gas or electric one (ignore, for the sake of this example, the possibility of owning a microwave in addition to a convection oven). Under analogous assumptions to those given, the utility of each type of oven is

$$U_g = \beta_1 \, PP_g + \beta_2 \, OC_g + e_g;$$

$$U_r = \beta_1 \, PP_r + \beta_2 \, OC_r + e_r;$$

$$U_m = \beta_1 \, PP_m + \beta_2 \, OC_m + e_m;$$

where the subscript m denotes microwave. Under the assumption that e_g, e_r, and e_m are each distributed independently extreme value, the probability that the household chooses a gas oven is

$$P_g = \frac{e^{\beta_1 \, PP_g + \beta_2 \, OC_g}}{e^{\beta_1 \, PP_g + \beta_2 \, OC_g} + e^{\beta_1 \, PP_r + \beta_2 \, OC_r} + e^{\beta_1 \, PP_m + \beta_2 \, OC_m}}. \tag{2.3}$$

The probabilities for electric and microwave ovens are analogous.

Expression (2.3) has the same numerator in the binary case of expression (2.2), but the denominator is larger by the quantity $\exp(\beta_1 \, PP_m + \beta_2 \, OC_m)$. Therefore, as one would expect in the real world, the probability of choosing a gas oven is lower when the possibility of buying a microwave oven is available than when it is not.

2.2   The Independence from Irrelevant Alternatives Property

Three properties of logit probabilities are discussed in section 2.1, namely, that they (1) range from zero to one, (2) sum to one over alternatives, and (3) are a sigmoid or S-shaped function of representative utility. Each of these properties is quite reasonable, and in fact the first two are logically necessary. Logit probabilities also exhibit a property, however, that, at least in some contexts, is not desirable. This is called the independence from irrelevant alternatives property, or the IIA property for short.

The IIA property has been the focus of considerable discussion in the literature and not a small amount of confusion. In the next pages, the basics of the IIA property are presented first, followed by a discussion of relatively recent concepts that place the IIA property in clearer perspective.

IIA Basics

Consider the ratio of the choice probabilities for two alternatives, i and k:

$$\frac{P_{in}}{P_{kn}} = \frac{e^{V_{in}}/\sum_{j \in J_n} e^{V_{jn}}}{e^{V_{kn}}/\sum_{j \in J_n} e^{V_{jn}}}$$

$$= \frac{e^{V_{in}}}{e^{V_{kn}}} = e^{V_{in}-V_{kn}}.$$

Note that the ratio of these two probabilities does not depend on any alternatives other than i and k. That is, the ratios of probabilities is necessarily the same no matter what other alternatives are in J_n or what the characteristics of other alternatives are. Since the ratio is independent from alternatives other than i and k, it is said to be independent from "irrelevant" alternatives, that is, alternatives other than those for which the ratio is calculated.

While this property is an accurate reflection of reality in some choice situations, it is clearly inappropriate in other situations. Consider, for example, the classic red bus/blue bus problem. Suppose there is a traveler who has a choice of going by auto or taking a blue bus and that both alternatives have the same representative utility. Because the representative utilities are equal, the choice probabilities are equal ($P_a = 1/2 = P_{bb}$, where a denotes auto and bb denotes blue bus) and the ratio of probabilities is one ($P_a/P_{bb} = 1$).

Now suppose that a red bus were introduced and that the traveler considered the red bus to be exactly like the blue bus. Consequently, the ratio of probabilities for taking the two differently colored buses is one ($P_{bb}/P_{rb} = 1$, where rb denotes red bus). However, since in the logit model the ratio P_a/P_{bb} is the same independent of the existence of other alternatives, this ratio remains constant at one. The only probabilities for which $P_a/P_{bb} = 1$ and $P_{bb}/P_{rb} = 1$ are $P_a = P_{bb} = P_{rb} = 1/3$, which are the probabilities that the logit model predicts.

In real life, however, we would expect the probability of taking an auto to remain the same when a new bus is introduced that is essentially the same as the old bus. We would also expect the original probability of taking bus to be split, after the introduction of the new bus, between the two buses. That is, we would expect $P_a = 1/2$ and $P_{bb} = P_{rb} = 1/4$. In this case, the logit model, because of its IIA property, overestimates the probability of taking either of the buses and underestimates the probability of taking an auto.

In cases like that of the red bus/blue bus, the IIA property of logit models is inappropriate. However, in situations in which the IIA property reflects reality, considerable advantages are gained by its employment. First, because of the IIA property, it is possible to estimate model parameters consistently on a subset of alternatives for each sampled decisionmaker. For example, in a situation with 100 alternatives, the researcher might (so as to reduce computer costs) estimate on a subset of 10 alternatives for each sampled person, with the person's chosen alternative included as well as 9 alternatives randomly selected from the remaining 99. Since relative probabilities within a subset of alternatives are unaffected by exclusion of alternatives not in the subset, exclusion of alternatives in estimation does not affect the consistency of the estimation. (Details of this type of estimation and its consistency are given in section 2.6.)

This fact has considerable practical importance. In analyzing choice situations for which the number of alternatives is large, estimating on a subset of alternatives can save substantial amounts of computer time and expense. At the extreme, the number of alternatives might be so large as to preclude estimation altogether (due to core capacity of computers) if it were not possible to utilize a subset of alternatives.

Another practical use of this ability to estimate on subsets of alternatives arises when a researcher is only interested in examining choices among a subset of alternatives and not among all alternatives. For example, consider a researcher who is interested in identifying the factors that contribute to a worker's choice of taking an auto or a bus to work. The full set of alternative modes includes walking, bicycling, etc., in addition to auto and bus. However, the researcher, if he believed the IIA property to be appropriate in this case, could estimate a model with only the alternatives of bus and auto included for each sampled person, thereby saving considerable time and money. Sampled workers who did not choose either auto or bus would be excluded from the sample (since their chosen alternatives are not in the estimation subset) and the model would be estimated on the remaining sampled workers.

The IIA property also allows the researcher to predict demand for alternatives that do not currently exist, such as the demand for a new make of car, a new mode of travel, a new product, and so on. Consider, for example, a researcher examining households' choices of make and model of auto. If the researcher thinks that the IIA property is appropriate in this setting, he can estimate a model describing the choice of make and model of auto using currently available makes and models in the estimation, and then use the estimated model to calculate the probability that a household would choose a make and model that will be introduced shortly.

The appropriateness of this procedure is conceptually related to the consistency of estimation on a subset of alternatives. If the full set of alternatives is considered to be all the currently available makes and models plus the soon-to-be-introduced make and model, then estimation on currently available makes and models is equivalent to estimating on a subset of alternatives, which, as discussed, provides consistent estimates of the model parameters.

IIA Revisited

Despite its practical advantages, the IIA property is a restriction that is not realistic in many situations. Recent work has indicated, however, that the IIA property in logit models is not as restrictive as it might at first seem, or, in particular, as indicated by the red bus/blue bus problem.

McFadden (1975) has shown that any model that specifies choice probabilities, including models that do not exhibit IIA, can be expressed in the **form** of logit models. That is, it is possible to express any choice probability as

$$P_{in} = \frac{e^{W_{in}}}{\sum_{j \in J_n} e^{W_{jn}}},$$

where W_{jn}, for all j in J_n, is some function of observed data.

The proof is simple. Let $P_{in}^* = f(z_{in}; z_{jn},$ for all $j \neq i; s_n)$ be the "true" model, where z_{in} is observed data relating to alternative i as faced by decisionmaker n, and s_n is a vector of characteristics of the decisionmaker. Note that this specification is completely general; in particular, choice probabilities that do not exhibit IIA are allowed. Taking logs,

$$\log P_{in}^* = \log f(z_{in}; z_{jn}, \text{ for all } j \neq i; s_n).$$

Now, define $W_{in} = \log P_{in}^*$ and evaluate logit probabilities based on W_{in}:

$$P_{in} = \frac{e^{W_{in}}}{\sum_{j \in J_n} e^{W_{jn}}} = \frac{e^{\log P_{in}^*}}{\sum_{j \in J_n} e^{\log P_{jn}^*}} = \frac{P_{in}^*}{\sum_{j \in J_n} P_{jn}^*} = P_{in}^*,$$

where the last equality is due to the fact that choice probabilities necessarily sum to one. This shows that logit probabilities, with the appropriate specification of W_{in}, equal the true probabilities. Stated another way, any choice model can, with an appropriate choice of W_{in}, be put into the logit form. This concept has given rise to the term "mother logit."

The logit model derived from the extreme value distribution, which exhibits the IIA property, is a special case of "mother logit." The term W_{in} in the mother logit model depends in general on all observed data including characteristics of alternatives other than i. However, V_{in} in equation (2.1), which can be called the standard logit model, depends only on character-istics of alternative i and of the decisionmaker; characteristics of alterna-tives other than i do not enter V_{in}. Therefore, when W_{in} depends only on characteristics of the decisionmaker and alternative i, mother logit becomes standard logit and exhibits IIA; otherwise, the mother logit model need not exhibit IIA.

What this discussion implies is that the logit specification can be used in situations for which IIA does not hold. All that is required is that additional variables be added to representative utility, in particular, variables that relate to alternatives other than the one for which the representative utility is designated.

An example of how this can be done, that is, of how adding terms to representative utility within the logit specification can enable the model to represent situations in which IIA does not hold, is provided by reexamining the red bus/blue bus problem. The representative utility of auto, red bus, and blue bus is assumed to be the same:

$$V_a = V_{bb} = V_{rb}.$$

As discussed, the standard logit model gives equal probabilities for all three alternatives, while we know that the true probabilities are .5 for auto and .25 each for blue bus and red bus. However, if the term $\ln(1/2)$ is added to the representative utility of the two bus alternatives, then the logit model gives the true probabilities. The probability of auto is

$$P_a = \frac{e^{V_a}}{e^{V_{bb} + \ln(1/2)} + e^{V_{rb} + \ln(1/2)} + e^{V_a}}$$

$$= \frac{e^{V_a}}{(e^{V_{bb}})(1/2) + (e^{V_{rb}})(1/2) + e^{V_a}}$$

$$= \frac{e^{V_a}}{2e^{V_a}}$$

$$= \frac{1}{2},$$

where the next to last equality is due to the fact that $V_{bb} = V_{rb} = V_a$. It can be similarly shown that $P_{bb} = P_{rb} = .25$. In summary, if appropriate terms are added to representative utility in the logit model, the red bus/blue bus "problem" is not a problem at all.

The difficulty, in general, is knowing what terms to add to representative utility to account for true probabilities not exhibiting IIA. In some cases, however, the researcher need not know the adjustment factor a priori, since it can be estimated. In the red bus/blue bus case, for example, the researcher need not know that $\ln(1/2)$ should be added to the representative utilities of the bus alternatives. Suppose the researcher estimates the model with all three alternatives in the choice set and includes a constant term in the specification of the representative utility of the bus alternatives; that is, suppose the researcher specified the representative utility of each alternative as

$$V_a^* = V_a;$$

$$V_{bb}^* = \alpha + V_{bb};$$

$$V_{rb}^* = \alpha + V_{rb}.$$

The estimation procedure would automatically estimate a value of α equal to $\ln(1/2)$. (This is due to the fact, explained in section 2.6, that the estimated value of a constant in the representative utility of each alternative is that at which the average estimated probability for each alternative exactly equals the share of sampled decisionmakers who actually chose that alternative. If the true shares for auto, blue bus, and red bus are .5, .25, and .25, respectively, and $V_a = V_{bb} = V_{rb}$, then the only value of α that would cause the estimated probabilities to equal these shares is $\ln(1/2)$.)

Using the logit model when the true probabilities do not exhibit IIA is not as problematic, therefore, as it at first appeared. There are three contexts, however, in which the problem still arises. First, in a situation like the red bus/blue bus case, if the researcher is estimating a model with all alternatives (three in the red bus/blue bus case) and does not include a constant in the representative utility of each alternative, then the estimation cannot incorporate the needed adjustment term. This implies that, whenever possible, the researcher should include constants in the representative utility of each alternative. Second, in a situation like the red bus/blue bus case, if the researcher estimates the model on a subset of alternatives (e.g., auto and blue bus) and then forecasts for a third alternative (e.g., red bus), then the estimated probability for the new alternative will not represent the true probability. This is because the representative utility of the new alternative will not incorporate the necessary adjustment. (If the researcher somehow knows the required adjustment factor, then he can apply it and calculate consistent probabilities for the new alternatives.) Third, if the situation is not like a red bus/blue bus case and an adjustment other than to the constant in representative utility is required to enable the logit specification to represent the true probabilities, then, unless the researcher can determine the necessary adjustments a priori, the estimated logit model will not represent the true probabilities.

2.3 Specification of Representative Utility

We turn now to several issues regarding the specification of representative utility. Since representative utility is usually assumed to be linear in parameters, this assumption is maintained through most of the section; nonlinear-in-parameters representative utility is discussed at the end of this section.

A linear-in-parameters representative utility function is written as

$$V_{in} = \beta w(z_{in}, s_n),$$

where w is a vector-valued function of the observed data and β is a vector of parameters. For notational simplicity the functional relation of the variables w to the observed data z_{in}, s_n can be suppressed by writing $V_{in} = \beta w_{in}$, where $w_{in} = w(z_{in}, s_n)$. The logit choice probabilities therefore become

$$P_{in} = \frac{e^{\beta w_{in}}}{\sum_{j \in J_n} e^{\beta w_{jn}}}, \qquad \text{for all} \quad i \text{ in } J_n.$$

Within this context, issues regarding the specification of representative utility are questions of what variables to enter as elements of w_{in}.

Alternative-Specific Constants

Recall that the utility that decisionmaker n obtains from alternative i in J_n is composed of a part observed by the researcher and a part not observed, $U_{in} = \beta w_{in} + e_{in}$. For a logit model, e_{in} is assumed to be distributed extreme value, which means it has zero mean. It will usually not be the case that the average of all unobserved factors that affect the decisionmaker's utility is zero. Suppose the average of e_{in} is α_i, a scalar parameter unknown to the researcher. Then the representative utility of alternative i can be expanded to include this constant:

$$U_{in} = \beta w_{in} + \alpha_i + e_{in}^*,$$

where $e_{in}^* = e_{in} - \alpha_i$ and hence has zero mean. The parameter α_i is then estimated along with the other parameters of the model (i.e., with β) in the manner described in section 2.6. Conceptually, it is similar to the intercept term in a regression, except that in the decomposition of utility the left-hand-side variable, U_{in}, is not observed.

Including an alternative-specific constant for each alternative serves two functions in addition to providing a zero mean for unobserved utility. First, as demonstrated in section 2.6, the estimated values for the alternative-specific constant are those at which the average probability over the estimation sample for each alternative exactly equals the proportion of decisionmakers in the sample that actually chose that alternative. That is, a model estimated with alternative-specific constants will exactly reproduce the observed shares in the estimation sample. Second, for reasons that are discussed in section 2.2, the inclusion of alternative-specific constants can mitigate, and in some cases remove, inaccuracies due to logit's independence of irrelevant alternatives property.

While one speaks of entering an alternative-specific constant for each alternative, in actuality the constant for one alternative is necessarily normalized to zero and so constants are estimated for, at most, one fewer alternative than there are available. This is not a restriction of the model, only a normalization whose motivation is an aspect of the following topic.

Differences in Representative Utility

A fundamental property of logit models is that only differences in representative utility affect the choice probabilities, not their absolute levels. Consider the probability of choosing alternative i. The standard expression for this probability is

$$P_{in} = \frac{e^{\beta w_{in}}}{\sum_{j \in J_n} e^{\beta w_{jn}}}.$$

The probability can equivalently be expressed in terms of the difference between each alternative's representative utility and the representative utility for any alternative in the choice set:

$$P_{in} = \frac{e^{\beta w_{in} - \beta w_{kn}}}{\sum_{j \in J_n} e^{\beta w_{jn} - \beta w_{kn}}},$$

where k is any alternative in J_n, including perhaps i. These two expressions are equal since

$$\frac{e^{\beta w_{in} - \beta w_{kn}}}{\sum_{j \in J_n} e^{\beta w_{jn} - \beta w_{kn}}} = \frac{e^{\beta w_{in}} \cdot e^{-\beta w_{kn}}}{\sum_{j \in J_n} e^{\beta w_{jn}} \cdot e^{-\beta w_{kn}}} = \frac{e^{\beta w_{in}}}{\sum_{j \in J_n} e^{\beta w_{jn}}}.$$

This fact has several implications. First, it allows the logit probabilities in binary choice situations to be expressed in a simplified form. Consider the choice between gas and electric water heaters. The probability of choosing a gas water heater is

$$P_g = \frac{e^{\beta w_g}}{e^{\beta w_g} + e^{\beta w_r}},$$

where the subscripts g and r denote gas and electricity, respectively, and the subscript n denoting decisionmaker is suppressed. This expression can be rewritten as

$$P_g = \frac{1}{1 + e^{\beta w_r - \beta w_g}},$$

which is the form used in most of the binary logit literature.

Second, since only differences in representative utility matter, alternative-specific constants cannot meaningfully be entered in each alternative; as stated, at least one must be normalized to zero. Consider a binary choice situation in which the representative utility of the two alternatives are written as

$$V_{1n} = \beta w_{1n} + \alpha_1;$$

$$V_{2n} = \beta w_{2n} + \alpha_2.$$

The probabilities that result from these representative utilities are exactly the same as those that result from

$$V_{1n} = \beta w_{1n} + \alpha_1^*;$$

$$V_{2n} = \beta w_{2n},$$

in which $\alpha_1^* = \alpha_1 - \alpha_2$. In fact, any pair of alternative-specific constants whose difference is $\alpha_1 - \alpha_2$ is equivalent.

It is impossible to estimate a constant for each alternative in a choice set since the choice probabilities depend only on differences in the constants and an infinite number of combinations of constants have the same differences. By convention, the constant for one alternative is set equal to zero. The constant for each other alternative is then interpreted as the difference between the average impact of unobserved factors for the two alternatives.

Third, since only differences in representative utility are relevant, variables that do not vary over alternatives cannot affect the choice probabilities. For example, consider the choice of make and model of car. Let representative utility for each alternative i in J_n be $V_{in} = \beta_1 \, PP_{in} + \beta_2 A_n$, where PP_{in} is the amount that person n must pay to purchase make/model i and A_n is the age of person n. In taking differences across alternatives, $V_{in} - V_{jn}$, the term $\beta_2 A_n$ drops out. The representative utility given is equivalent in terms of the decisionmaker's choices to $V_{in} = \beta_1 \, PP_{in}$. Simply adding a constant to the utility of each alternative does not change the decisionmakers choices or, consequently, the choice probabilities.

If the researcher believes that a factor that does not vary over alternatives (e.g., any characteristic of the decisionmaker) affects the decisionmaker's choices, then it must be entered into representative utility in a meaningful fashion. In particular, it must interact with a variable that varies over alternatives.

In the example of the choice of make and model of car, the researcher might think that households with more members are more likely to purchase large cars because they value the extra room more than smaller families. This effect can be captured in the model by (1) defining a dummy variable that is one for large makes and models, then (2) interacting household size with this dummy variable, and finally (3) entering the interaction variable in representative utility:

$$V_{in} = \beta_1 \, PP_{in} + \beta_2 M_n D_i,$$

where D_i is one if i is a large car and zero otherwise, and M_n is the number of members in household n. The coefficient β_2 represents a preference for large cars that increases with household size.

Another example is useful. Consider a household's choice of how many cars to own, with the alternatives being 0, 1, or 2. Suppose the only factor affecting this choice that the researcher observes is the number of members in the household, again labeled M_n for household n. Suppose further that the researcher feels that M_n affects the representative utility for each alternative differently, so that

$V_{0n} = \beta_0 M_n;$

$V_{1n} = \beta_1 M_n;$

$V_{2n} = \beta_2 M_n;$

where V_{0n}, V_{1n}, and V_{2n} are the representative utility of owning no, one, and two cars, respectively, and β_0, β_1, and β_2 are scalar parameters.

Recognizing that only differences in representative utility are relevant, two reformulations are necessary. First, one of the parameters β_0, β_1, or β_2 must be normalized to zero for reasons that are analogous to the normalization of one alternative-specific constant. An equivalent, normalized set of representative utilities is

$V_{0n} = 0;$

$V_{1n} = \beta_1^* M_n;$

$V_{2n} = \beta_2^* M_n;$

where $\beta_1^* = (\beta_1 - \beta_0)$ and $\beta_2^* = (\beta_2 - \beta_0)$. Second, even though M_n does not vary over alternatives, it enters with a different coefficient in each alternative. This is equivalent to M_n being interacted with dummy variables for each alternative. That is, an equivalent expression for representative utilities that explicitly recognizes this interaction is

$V_{in} = \beta_1^* M_n D_i^1 + \beta_2^* M_n D_i^2, \qquad i = 0, 1, 2,$

where D_i^1 equals one when $i = 1$ and zero otherwise, and D_i^2 equals one when $i = 2$ and zero otherwise. Note that since β_0 is zero by normalization, no variable is included that interacts M_n with a dummy for the alternatives of owning no cars.

The parameters β_1^* and β_2^* reflect the difference in the impact of M_n on representative utility for the alternative of owning one or two cars, respectively, compared with that of owning no cars. If β_1^* is positive, then increasing the number of members in the household increases the probability of owning one car relative to the probability of owning no car. If β_2^* is also positive, increasing M_n also increases the probability of owning two cars over owning none. Whether the probability of owning two cars increases relative to the probability of owning one car depends on whether β_2^* is larger than β_1^*. If β_2^* is greater than β_1^*, increasing the number of household members increases the probability of owning two cars over one and the probability of owning one car over none.

Taste Variation

The value, or importance, that decisionmakers place on each characteristic of the alternatives varies, in general, over decisionmakers. As discussed, for example, the size of a car was presumed to be more important to households with many members than smaller households. Other examples are readily identifiable. Low income households are probably more concerned about the purchase price of a good, relative to its other characteristics, than higher income households; younger decisionmakers might care more about the horsepower of a car than older people (or vice versa); in choosing a neighborhood to live in, households with young children will be more concerned about the accessibility and quality of schools than those without children; and so on. In addition, decisionmakers' tastes vary for reasons that are not observable or identifiable, just because people are different.

Logit models can capture taste variations, but only within limits. In particular, tastes that vary systematically with respect to observed variables can be incorporated in logit models, while tastes that vary with unobserved variables, or purely randomly, cannot be handled. The following example will demonstrate the distinction.

Consider households' choices among makes and models of cars to buy. Suppose, for simplicity, that the only two characteristics of cars that the researcher observes is the purchase price (PP_i for make/model i) and inches of shoulder room (SR_i).[2] The value that different households place on these two characteristics varies over households, and so total utility can be written as

$$U_{in} = \alpha_n SR_i + \beta_n PP_i + e_{in}, \tag{2.4}$$

where α_n and β_n are parameters specific to household n.

The parameters vary over households reflecting differences in taste. Suppose, for example, that the value of shoulder room varies with the number of members in the household (M_n) but nothing else:

$$\alpha_n = \rho M_n,$$

so that as M_n increases, the value of should room, α_n, also increases. Similarly, suppose the importance of purchase price is inversely related to income (I_n), so that low income households place larger importance on purchase price:

$$\beta_n = \theta/I_n.$$

Substituting these relations into (2.4) produces

$$U_{in} = \rho(M_n \mathrm{SR}_i) + \theta(\mathrm{PP}_i/I_n) + e_{in}.$$

Under the assumption that each e_{in} is an independently distributed extreme value, a standard logit model obtains with two variables entering representative utility, both of which are interactions of a vehicle characteristic with a household characteristic.

Other specifications for the variation in tastes can be substituted. For example, the value of shoulder room might be assumed to increase with household size, but at a decreasing rate, so that $\alpha_n = \rho M_n + \phi M_n^2$, where ρ is expected to be positive and ϕ negative. Then $U_{in} = \rho(M_n \mathrm{SR}_i) + \phi(M_n^2 \mathrm{SR}_i) + \theta(\mathrm{PP}_i/I_n) + e_{in}$, which results in a standard logit model with three variables entering representative utility.

The limitation of the logit model arises when we attempt to allow tastes to vary with respect to unobserved variables or purely randomly. Suppose, for example, that the value of shoulder room varied with household size plus some other factors (e.g., size of the people themselves, or frequency with which the household travels together) that are unobserved by the researcher and hence considered random:

$$\alpha_n = \rho M_n + \mu_n,$$

where μ_n is a random variable. Similarly, the importance of purchase price consists of its observed and unobserved components:

$$\beta_n = \theta(1/I_n) + \eta_n.$$

Substituting into (2.4) produces

$$U_{in} = \rho(M_n \mathrm{SR}_i) + \mu_n \mathrm{SR}_i + \theta(\mathrm{PP}_i/I_n) + \eta_n \mathrm{PP}_i + e_{in}.$$

Since μ_n and η_n are not observed, the terms $\mu_n \mathrm{SR}_i$ and $\eta_n \mathrm{PP}_i$ become part of the unobserved component of utility,

$$U_{in} = \rho(M_n \mathrm{SR}_i) + \theta(\mathrm{PP}_i/I_n) + \tilde{e}_{in},$$

where $\tilde{e}_{in} = \mu_n \mathrm{SR}_i + \eta_n \mathrm{PP}_i + e_{in}$. The new error term $\tilde{e}_{in}$ cannot possibly be distributed independently, identically random as required for the logit formulation. Since μ_n and η_n are constant over alternatives for each decisionmaker, $\tilde{e}_{in}$ is necessarily correlated over alternatives, violating the independence assumption (i.e., $\text{cov}(\tilde{e}_{in}, \tilde{e}_{jn}) \neq 0$ for $j \neq i$). Furthermore, since SR_i and PP_i vary across alternatives, the variance of $\tilde{e}_{in}$ will vary over alternatives, violating the assumption of identically distributed errors (i.e., $\text{Var}(\tilde{e}_{in}) \neq \text{Var}(\tilde{e}_{jn})$ for $j \neq i$).

This example demonstrates the general point that when tastes vary systematically in the population in relation to observed variables, the variation can be incorporated in logit models. However, if taste variation is random, logit is inappropriate. A probit model, discussed in chapter 3, should be used instead.

Utility Theory as a Specification Tool

The researcher decides what variables to enter in representative utility on the basis of a priori information, both formal and informal. The researcher must decide not just which factors affect the choice probabilities, but how to enter them, that is, what types of interaction terms to specify and by what arithmetic operations, if any, to transform the variables (e.g., log, squared terms). It is often difficult to know the implications of various specifications of representative utility and to determine whether and how, for example, one specification is intrinsically different from another. In these situations, utility theory can often be a useful aid for interpreting and motivating specifications. The appropriate application of utility theory is different in each choice situation. However, an example will illustrate the point of how utility theory can aid in specifying variables to enter representative utility.

In logit models of workers' choice of mode (auto, bus, rail, etc.) for commuting, the wage of the worker often enters as an explanatory variable. In some cases (Train, 1980a, for example) the cost of travel is divided by the worker's wage to reflect the presumption that a worker with a high wage is less concerned about cost than a worker with a low wage. In other cases (McFadden, 1974, for example) travel time is multiplied by the worker's wage to reflect the presumption that a worker with a high wage is more concerned with lost time than a worker with a low wage.

Representative utility is assumed in both specifications to be of the form

$$V_{in} = \beta_n t_{in} + \theta_n c_{in},$$

where t_{in} is the time that it would take person n to travel to work by mode i, c_{in} is the cost of travel by mode i for person n, and β_n and θ_n are parameters specific to person n. With this formulation, the value of money **relative** to time is θ_n/β_n.

In the first specification, the parameters are assumed to vary as

$$\beta_n = \beta^A;$$

$$\theta_n = \theta^A/w_n;$$

where w_n is the wage of person n and β^A and θ^A are parameters constant over all people. The relative value of money compared with time therefore becomes $\theta^A/\beta^A w_n$. In the second specification

$$\beta_n = \beta^B w_n;$$

$$\theta_n = \theta^B;$$

so that the value of money relative to time is $\theta^B/\beta^B w_n$.

The relative value of time and money depends on wage in the same way in these two specifications. The question therefore arises: How are the two specifications different, or are they essentially the same? Does it matter which specification the researcher uses?

To address this question, the neoclassical theory of the tradeoff between goods and leisure is used to derive representative utility for workers' mode choice models. It is shown through this derivation that the two specifications have quite different implications regarding the worker's tradeoff between goods and leisure and that the shape of the worker's indifference mapping for goods and leisure determines the manner in which wage should enter representative utility.

Under the standard treatment of the goods/leisure tradeoff, a worker chooses how many hours to work and in doing so determines how many goods he can consume and how much leisure he has. For every extra hour worked, the worker has one less hour of leisure but can purchase more goods with the money earned in that hour. The worker values both goods and leisure and has a utility function that reflects his preferences regarding various combinations of goods and leisure. The worker chooses the amount to work that maximizes his utility subject to the constraints that (1) his leisure time is necessarily the total time available (24 hours per day) minus the amount worked and (2) the value of the goods he consumes is equal to the value of his wage earnings plus any unearned income.

The standard theory is expanded as follows to allow for the worker choosing a mode to work as well as the number of hours to work. Let the utility function be $U = U(G, L)$, where G is goods and L is leisure. Assuming the price index for goods is constant and normalized to one, the worker faces the constraints that

$$G = V + wW - c;$$

$$L = T - W - t;$$

where V is unearned income (i.e., not related to amount worked), W is the number of hours worked, w is the hourly wage rate, c is the cost of travel to work (which takes values c_i for each mode i), T is the total number of hours available, and t is the time required for travel to work (which takes value t_i for each mode).

We can determine the number of hours that the worker would choose to work **conditional** upon a particular mode being used to travel to work, and then examine the choice of mode. Given mode i, the worker chooses the number of hours to work that maximizes U subject to

$$G = V + w \cdot W - c_i; \tag{2.5}$$

$$L = T - W - t_i. \tag{2.6}$$

Substituting the maximizing value of W into U gives the utility that could be obtained given that mode i is chosen, labeled U_i^*. The worker then chooses the mode with the highest U_i^*.

Let us consider two polar cases for the $U(G, L)$. We shall find that the two specifications of representative utility used in mode choice models arise from these two cases.

CASE A: LET $U = \alpha_1 \log G + \alpha_2 L$ With this utility function, the worker will respond to additional unearned income by reducing the number of hours worked and not by consuming additional goods (to be shown as an intermediate result).

Substituting the constraints (2.5) and (2.6) into the utility function, we have

$$U_i = \alpha_1 \log(V + wW - c_i) + \alpha_2(T - W - t_i). \tag{2.7}$$

Maximizing U_i with respect to W,

$$\partial U_i/\partial W = \alpha_1 w/(V + wW - c_i) - \alpha_2 = 0,$$

so that the utility maximizing number of hours to work is

$$W = (\alpha_1/\alpha_2) + (c_i/w) - (V/w). \tag{2.8}$$

Substituting this into (2.5), we know that the utility maximizing amount of goods consumed is

$$G = V + w((\alpha_1/\alpha_2) + (c_i/w) - (V/w)) - c_i = w\alpha_1/\alpha_2.$$

Note that utility maximizing G does not vary with unearned income V, but that utility maximizing W decreases with V, implying that if a worker with the utility function given above were given additional unearned income, he would respond by reducing his work hours (i.e., increasing leisure) and not increasing consumption.

Substituting the utility maximizing W into the utility function (i.e., substituting (2.8) into (2.7)) gives

$$U_i^* = \alpha_1 \log(V + w((\alpha_1/\alpha_2) + (c_i/w) - (V/w)) - c_i)$$

$$+ \alpha_2(T - (\alpha_1/\alpha_2) - (c_i/w) + (V/w) - t_i)$$

$$= \alpha_1 \log(w\alpha_1/\alpha_2) + \alpha_2 T - \alpha_1 + (\alpha_2 V/w) - \alpha_2((c_i/w) + t_i).$$

In the choice of mode, all terms that do not vary over i drop out (since only difference in utility matter), and so

$$U_i^* = -\alpha_2((c_i/w) + t_i).$$

In this case, the correct specification of representative utility is for cost to be divided by wage and time not to be interacted.

CASE B: LET $U = \alpha_1 G + \alpha_2 \log L$ Using analogous steps to those for case A, we can show that (1) this U implies that the worker would consume all additional unearned income in goods and would not reduce the number of hours worked at all and (2) the maximum utility that the worker can receive conditional upon mode i is

$$U_i^* = \alpha_1 V + \alpha_1 Tw - \alpha_2 - \alpha_1(t_i w + c_i) + \alpha_2 \log((\alpha_2/\alpha_1)w).$$

The representative utility in the choice of mode includes only those terms that vary over modes and therefore takes the form

$$U_i^* = -\alpha_1(t_i w + c_i);$$

that is, time is multiplied by wage and cost is not interacted.

These two cases show that if the researcher believes that a worker would respond to additional unearned income by working fewer hours (i.e., that $U = \alpha_1 \log G + \alpha_2 L$ reflects workers' preferences), then he should enter cost divided by wage. On the other hand, if he feels that workers would purchase additional goods and not reduce work hours (i.e. if $U = \alpha_1 G + \alpha_2 \log L$), then he should enter time multiplied by wage.

Nonlinear-in-Parameters Representative Utility

Thus far in this section, representative utility has been assumed to be linear in parameters. This assumption is maintained in the great majority of applications. Since, under fairly general conditions, any parametric function can be approximated arbitrarily closely by a function that is linear in parameters, the assumption does not necessarily introduce significant errors.

In some situations, however, it is useful to specify representative utility as not being linear in parameters. Estimation is more difficult and computer routines are not as widely available for logit models with nonlinear-in-parameters representative utility. However, the additional accuracy or information obtained might warrant the additional effort and expense.

Such cases arise when the form of representative utility can be determined theoretically and contains parameters that enter nonlinearly but nevertheless are interesting or important to estimate. Two examples will illustrate this point.

Example 1   In the previous example concerning the goods/leisure tradeoff, the conclusion was reached that (1) if the researcher believed that workers would respond to additional unearned income by reducing the amount they worked but not consuming more goods, then representative utility in a mode choice model should be $-\alpha_1((c_i/w) + t_i)$, where c_i and t_i are the time and cost of mode i, respectively, and w is the wage of the worker; however, (2) if the researcher felt that workers would consume any additional income in goods and not work less, then the appropriate representative utility is $-\alpha_1(c_i + wt_i)$.

It is probably the case, however, that neither of these two extreme situations accurately describe workers' behavior. If given additional unearned income, workers would probably consume somewhat more goods and reduce somewhat the number of hours they worked. The same type of analysis as given above for the extreme cases can be used to construct a more realistic in-between case. In particular, suppose, using the same notation, that workers' preferences regarding goods and leisure are represented by a utility function of the form

$$U = (1 - \beta)\log G + \beta \log L.$$

With this utility function, workers respond to additional unearned income by consuming more goods and working less. It can be shown (see Train and McFadden, 1978, for details) that the representative utility entering a mode choice model, given this utility function for goods and leisure, is

$$U_i = \alpha((c_i/w^\beta) + w^{1-\beta}t_i).$$

That is, the cost of travel is divided by w^β and travel time is multiplied by $w^{1-\beta}$. This is a generalization of the polar cases described, since (1) as β approaches one, U_i becomes $-\alpha((c_i/w) + t_i)$, and (2) as β approaches zero, U_i becomes $-\alpha(c_i + wt_i)$. Estimating the general form of U_i, even though β enters nonlinearly, is valuable since it is more realistic on theoretical grounds and the estimated value of β provides information on workers' preference mapping for goods and leisure.

Example 2 Logit models have been used to describe urban travelers' choice of destination conditional upon their deciding to take a trip within the metropolitan area in which they live. Generally, the metropolitan area is partitioned into zones, and models are specified for the probability that a person taking a trip within the city will choose to go to a particular zone. Representative utility for each zone depends in these models on the time and cost of travel to the zone plus a variety of variables, such as residential population and retail employment in the zone, that reflect reasons that travelers would want to visit the zone. These latter variables are called "attraction" variables; label them by the vector a_i for zone i. Since it is these attraction variables that give rise to parameters entering nonlinearly, assume for simplicity that representative utility depends only on these variables, so that

$$V_{in} = f(a_i, \beta),$$

where β is a vector of parameters.

The difficulty in specifying representative utility (that is, in determining f) comes in recognizing that, since zonal definitions are largely arbitrary, an accurate model would not be sensitive to different zonal definitions. In particular, if two zones are combined, it would be desirable for the model to predict a probability of choosing the combined zone that is equal to the sum of the probabilities that it predicted of choosing each of the two original zones. This consideration places restrictions on the form that V_{in} can take. Consider zones i and k, which, when combined, are labeled zone c. Since population and employment in the combined zone is the sum of that in the two original zones, we have $a_c = a_i + a_k$. Also, in order for the model to give the same probabilities for choosing these zones before and after merger, V_{in} must be specified such that

$$P_{in} + P_{kn} = P_{cn};$$

$$\left(e^{V_{in}} + e^{V_{kn}}\right) \bigg/ \left(e^{V_{in}} + e^{V_{kn}} + \sum_{\substack{j \in J \\ j \neq i,k}} e^{V_{jn}}\right) = \left(e^{V_{cn}}\right) \bigg/ \left(e^{V_{cn}} + \sum_{\substack{j \in J \\ j \neq i,k}} e^{V_{jn}}\right).$$

This equality holds only if

$$\exp(V_{in}) + \exp(V_{kn}) = \exp(V_{cn}). \tag{2.9}$$

If we let $V_{in} = \ln(\beta a_i)$ for all i, then relation (2.9) holds given that $a_i + a_k = a_c$.

Therefore, to specify a destination choice model that is not sensitive to the definition of zones, representative utility must be specified with parameters inside a log operation. Special computer routines have been written to estimate such parameters.

2.4   Derivatives and Elasticities of Choice Probabilities

Since choice probabilities are a function of observed variables, it is often useful to know the extent to which these probabilities change in response to a change in some observed factor. For example, in a household's choice of make and model of car to buy, a natural question is to what extent will the probability of choosing a given car increase if the vehicle's fuel efficiency is improved. From a competing manufacturers point of view, a related question is to what extent will the probability of choosing a given car decrease if the fuel efficiency of a competing make and model improves.

To address these questions, derivatives of the choice probabilities are calculated. The change in the probability of choosing alternative i given a change in an observed factor, y_{in}, entering the representative utility of alternative i (and holding the representative utility of other alternatives constant) is

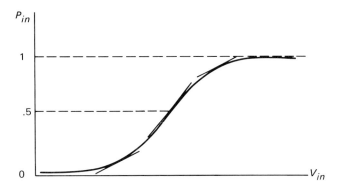

Figure 2.2
Slope of the logit curve.

$$\frac{\partial P_{in}}{\partial y_{in}} = \frac{\partial \left[(e^{V_{in}})(\sum_{j \in J_n} e^{V_{jn}})^{-1} \right]}{\partial y_{in}}$$

$$= \left(\frac{\partial V_{in}}{\partial y_{in}} \right)(e^{V_{in}})(\sum e^{V_{jn}})^{-1} - (e^{V_{in}})(\sum e^{V_{jn}})^{-2}(e^{V_{in}}) \left(\frac{\partial V_{in}}{\partial y_{in}} \right)$$

$$= \frac{\partial V_{in}}{\partial y_{in}}(P_{in} - P_{in}^2)$$

$$= \left(\frac{\partial V_{in}}{\partial y_{in}} \right) P_{in}(1 - P_{in}).$$

Usually V_{in} is linear in the observed variables, with parameters as coefficients. If the coefficient of y_{in} is the scalar β_y, then $\partial V_{in}/\partial y_{in} = \beta_y$ and $\partial P_{in}/\partial y_{in} = \beta_y P_{in}(1 - P_{in})$. This derivative is particularly easy to evaluate. Note that, since β_y is constant, the derivative is largest when $P_{in} = 1 - P_{in}$, which occurs when $P_{in} = 1/2$, and becomes smaller as P_{in} approaches zero or one. This fact is a natural result of the sigmoid shape of the logit function. Consider figure 2.2. The derivative of the choice probability at any level of y_{in} is the slope of the probability curve at that point. This slope is obviously highest at $P_{in} = 1/2$ and becomes lower as P_{in} moves in either direction away from 1/2.

Stated intuitively, the effect of a change in an observed variable is highest when the choice probabilities indicate a high degree of uncertainty regarding the choice; as the choice becomes more certain (i.e., the probabilities approach zero or one), the effect of a given change in an observed variable lessens.

One can also determine the extent to which the probability of choosing a particular alternative changes when an observed variable relating to **another** alternative changes. Let y_{jn} denote an attribute of alternative j (e.g., the fuel efficiency of vehicle j). How does the probability of choosing alternative i change as the y_{jn} increases?

$$\frac{\partial P_{in}}{\partial y_{jn}} = \frac{\partial (e^{V_{in}})(\sum_{j \in J_n} e^{V_{jn}})^{-1}}{\partial y_{jn}}$$

$$= -(e^{V_{in}})(\sum e^{V_{jn}})^{-2}(e^{V_{jn}})\frac{\partial V_{jn}}{\partial y_{jn}}$$

$$= -(\partial V_{jn}/\partial y_{jn})P_{in}P_{jn}.$$

In the case of V_{jn} being linear in observed variables, with a scalar coefficient β_y for y_{jn}, then

$$\partial P_{in}/\partial y_{jn} = -\beta_y P_{in}P_{jn}.$$

If y_{jn} is a desirable attribute such that β_y is positive, then increasing y_{jn} decreases the probability of choosing each alternative other than j. Furthermore, the decrease in probability is proportional to the value of the probability before y_{jn} was changed.

This latter fact is a property of logit models that can be undesirable in some situations. For example, consider a traveler's choice among auto, bus, and rail. If the probability of taking an auto is .60 and bus and rail each have a .20 probability, then an improvement in the attributes of bus travel (e.g., a reduction in its price) would reduce the probability of taking an auto three times as much as the probability of going by rail. If in reality most of the additional bus probability is drawn from the rail mode, then the standard logit model is inappropriate. The underlying problem in this situation is the independence of irrelevant alternatives (IIA) property of logit models, which is discussed in section 2.2. The solution is to take one of the corrective measures indicated in that discussion or to utilize a model, such as probit or GEV, as described in chapters 3 and 4, respectively, that does not exhibit the IIA property.

A logically necessary aspect of derivatives of choice probabilities is that, when an observed variable changes, the changes in the choice probabilities sum to zero. This is a necessary consequence of the fact that the probabilities must sum to one before and after the change; it is demonstrated as follows:

$$\sum_{i \in J_n} \frac{\partial P_{in}}{\partial y_{jn}} = \left(\frac{\partial V_{jn}}{\partial y_{jn}}\right) P_{jn}(1 - P_{jn}) + \sum_{\substack{i \in J_n \\ i \neq j}} \left(-\frac{\partial V_{jn}}{\partial y_{jn}}\right) P_{jn} P_{in}$$

$$= \left(\frac{\partial V_{jn}}{\partial y_{jn}}\right) P_{jn} \left[(1 - P_{jn}) - \sum_{\substack{i \in J_n \\ i \neq j}} P_{in}\right]$$

$$= \left(\frac{\partial V_{jn}}{\partial y_{jn}}\right) P_{jn} [(1 - P_{jn}) - (1 - P_{jn})]$$

$$= 0.$$

In practical terms, if one alternative is improved so that its probability of being chosen increases, the additional probability is necessarily "drawn" from other alternatives. That is, to increase the probability of one alternative necessitates decreasing the probability of another alternative. While obvious, this fact is often forgotten by planners who want to improve demand for one alternative without reducing demand for other alternatives.[3]

Economists often measure response by elasticities rather than derivatives, since elasticities are normalized for the variables' units. An elasticity is the percent change in one variable that is associated with a percent change in another variable. The elasticity of choice probabilities with respect to observed factors affecting the probabilities are now given. The elasticity of P_{in} with respect to y_{in}, a variable entering the utility of alternative i, is

$$E_{iy_i} = (\partial P_{in}/\partial y_{in})(y_{in}/P_{in})$$

$$= (\partial V_{in}/\partial y_{in}) P_{in}(1 - P_{in})(y_{in}/P_{in})$$

$$= (\partial V_{in}/\partial y_{in}) y_{in}(1 - P_{in}).$$

If representative utility is linear in y_{in}, with coefficient β_y, then

$$E_{iy_i} = \beta_y y_{in}(1 - P_{in}).$$

The elasticity of P_{in} with respect to a variable entering alternative $j \neq i$, called a cross-elasticity, is calculated as

$$E_{iy_j} = -(\partial V_{jn}/\partial y_{jn}) y_{jn} P_{jn},$$

which in the case of linear utility reduces to

$$E_{iy_j} = -\beta_y y_{jn} P_{jn}.$$

2.5   Average Probabilities, Derivatives, and Elasticities

Different individuals facing the same set of alternatives will, in general, have different representative utility for each alternative, because the characteristics of each alternative vary over people (e.g., the time required to travel to work by auto varies by place of home and place of work) and because individuals' characteristics (such as income, age, etc.) vary in the population. Decisionmakers with different representative utility for each alternative will have different choice probabilities. And, given that derivatives and elasticities depend on the choice probabilities, different individuals will be predicted to respond differently to changes in factors entering representative utility.

Usually a researcher is interested in the average probability or average response within a population, rather than the probability or response of any one individual. Methods for predicting population behavior with qualitative choice models are discussed in detail in chapter 6. It is useful at this point, however, to introduce the most straightforward and widely used method and to warn against an erroneous method that is nevertheless common.

Suppose the researcher has a random or stratified random[4] sample of individuals drawn from a population. Aggregate, or population, variables are predicted by taking the weighted average of the variables calculated for each individual. For example, to calculate the average probability in the population for a particular alternative, choice probabilities are calculated for each individual on the basis of the individual's characteristics and the characteristics of the alternatives as faced by the individual. The average probability for alternative i is then estimated as

$$\bar{P}_i = \sum_n w_n P_{in},$$

where w_n is sampling weight associated with individual n, and the summation is over all sampled individuals. If the sample is purely random, then w_n is the same for all sampled individuals and equals $1/N$, where N is the sample size. For stratified random samples, w_n varies over strata.

The number of individuals in the population predicted to choose alternative i is estimated as the average probability for alternative i times the population size:

$$N_i = M\bar{P}_i,$$

where M is the number of decisionmakers in the population and N_i is the estimated number that will choose alternative i. Average derivatives and elasticities are calculated similarly as the weighted average of individual derivatives and elasticities.

An alternative method of estimating average probabilities and responses is common but not consistent. Instead of calculating the probabilities and responses for a sample of decisionmakers and then taking averages, this alternative approach is to calculate probabilities and responses for an **average** decisionmaker and consider these to be in some way representative of average population behavior. For example, consider a mode choice model in which each traveler chooses between auto and transit on the basis of the cost and time associated with each. A consistent way to estimate the average probability of auto is to determine the times and costs faced by each person in a sample, calculate the probability of choosing auto for each person, and take the weighted average of these probabilities. The simpler, but inconsistent method, is to calculate the average cost and time associated with each mode and determine the probability of choosing auto given these average costs and times.

The inconsistency of this approach results from the fact that the choice probabilities, derivatives, and elasticities are nonlinear functions of the observed data and, as is well known, the average value of a nonlinear function over a range of data is not equal to the value of the function evaluated at the average of the data. The point can be made visually. Consider figure 2.3, which gives the probabilities of choosing a particular alternative for two individuals with representative utility for this alternative of a and b (assuming the representative utility of other alternatives is the same for the two individuals). The average probability is the average of the probabilities for the two individuals, namely, $(P_a + P_b)/2$. The probability evaluated at the average representative utility is given by the point on the logit curve above $(a + b)/2$. As shown for this case, the average probability is above the probability at the average representative utility. In general, the probability evaluated at the average utility underestimates the average probability when the individuals' choice probabilities are low and overestimates when they are high.

Estimating average responses by calculating derivatives and elasticities at the average representative utility is usually even more problematic than for average probabilities. Consider figure 2.4, depicting two individuals with representative utility a and b. The derivative of the choice probability

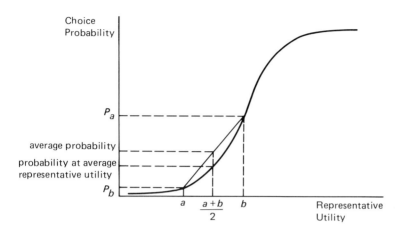

Figure 2.3
Difference between average probability and probability calculated at average representative utility.

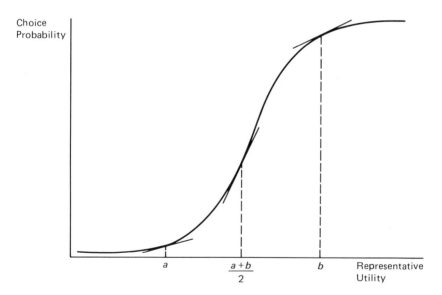

Figure 2.4
Difference between average response and response calculated at average representative utility.

for a change in representative utility is small for both of these individuals (the slope of the logit curve above a and b). Consequently, the average derivative is also small. However, the derivative at the average representative utility is very high (the slope above $(a + b)/2$). Estimating average responses in this way can be seriously misleading. In fact, Talvitie (1976) has found, in a mode choice situation, that elasticities at the average representative utility can be as much as two to three times greater or less than the average of individual elasticities.

2.6   Estimation

In order to calculate the choice probabilities for a particular decisionmaker the researcher must (unless a priori information is utilized) estimate the value of the parameter vector β. If the researcher does not intend to predict decisionmakers' choices, he might nevertheless be interested in knowing the value of β for other reasons. For example, suppose an auto manufacturer considers the utility consumers obtain from a make and model of vehicle to be $-\beta_1 \, \text{PP} + \beta_2 \, \text{FE}$ plus a term for unobserved factors, where PP is the purchase price of the vehicles and FE is its fuel efficiency. This manufacturer could use information on the relative value of β_1 and β_2 to decide whether to incorporate into the vehicle that he produces a device that would increase its fuel efficiency but also increase its price.

Standard Estimation on Exogenous Sample

Assume that the researcher observes the choices of a sample of decision-makers, along with the characteristics of each decisionmaker and each alternative faced by the decisionmaker. Consider first the situation in which the sample is exogenously drawn, that is, is either random or stratified random with the strata defined on factors that are exogenous to the choice being analyzed. If the sampling procedure is related to the choice being analyzed (for example, if mode choice is being examined and the sample is drawn by selecting people on buses and pooling them with people selected at toll booths), then more complex estimation procedures are generally required, as described later in this section.

The parameter vector β is estimated by maximum likelihood methods, which can be described as follows for exogenously chosen samples. (For readers who are unfamiliar with maximum likelihood estimation, a straightforward discussion is given on pages 69–71 of the widely used econometrics text by Pindyck and Rubinfeld, 1981.) Consider one sampled decisionmaker, labeled n. The probability of person n choosing the alternative that he was actually observed to choose is

$$\prod_{i \in J_n} P_{in}^{\delta_{in}},$$

where δ_{in} is one if person n chose alternative i, and zero otherwise. Note that since $\delta_{in} = 0$ for all nonchosen alternatives and $P_{in}^0 = 1$, this term is simply the probability of the chosen alternative.

Consider now the entire sample. Since each decisionmaker's choice is independent of that of other decisionmakers, the probability of each person in the sample choosing the alternative that he was observed actually to choose is

$$L = \prod_{n \in N} \prod_{i \in J_n} P_{in}^{\delta_{in}}, \tag{2.10}$$

where N is the set of decisionmakers in the sample. This expression is simply the probability of each person's chosen alternative multiplied across all people in the sample.

Each P_{in} in expression (2.10) is a function of β and the observed data. Holding the observed data fixed, L can therefore be considered a function of β and written $L(\beta)$. In particular, it is the likelihood function for β, giving for each value of β the probability that the sampled decisionmakers would choose the alternatives that they actually did choose. The value of β that gives the highest such probability, that is, that maximizes the likelihood function, is called the maximum likelihood estimate of β. Under fairly general conditions, this estimator is consistent and efficient, as is usually the case with maximum likelihood estimators (see McFadden, 1973).

Rather than deal with the likelihood function itself, it is usually easier to maximize the log of the likelihood function. (Since the log operation is a monotonic function, the value of β that maximizes $L(\beta)$ will also maximize the log of $L(\beta)$.) This log likelihood function, designated LL, is written as

$$LL(\beta) = \sum_{n \in N} \sum_{i \in J_n} \delta_{in} \log P_{in}. \tag{2.11}$$

Recalling that δ_{in} is zero for nonchosen alternatives, $LL(\beta)$ is simply the log of the probability of the chosen alternative of each person, summed over all sampled decisionmakers. The estimate of β is that which maximizes this sum. (Note that, since L is a probability and consequently cannot exceed one, LL is always negative, since the log of one is zero. Therefore, maximizing LL is the same as minimizing its magnitude, a point that often causes confusion.) Several computer software packages are available that perform this maximization specifically in the context of logit models.

Given that the estimated value of β is that which maximizes $LL(\beta)$, we can easily demonstrate that the estimated values of alternative-specific constants are those that equate the average probability for each alternative with the share of decisionmakers in the sample who actually chose that alternative. For ease of notation, consider a binary choice situation in which the representative utility of choosing the first alternative is zero by normalization and the representative utility of the second alternative is $\alpha + V_n$, where α is a constant and V_n varies over n (with its dependence on parameters suppressed in this notation). Then

$$P_{1n} = \frac{1}{1 + e^{\alpha + V_n}} \quad \text{and} \quad P_{2n} = \frac{e^{\alpha + V_n}}{1 + e^{\alpha + V_n}}.$$

Let δ_n equal one if person n chose alternative one and zero if person n chose alternative two (hence, $1 - \delta_n$ equals one if alternative two is chosen). The log likelihood function in this case is

$$LL = \sum_n [\delta_n \log P_{1n} + (1 - \delta_n) \log P_{2n}]$$

$$= \sum_n \left[\delta_n \log \left(\frac{1}{1 + e^{\alpha + V_n}} \right) + (1 - \delta_n) \log \left(\frac{e^{\alpha + V_n}}{1 + e^{\alpha + V_n}} \right) \right]$$

$$= \sum_n [-\delta_n \log(1 + e^{\alpha + V_n}) + (1 - \delta_n)(\alpha + V_n)$$

$$\quad - (1 - \delta_n) \log(1 + e^{\alpha + V_n})]$$

$$= \sum_n [(1 - \delta_n)(\alpha + V_n) - \log(1 + e^{\alpha + V_n})].$$

To maximize LL with respect to α, we take the derivative of LL with respect to α, equate the derivative to zero, and solve for α:

$$\frac{\partial LL}{\partial \alpha} = \sum_n \left[(1 - \delta_n) - \frac{e^{\alpha + V_n}}{1 + e^{\alpha + V_n}} \right]$$

$$= \sum_n [(1 - \delta_n) - P_{2n}]$$

$$= \sum_n [(1 - \delta_n) - (1 - P_{1n})] = \sum_n P_{1n} - \delta_n = 0.$$

Therefore,

$$\sum_n \delta_n = \sum_n P_{1n},$$

and

$$\frac{1}{N}\sum_n \delta_n = \frac{1}{N}\sum_n P_{1n},$$

where N is the total sample size. That is, the value of α that maximizes the log likelihood function (that is, the estimated value of α) is that which equates the average probability for each alternative $((1/N)\sum P_{1n})$ with the share of sampled decisionmakers who chose that alternative $((1/N)\sum \delta_n)$.

Though the proof is more tedious, the same result applies in the multinomial case. That is, if a constant is included in the representative utility of each alternative (except, of course, for one alternative, whose constant is normalized to zero; see section 2.3), then the estimated values of these constants are such that the average probability for each alternative equals the share of sampled decisionmakers who actually chose that alternative. This fact has considerable practical importance—for example (see in section 2.2), the mitigation of the ill effects of the independence from irrelevant alternatives property not holding for the choice situation being examined.

Estimation on a Subset of Alternatives

In some situations, the number of alternatives facing the decisionmaker is so large that estimating model parameters is very expensive or even impossible (due perhaps to core capacity limitations of the researcher's computer). As mentioned in the discussion of the independence from irrelevant alternatives property, estimation can be performed on a subset of alternatives and not lose consistency. For example, a researcher examining a choice situation that involves 100 alternatives can estimate on a subset of 10 alternatives for each sampled decisionmaker, with the person's chosen alternative included as well as 9 alternatives randomly selected from the remaining 99.

In general, estimation with a subset of alternatives for each sampled decisionmaker proceeds as if each decisionmaker actually faced only the alternatives in the subset. Denote the subset of alternatives selected for person n as K_n, which can be the same or different for different persons. Label the set of sampled individuals who actually chose an alternative within their subset as M. A "quasi" log likelihood function is constructed as

$$QLL(\beta) = \sum_{n \in M} \sum_{i \in K_n} \delta_{in} \log \tilde{P}_{in},$$

where

$$\tilde{P}_{in} = \frac{e^{V_{in}}}{\sum_{j \in K_n} e^{V_{jn}}}.$$

This is the same as the log likelihood function given in equation (2.11) except (1) the subset of alternatives K_n replaces, for each sampled person, the complete set J_n in both the calculation of the probabilities and in the summation within the function, and (2) only the sampled persons in subset M are included in the summation rather than all sampled persons (that is, those whose chosen alternative is not in their subset of alternatives are excluded). Since, in accordance with the independence from irrelevant alternatives property, relative probabilities within a subset of alternatives are unaffected by exclusion of alternatives not in the subset, maximization of $QLL(\beta)$ provides a consistent estimate of β. However, since information is excluded from $QLL(\beta)$ that $LL(\beta)$ incorporates (i.e., information on alternatives not in each subset and on decisionmakers whose chosen alternatives are not in their subsets), the value of β that maximizes $QLL(\beta)$ is not an efficient estimator.

Estimation with Choice Based Samples

In some situations, a sample drawn on the basis of exogenous factors would include few people who have chosen particular alternatives. For example, in the choice of water heaters, a random sample of housholds in most areas would include only a small proportion who had chosen solar water heating systems. If the researcher is particularly interested in factors that affect the penetration of solar devices, estimation on a random sample of households would require a very large total sample size.

In situations such as these, the researcher might instead select the sample, or part of the sample, on the basis of the choice being analyzed. For example, the researcher examining water heaters might supplement a random sample of households with households that are known (perhaps through sales records at stores if the researcher has access to these records) to have recently installed solar water heater systems.

Samples selected on the basis of decisionmakers' choices can be purely choice based or a hybrid of choice based and exogenous. For a purely choice based sample, the population is divided into those that choose each alternative and decisionmakers within each group are drawn randomly, though at different rates. For example, a researcher who is examining the choice of home location and is interested in identifying the factors that contribute to people choosing one particular community might draw randomly from within that community at the rate of one out of N households, and draw randomly from all other communities at a rate of one out of M, where M is larger than N. A hybrid sample is like the one drawn by the researcher interested in solar water heating, in which an exogenous sample is supplemented with a sample drawn on the basis of the households' choices.

Estimation of model parameters with samples drawn at least partially on the basis of the decisionmaker's choice is fairly complex in general, and varies with the exact form of the sampling procedure. For interested readers, details are given by Ben-Akiva and Lerman (1985).

One result, however, is particularly significant, since it allows researchers to use choice based samples without becoming involved in complex estimation procedures. This result can be stated as follows. If the researcher is using a purely choice based sample and includes an alternative-specific constant in the representative utility for each alternative, then estimating the model parameters **as if** the sample were exogenous produces consistent estimates for all the model parameters except the alternative-specific constants. Furthermore, these constants are biased by a known factor and can therefore be adjusted so that the adjusted constants are consistent. In particular, the expectation of the estimated constant for alternative i, labeled $\hat{\alpha}_i$, is related to the true constant α_i^*,

$$E(\hat{\alpha}_i) = \alpha_i^* - \ln(A_i/S_i),$$

where A_i is the proportion of decisionmakers in the population that choose alternative i and S_i is the proportion in the choice based sample that choose alternative i. Consequently, if A_i is known (that is, if population shares are known for each alternative), then a consistent estimate of the alternative-specific constant is the estimated constant $\hat{\alpha}_i$ plus $\ln(A_i/S_i)$.

2.7 Goodness of Fit

A statistic, called the likelihood ratio index, is often used with qualitative choice models to measure how well the model fits the data. Stated more precisely, the statistic measures how well the model, with its estimated parameters, performs compared with a model in which all the parameters are zero (which is usually equivalent to having no model at all). This comparison is made on the basis of the log likelihood function, evaluated at both the estimated parameters and at zero for all parameters.

The likelihood ratio index is defined as

$$\rho = 1 - (LL(\beta^*)/LL(0)),$$

where $LL(\beta^*)$ is the value of the log likelihood function at the estimated parameters and $LL(0)$ is its value when all the parameters are set equal to zero. If the estimated parameters do no better, in terms of the likelihood function, than zero parameters (that is, if the estimated model is no better than no model), then $LL(\beta^*) = LL(0)$ and so $\rho = 0$. This is the lowest value that ρ can take (since if $LL(\beta^*)$ is less than $LL(0)$, then β^* would not be the maximum likelihood estimate).

At the other extreme, suppose the estimated model were so good that each sampled decisionmaker's choice could be predicted perfectly. In this case, the likelihood function at the estimated parameters would be one, since the probability of observing the choices that were actually made is one. And, since the log of one is zero, the log likelihood function would be zero at the estimated parameters. With $LL(\beta^*) = 0$, $\rho = 1$. This is the highest value that ρ can take.

In summary, the likelihood ratio index ranges from zero, when the estimated parameters are no better than zero parameters, to one, when the estimated parameters allow for perfectly predicting the choices of the sampled decisionmakers.

It is important to note that the likelihood ratio index is not at all similar in its interpretation to the R-squared used in regression, despite both statistics having the same range. R-squared indicates the percent of the variation in the dependent variable that is "explained" by the estimated model. The likelihood ratio has no intuitively interpretable meaning for values between the extremes of zero and one. It is the percent increase in the log likelihood function above the value taken at zero parameters (since $\rho = 1 - (LL(\beta^*)/LL(0)) = (LL(0) - LL(\beta^*))/LL(0))$. However, the meaning of such a percent increase is not clear. In comparing two models estimated on the same data and with the same set of alternatives (such that $LL(0)$ is the same for both models), it is usually valid to say that the model with the higher ρ fits the data better. But this is saying no more than that increasing the value of the log likelihood function is preferable. Two models estimated on samples that are not identical or with a different set of alternatives for any sampled decisionmaker cannot be compared via their likelihood ratio index values.

Another goodness-of-fit statistic that is sometimes used, but is of even less value than the likelihood ratio index, is the "percent correctly predicted." This statistic is calculated by identifying for each sampled decisionmaker the alternative with the highest probability, based on the estimated model, and determining whether or not this was the alternative that the decision-maker actually chose; the percent of sampled decisionmakers for which the highest probability alternative and the chosen alternative are the same is called the percent correctly predicted.

This statistic, while popular in the early applications of qualitative choice models, incorporates a notion that is opposed to the meaning of proba-bilities and the purpose of specifying choice probabilities. The statistic is based on the idea that the decisionmaker is predicted by the researcher to choose the alternative for which the model gives the highest probability. Recall from section 1.3, however, that the researcher does not have enough information to predict the decisionmaker's choice; he has only enough information to state the probability that the decisionmaker will choose each alternative. In stating choice probabilities, the researcher is saying that if the choice situation were repeated numerous times, each alternative would be chosen a certain proportion of the time. This is quite different from saying that the alternative with the highest probability will be chosen each time.

An example might be useful. Suppose an estimated model predicts choice probabilities of .75 and .25 in a two-alternative situation. Those proba-bilities mean that if the situation were repeated 100 times, the researcher's best predictions of how many times each alternative would be chosen are 75 and 25. However, the percent correctly predicted statistic is based on the notion that the best prediction in each situation is the alternative with the highest probability. With 100 repetitions, this notion would predict that one alternative would be chosen all 100 times and the other alternative never chosen. This misses the point of probabilities and seems to imply that the researcher has perfect information.

2.8   Hypothesis Testing

A likelihood ratio test is a very general test that is used in nearly all contexts. (The one major exception is for testing hypotheses on individual parameters for which standard t-tests are performed.) Consider a null hypothesis H that can be expressed as constraints on the values of the parameters. Two of the most common such hypotheses are (1) several parameters being zero, and (2) two or more parameters being equal to each other. The constrained maximum likelihood estimate of the parameters (labeled β^H) is that value of β that gives the highest value of LL without violating the constraints of the null hypothesis H. For example, if H is the hypothesis that the first two elements of N-tuple β are equal, then β^H is the value of β that, out of the set of all N-tuples whose first two elements are equal, results in the highest value of the likelihood function.

Define the ratio of likelihoods, $R = L(\beta^H)/L(\beta^*)$, where $L(\beta^H)$ is the (constrained) maximum value of the likelihood function under the null hypothesis H and $L(\beta^*)$ is the unconstrained maximum of the likelihood function. As in likelihood ratio tests for models other than those of qualitative choice, the test statistic defined as $-2 \log R$ is distributed chi-squared with degrees of freedom equal to the number of restrictions implied by the null hypothesis. Therefore, the test statistic is $-2(LL(\beta^H) - LL(\beta^*))$. Since the log likelihood is always negative, this is simply two times the (magnitude of the) difference between the constrained and unconstrained maximums of the log likelihood function. If this value exceeds the critical value of chi-squared with the appropriate degrees of freedom, then the null hypothesis is rejected.

Examples

NULL HYPOTHESIS I: THE COEFFICIENTS OF SEVERAL EXPLANATORY VARIABLES ARE ZERO   To test this hypothesis, estimate the model twice: once with these explanatory variables included and a second time without them (since excluding the variables forces their coefficients to be zero). Observe the maximum value of the log likelihood function for each estimation; two times the difference in these maximum values is the value of the test statistic. Compare the test statistic with the critical value of chi-squared with degrees of freedom equal to the number of explanatory variables excluded from the second estimation.

NULL HYPOTHESIS II: THE COEFFICIENTS OF THE FIRST TWO VARIABLES ARE THE SAME   To test this hypothesis, estimate the model twice: once with each of the explanatory variables entered separately including the first two; then with the first two variables replaced by one variable that is the **sum** of the two variables (since summing the variables forces their coefficients to be equal). Observe the maximum value of the log likelihood function for each of the estimations. Multiply the difference in these maximum values by two and compare this figure with the critical value of chi-squared with one degree of freedom.

2.9 Derivation of Logit Probabilities

It was stated without proof in section 2.1 that if the utility of alternative i is decomposed into observed and unobserved parts $U_{in} = V_{in} + e_{in}$ and each e_{in} is independently identically distributed in accordance with the extreme value distribution, then the choice probabilities have the logit form

$$P_{in} = \frac{e^{V_{in}}}{\sum_j e^{V_{jn}}}$$

This statement is demonstrated as follows.

Under the extreme value distribution, the density function for each e_{in} is

$$\exp(-e_{in}) \cdot \exp(-e^{-e_{in}}),$$

with a cumulative distribution of

$$\exp(-e^{-e_{in}}).$$

The probability that alternative i is chosen is

$$P_{in} = \text{Prob}(V_{in} + e_{in} > V_{jn} + e_{jn}, \text{ for all } j \text{ in } J_n, j \neq i).$$

Rearranging terms within the parentheses, we can write

$$P_{in} = \text{Prob}(e_{jn} < e_{in} + V_{in} - V_{jn}, \text{ for all } j \text{ in } J_n, j \neq i). \tag{2.12}$$

Suppose, for the moment, that e_{in} takes a particular value, say, s. The probability that alternative i is chosen is then the probability that each e_{jn} is less than $s + V_{in} - V_{jn}$, respectively, for all j in $J_n, j \neq i$. The probability that $e_{in} = s$ and, simultaneously, that $e_{jn} < s + V_{in} - V_{jn}$, for all j in $J_n, j \neq i$, is the density of e_{in} evaluated at s times the cumulative distribution for each e_{jn} except e_{in} evaluated at $s + V_{in} - V_{jn}$. From the extreme value distribution, this is

$$e^{-s} \exp(-e^{-s}) \prod_{\substack{j \in J_n \\ j \neq i}} \exp(-e^{-(s+V_{in}-V_{jn})}).$$

Since $V_{in} - V_{in} = 0$, this expression can be rewritten as

$$e^{-s} \prod_{j \in J_n} \exp(-e^{-(s+V_{in}-V_{jn})}). \tag{2.13}$$

The random variable e_{in} need not equal s, however; it can take any value within its range. The right-hand side of equation (2.12) is, therefore, the sum of expression (2.13) over all possible values of s. That is, since e_{in} is continuous, equation (2.12) becomes

$$P_{in} = \int_{s=-\infty}^{\infty} e^{-s} \prod \exp(-e^{-(s+V_{in}-V_{jn})}) \, ds.$$

Our task in deriving the choice probabilities is to evaluate this integral. Collecting terms in the exponent of e,

$$P_{in} = \int_{s=-\infty}^{\infty} e^{-s} \exp\left\{-\sum_{j \in J_n} e^{-(s+V_{in}-V_{jn})}\right\} ds$$

$$= \int_{s=-\infty}^{\infty} e^{-s} \exp\left\{-e^{-s} \sum_{j \in J_n} e^{-(V_{in}-V_{jn})}\right\} ds.$$

Let $e^{-s} = t$. Then $-e^{-s} \, ds = dt$ and $ds = -(dt/t)$. Note that as s approaches infinity, t approaches zero, and as s approaches negative infinity, t becomes infinitely large. Using these new terms,

$$P_{in} = \int_{\infty}^{0} t \exp\left\{-t \cdot \sum_{j \in J_n} e^{-(V_{in}-V_{jn})}\right\} (-dt/t)$$

$$= \int_{0}^{\infty} \exp\left\{-t \cdot \sum_{j \in J_n} e^{-(V_{in}-V_{jn})}\right\} dt$$

$$= \frac{\exp\left\{-t \cdot \sum_{j \in J_n} e^{-(V_{in}-V_{jn})}\right\}}{-\sum_{j \in J_n} e^{-(V_{in}-V_{jn})}} \Bigg|_{0}^{\infty}$$

$$= \frac{1}{\sum_{j \in J_n} e^{-(V_{in}-V_{jn})}} = \frac{e^{V_{in}}}{\sum_{j \in J_n} e^{V_{jn}}},$$

as required.

3 Probit

3.1 Functional Form of Choice Probabilities

The restrictions of the logit model, particularly the IIA property, are due to the assumption that the unobserved components of utility are independently and identically distributed. Let the utility that person n obtains from alternative i, labeled U_{in}, be decomposed into an observed part V_{in} and an unobserved part e_{in} for all i in the choice set J_n. Then, for the logit model, any e_{in} and e_{jn}, $i \neq j$, are assumed to have the same distribution, with the same mean and variance, and also to be uncorrelated. These random variables being uncorrelated means that any factor that the researcher does not observe that affects the utility of alternative i does **not** affect the utility of alternative j. The two terms e_{in} and e_{jn} having the same variance means that the unobserved factors that affect the utility of alternative i have the same variation as the different (due to zero correlation) unobserved factors that affect the utility of alternative j. In the real world, these assumptions will seldom actually hold.

The probit model is derived by relaxing these assumptions about the unobserved components of utility. In particular, these unobserved components are assumed, instead of independent, identical extreme values, to be distributed jointly normal, with a general variance-covariance matrix. The critical change here is not from the extreme value distribution to the normal, since these two distributions for a single random variable are practically the same. The important distinction is that, with the **joint** normal distribution, each e_{in}, for all i in J_n, can have a different variance and can be correlated with other e_{jn}, j in J_n, $j \neq i$.

The probit choice probabilities are derived from the assumption of jointly normal unobserved utility components. As usual, utility is decomposed into observed and unobserved parts:

$$U_{in} = V_{in} + e_{in}, \qquad \text{for all } i \text{ in } J_n.$$

Consider the vector composed of each e_{in} for all i in J_n; label this vector $\tilde{e}_n$. We assume that $\tilde{e}_n$ is distributed normal with a mean vector of zero and variance-covariance matrix denoted Ω_n whose elements are parameters that are either specified a priori or estimated by the researcher. That is, the density function of $\tilde{e}_n$ is

$$\phi(\tilde{e}_n) = (2\pi)^{-\frac{1}{2}m_n}|\Omega_n|^{-\frac{1}{2}}\exp\left[-\tfrac{1}{2}\tilde{e}_n\Omega_n^{-1}\tilde{e}_n\right],$$

where $|\Omega_n|$ is the determinate of Ω_n and m_n is the number of alternatives in J_n.

Recall that the probability of choosing alternative i is the probability that the utility associated with alternative i is higher than that of any other alternative:

$P_{in} = \text{Prob}(V_{in} + e_{in} > V_{jn} + e_{jn}, \text{ for all } j \text{ in } J_n, j \neq i).$

Rearranging,

$P_{in} = \text{Prob}(e_{jn} < e_{in} + V_{in} - V_{jn}, \text{ for all } j \text{ in } J_n, j \neq i).$

To evaluate this expression suppose first that e_{in} is given. Then the right-hand side of this expression is the probability that the random variable e_{jn} is below the known value $e_{in} + V_{in} - V_{jn}$, for all j in $J_n, j \neq i$. That is, for given e_{in}, the expression is simply the cumulative distribution of e_{jn} evaluated at $e_{in} + V_{in} - V_{jn}$, for all j in J_n, j in i. Since a cumulative distribution is the integral of the density function, the probability of choosing alternative i given a particular value of e_{in}, labeled $P_{in}(e_{in})$, is simply the density of the random vector $\tilde{e}_n$ integrated from negative infinity to $e_{in} + V_{in} - V_{jn}$ for each element j in $J_n, j \neq i$:

$$P_{in}(e_{in}) = \int_{e_{1n}=-\infty}^{e_{in}+V_{in}-V_{1n}} \int_{e_{2n}=-\infty}^{e_{in}+V_{in}-V_{2n}}$$
$$\cdots \int_{e_{m_nn}=-\infty}^{e_{in}+V_{in}-V_{m_nn}} \phi(\tilde{e}_n)\, de_{m_nn} \cdots de_{2n}\, de_{1n}, \tag{3.1}$$

where the "$\cdots$" is over all elements e_{jn} in the vector $\tilde{e}_n$ except e_{in}, which is set equal to its given value.

In actuality, the value of e_{in} is not given. Consequently, the probability of choosing alternative i is the probability of choosing it for any given value of e_{in} integrated over all possible values of e_{in}. That is,

$$P_{in} = \int_{e_{in}=-\infty}^{\infty} P_{in}(e_{in})\phi(\tilde{e}_n)\, de_{in}. \tag{3.2}$$

Substituting (3.1) into (3.2) gives

$$P_{in} = \int_{e_{in}=-\infty}^{\infty} \int_{e_{1n}=-\infty}^{e_{in}+V_{in}-V_{1n}} \int_{e_{2n}=-\infty}^{e_{in}+V_{in}-V_{2n}}$$
$$\cdots \int_{e_{m_nn}=-\infty}^{e_{in}+V_{in}-V_{m_nn}} \phi(\tilde{e}_n)\, de_{m_nn} \cdots de_{2n}\, de_{1n}\, de_{in}, \tag{3.3}$$

where both the parameters entering V_{in} and those entering the variance-covariance matrix Ω_n are determined in estimation or specified a priori by the researcher.

The probit choice probabilities being in such complex form is the main disadvantage of the model. In particular, estimation of probit models is very expensive because of the complexity of the choice probabilities. To evaluate a log likelihood function (defined in section 2.6) using these choice probabilities, numerous integrations are required for each sampled decision-maker; and to find the value of the parameters that maximizes the function, these numerous integrals must be evaluated numerous times. Several alternative methods of estimating probit models have been proposed, based on Monte Carlo methods and approximations (see section 3.4 for a discussion of these). However, it still remains that estimating a probit model with more than a few alternatives and a few explanatory variables is prohibitively expensive.

There are situations, however, in which the probit model, if the expense of estimation can be borne, is very useful. Two of these are discussed in the following sections.

3.2 Taste Variation

Suppose utility can be decomposed into a linear-in-parameters part that depends only on observed data, plus an unobserved part. Assume further that the parameters are not fixed, but rather vary randomly over decision-makers. This is represented as follows:

$$U_{in} = \beta_n w_{in} + e_{in};$$
$$\beta_n = \bar{\beta} + \tilde{\beta}_n;$$

where

w_{in} is a vector-valued function of observed data,
β_n is a vector of coefficients of w_{in} for person n, unknown to the researcher,
$\bar{\beta}$ is the mean of β_n over all persons, and
$\tilde{\beta}_n$ is the deviation of the coefficient vector of person n from the mean coefficients (i.e., $\tilde{\beta}_n \equiv \beta_n - \bar{\beta}$).

Substituting the equation for β_n,

$$U_{in} = \bar{\beta} w_{in} + \tilde{\beta}_n w_{in} + e_{in}.$$

The last two terms on the right-hand side are both unobserved (since $\tilde{\beta}_n$ is unobserved); denote their sum as η_{in} to obtain

$$U_{in} = \bar{\beta} w_{in} + \eta_{in}.$$

If both $\tilde{\beta}_n$ and e_{in} are normally distributed, then η_{in} is also normally distributed, and the choice probabilities, stated in terms of $\bar{\beta} w_{in}$, are probit. Estimation of the model provides values for $\bar{\beta}$ and the variance-covariance matrix for η.

For example, consider a two-alternative choice situation in which one explanatory variable enters the representative utility of each alternative. In this case,

$$U_{1n} = \beta_n y_{1n} + e_{1n};$$

$$U_{2n} = \beta_n y_{2n} + e_{2n};$$

where y_{1n} and y_{2n} are the values that the explanatory variable y takes for person n in each of the two alternatives (e.g., y could be the cost of obtaining the alternative). Assume that β_n is normally distributed with mean $\bar{\beta}$ and variance σ_β^2. Assume further that e_{1n} and e_{2n} are independently normally distributed each with zero mean and variance σ_e^2. (The assumption of independence simplifies the example but is not necessary.) With these assumptions, utility can be expressed as

$$U_{1n} = \bar{\beta} y_{1n} + \eta_{1n};$$

$$U_{2n} = \bar{\beta} y_{2n} + \eta_{2n};$$

where η_{1n} and η_{2n} are jointly normally distributed. The η have zero mean:

$$E(\eta_{in}) = E(\tilde{\beta}_n y_{in} + e_{in}) = 0, \qquad i = 1, 2.$$

The variance-covariance matrix for η is determined as follows. The variance of each is

$$V(\eta_{in}) = V(\tilde{\beta}_n y_{in} + e_{in})$$

$$= y_{in}^2 \sigma_\beta^2 + \sigma_e^2, \qquad i = 1, 2,$$

given that $\tilde{\beta}_n$ and e_{in} are uncorrelated. Their covariance is

$$E(\eta_{1n} \cdot \eta_{2n}) = E((\tilde{\beta}_n y_{1n} + e_{1n})(\tilde{\beta}_n y_{2n} + e_{2n}))$$

$$= E(\tilde{\beta}_n^2 y_{1n} y_{2n} + e_{1n} e_{2n} + e_{1n} \tilde{\beta}_n y_{1n} + e_{2n} \tilde{\beta}_n y_{2n})$$

$$= y_{1n} y_{2n} \sigma_\beta^2,$$

since e_{1n} and e_{2n} are uncorrelated and $\tilde{\beta}_n$ is uncorrelated with either e. Therefore, in this example

$$\Omega_n = \begin{bmatrix} y_{1n}^2\sigma_\beta^2 + \sigma_e^2 & y_{1n}y_{2n}\sigma_\beta^2 \\ y_{1n}y_{2n}\sigma_\beta^2 & y_{2n}^2\sigma_\beta^2 + \sigma_e^2 \end{bmatrix}$$

$$= \sigma_\beta^2 \begin{bmatrix} y_{1n}^2 & y_{1n}y_{2n} \\ y_{1n}y_{2n} & y_{2n}^2 \end{bmatrix} + \sigma_e^2 \begin{bmatrix} 1 & 0 \\ 0 & 1 \end{bmatrix}.$$

One last step is required for estimation. Note that decisionmakers' choices are not affected by a multiplicative transformation of utility: U_{in} is larger than U_{jn} for all $j \neq i$ if and only if U_{in}/λ is larger than U_{jn}/λ for all $j \neq i$. Consequently, the model $U_{in} = \bar{\beta}y_{in} + \eta_{in}$, where $\text{Var}(\eta_{in}) = y_{in}^2\sigma_\beta^2 + \sigma_e^2$, is equivalent to the model $U_{in}^* = (\bar{\beta}/\sigma_e)y_{in} + \eta_{in}^*$, where $\text{Var}(\eta_{in}^*) = y_{in}^2(\sigma_\beta/\sigma_e)^2 + 1$. Since any set of parameters $\bar{\beta}$, σ_β^2, and σ_e^2 that have the same ratios result in the same utility specification, a normalization is applied for estimation. A convenient normalization for this case is $\sigma_e^2 = 1$. Under this normalization,

$$\Omega_n = \sigma_\beta^2 \begin{bmatrix} y_{1n}^2 & y_{1n}y_{2n} \\ y_{1n}y_{2n} & y_{2n}^2 \end{bmatrix} + \begin{bmatrix} 1 & 0 \\ 0 & 1 \end{bmatrix}.$$

The values of y_{1n} and y_{2n} are observed by the researcher. The parameters σ_β^2 and $\bar{\beta}$ are determined through estimation of the model on a sample of decisionmakers. Thus, the researcher learns both the mean $(\bar{\beta})$ and the variance (σ_β^2) of the random coefficients of the observed variables entering utility.

3.3   Nonindependence from Irrelevant Alternatives

Independence or nonindependence from irrelevant alternative only becomes an issue in situations of three or more alternatives (since with only two alternatives there is no other alternative for the ratio of the two probabilities to be independent or nonindependent from). Consider a simple three-alternative case in which a home buyer can choose among purchase-money mortgages offered by three different lending institutions. One of the mortgages has a fixed interest rate, while the other two have variable rates. In this situation, it is unrealistic to expect the choice probabilities to exhibit IIA. Improving the characteristics of one variable rate loan (i.e., decreasing its initial interest rate) would be expected to reduce the probability of the other variable rate loan much more (proportionately) than the probability of the fixed rate loan, since the (unobserved) concern about risk that is associated with variable rate loans must be overcome in switching from a fixed to a variable rate loan but not (or not to the degree) in switching between two kinds of variable rate loans.

This situation can be modeled by probit with the source of non-IIA explicitly incorporated. Label the fixed rate loan as F and the two variable rate loans as VA and VB. Suppose the utility of homebuyer n associated with each loan depends on the initial interest rate of the loan (I_{in}, which is different for each of the three loans and varies over homebuyers on the basis of their credit worthiness) and the maximum possible increase in the interest rate (M_{in}, which is zero for the fixed rate loan and positive but perhaps different for each of the two variable rate loans). In addition, assume that utility depends on two unobserved factors: the homebuyer's perception of, and concern about, the degree of risk associated with the possibility of increased mortgage payments (labeled R_{in}, which is zero for the fixed rate loan and varies randomly for each of the two variable rate loans), and the homebuyer's perception of the ease of dealing with each institution (labeled η_i and depending on the location, reputation, and so on of each institution). With linear-in-parameters utility and suppressing alternative-specific constants for notational simplicity, we have

$$U_{in} = \alpha I_{in} + \beta M_{in} + e_{in}, \qquad i = \text{F, VA, VB,}$$

where $e_{in} = -R_{in} + \eta_{in}$ and the negative sign before R_{in} reflects the fact that risk is undesirable.

One would expect R_{in} to be correlated over the two variable rate loans: if the homebuyer thinks interest rates will rise and is concerned about the ability to keep up payments with an increased loan rate, then the concern would be applicable for both the variable rate loans.[1] Thus, even if η_{in} is independent across alternatives, the entire unobserved component of utility, e_{in}, is correlated.

Let η_{in} be distributed independently identically normal with zero mean and variance ω^2 and not correlated with R_{in}. Also let R_{in} be normally distributed for each of the two variable rate loans, with zero mean, variance σ^2 for each loan, and a covariance across the variable rate loans of σ^2_{AB}. (R_{in} for the fixed rate loan is nonstochastically zero.) Then the unobserved component of utility is also normally distributed with zero mean and variance-covariance

$$\Omega_n = \begin{bmatrix} 0 & 0 & 0 \\ 0 & \sigma^2 & \sigma^2_{AB} \\ 0 & \sigma^2_{AB} & \sigma^2 \end{bmatrix} + \omega \begin{bmatrix} 1 & 0 & 0 \\ 0 & 1 & 0 \\ 0 & 0 & 1 \end{bmatrix}.$$

Estimation of probit choice probabilities provides values of the coefficients α and β in the observed component of utility as well as the variance and covariance of the perceived risk associated with each variable rate loan.[2] The more general case in which the variance of e_{in} and R_{in} is different for each loan, and in which η_{in} is correlated over alternatives, can also be specified.

3.4 Estimation

The most straightforward (at least theoretically) way to estimate parameters in a probit model is through maximum likelihood techniques. The log likelihood function, defined in section 2.6 for logit models, is

$$LL = \sum_{n \in N} \sum_{i \in J_n} \delta_{in} \log P_{in}, \tag{3.4}$$

where δ_{in} equals one if decisionmaker n chose alternative i and zero otherwise, and N is the total number of decisionmakers in the sample. Substitution of the formula for probit choice probabilities, i.e., expression (3.3) into (3.4), gives LL as an explicit function of the parameter vector β entering representative utility, and the parameters entering the variance-covariance matrix, Ω_n, of the unobserved component of utility. The values of these two sets of parameters that maximize LL are, under fairly general conditions, consistent and efficient.

As mentioned, however, calculating probit probabilities for any given parameters involves numerous integrations; and these integrations must be performed numerous times in the search for the maximizing parameter values. Consequently, estimation of probit models with more than just a few alternatives and few explanatory variables is extremely expensive with standard maximum likelihood methods.

For this reason, alternative estimation methods have been developed. Two are particularly prominent: (1) a method based on an approximation by C. Clark and (2) a Monte Carlo method that utilizes randomly generated values for the unobserved component of utility. Each of the methods will now be discussed.

Estimation with the Clark Approximation

Clark (1961) demonstrated that the maximum of two normally distributed variables is distributed approximately normal. As will be shown, using this approximation reduces the number of integrals that must be evaluated in the calculation of probit choice probabilities to only one. Since the exact formula for choice probabilities in a situation of K alternatives involes K integrals, this approximation can considerably reduce the cost of estimating probit models.

Consider a choice situation with three alternatives labeled 1, 2, and 3. Denote the vector of utilities associated with these alternatives (U_1, U_2, U_3), assumed to be distributed jointly normal with mean vector (V_1, V_2, V_3) and variance-covariance matrix Ω, where the subscript denoting decisionmaker is suppressed for simplicity. Consider the choice probability for alternative 3. By equation (3.3), the formula for P_3 involves three integrals. However, using Clark's approximation, P_3 can be approximated by a formula with only one integral.

Define $z = \max(U_1, U_2)$. Since U_1 and U_2 are normal, it is possible to derive the mean and variance of z and the covariance of z with U_3. Label these variables as follows:

$E(z) = V_z;$

$\text{Var}(z) = \sigma_z^2;$

$\text{cov}(z, U_3) = \sigma_{z3}^2.$

Though the maximum of two normally distributed variables is not itself normally distributed, Clark showed that treating the maximum as if it is normally distributed does not introduce substantial error. That is, $z \overset{.}{\sim} N(V_z, \sigma_z^2)$ with covariance of σ_{z3}^2 with U_3.

By definition, $P_3 = \text{Prob}(U_3 > z)$. That is, the probability of choosing alternative 3 is the probability that U_3 is greater than the maximum of U_1 and U_2, and hence is greater than both. Rearranging, $P_3 = \text{Prob}(z - U_3 < 0)$. Since U_3 is normally distributed and z is approximately so, $z - U_3$ is also approximately normally distributed, with mean $V_z - V_3$ and variance $\sigma_z^2 + \sigma_3^2 - 2\sigma_{z3}^2$, where σ_3^2 is the variance of U_3. Therefore,

$$P_3 = \text{Prob}(z - U_3 < 0) = \int_{s=-\infty}^{0} \phi\left(\frac{s - (V_z + V_3)}{\sqrt{\sigma_z^2 + \sigma_3^2 - 2\sigma_{z3}^2}}\right) ds,$$

where ϕ is the standard normal density. Approximated in this way, P_3 involves only one integral.

The procedure can be applied recursively when more than three alternatives are involved. Consider a situation with four alternatives labeled 1, 2, 3, and 4. Define $z = \max(U_1, U_2)$ and $y = \max(U_1, U_2, U_3)$. By definition $y = \max(z, U_3)$. Since U_1 and U_2 are normal, z is approximately normal; then, since U_3 is normal and z is approximately normal, y is also approximately normal. The probability of choosing alternative 4 is $P_4 = \text{Prob}(U_4 > y) = \text{Prob}(y - U_4 < 0)$. Since y is approximately normal and U_4 is normal, their difference is approximately normal, and P_4 is simply the density of this approximately normal variable integrated from negative infinity to zero. Instead of performing four integrations as required by expression (3.3), P_4 can be approximated by a formula with only one integral. Situations with more alternatives are handled analogously. For a more detailed discussion, see Daganzo, Bouthelier, and Sheffi (1977).

Monte Carlo Method

The Monte Carlo method approximates the probit choice probabilities by simulating the choices of each decisionmaker under numerous, randomly generated values for unobserved utility.

The process begins by the researcher specifying particular values of the parameters entering V_{in} and the variance-covariance matrix of the vector $\tilde{e}_n$ (consisting of elements e_{in} for all i in J_n). Given the joint distribution of the vector $\tilde{e}_n$ (including values for the parameters entering this matrix), a random number generator produces a realization of this vector. Adding this realization to the observed component of utility (calculated at given values of the parameters entering V_{in}) gives total utility. Comparing total utility across alternatives identifies the alternative that has the highest total utility.

Choice probabilities are then approximated by repeating this process numerous time with the parameters held constant. In each randomly generated realization of unobserved utility, one of the alternative has highest utility. The proportion of times alternative i has the highest utility is an estimate of P_{in}. Obviously, as the number of repetitions increases, this proportion can be expected to become arbitrarily close to P_{in}. Since the distribution of $\tilde{e}_n$ depends on the parameters entering Ω_n and the value of representative utility depends on the parameters entering V_{in}, the Monte Carlo estimate of P_{in} depends on these parameters.

Choice probabilities calculated in this way for the given parameter values are then entered into the log likelihood function to determine the value of the function at the given values of the parameters. The entire process is then repeated for various different parameter values specified by the researcher. The parameters that result in the highest value of the log likelihood function are taken as the parameter estimates.

While both the Monte Carlo method and that based on the Clark approximation are less expensive than the standard maximum likelihood estimation of probit models, they do not completely solve the problem of probit estimation. The Clark approximation has been found in some situations to be very inaccurate. Especially bothersome is the fact that, in most cases, the researcher does not know the degree of inaccuracy unless standard maximum likelihood estimation is performed for comparison, in which case the approximation method is redundant. The Monte Carlo method does not necessarily entail the accuracy problems of the Clark approximation method, since the true probabilities can be approximated to any degree of accuracy by simply generating a sufficiently large number of realizations of unobserved utility for each sampled decisionmaker. Unfortunately, in most cases, when the number of repetitions is increased sufficiently to assure accuracy, the expense of the Monte Carlo method is not appreciably lower than that of the standard maximum likelihood method. For more details on estimation of probit models see Daganzo (1979) and Lerman and Manski (1981).

4 GEV

4.1 Functional Form of Choice Probabilities in Simple Cases

In some situations, independence from irrelevant alternatives (IIA) holds for some pairs of alternatives but not all. Logit is inappropriate in these situations since it assumes there is IIA between each pair of alternatives; however, a probit approach, even if feasible, might be unduly complex and expensive since it does not exploit the fact that IIA holds for some pairs of alternatives. Another qualitative choice model, called GEV for reasons to be described, is designed to handle situations like these.

A type of GEV model is used when the set of alternatives faced by a decisionmaker can be partitioned into subsets such that the ratio of probabilities for any two alternatives that are in the same subset is independent of the existence or characteristics of other alternatives. An example can best explain how to determine whether a set of alternatives can be so partitioned. Suppose the set of alternatives available to a worker for his commute to work consists of driving an auto alone, carpooling, taking the bus, and taking rail. If any one alternative were removed, the probabilities of the other alternatives would increase (e.g., if the worker became injured and could not drive an auto, then the probability of carpooling, bus, and rail would increase). The relevant question in partitioning these alternatives is, By what proportion would each probability increase when an alternative is removed? Suppose the changes in probabilities occur as set forth in table 4.1. Note that

- When the auto alone alternative is removed, the bus and rail probabilities increase by the same proportion, and consequently the ratio of their probabilities stays constant. That is, the ratio of bus and rail probabilities is independent of the existence of the auto alone alternative. However, the carpool probability increases more, proportionately, than either the bus or rail probability, meaning that the ratio of the carpool probability to either the bus or rail probability when the auto alone alternative is included differs from this ratio when it is removed. Therefore, the ratio of the carpool probability to either the bus or rail alternative is **not** independent of the existence of the auto alternative.
- Similarly, the change in probabilities that occurs when the carpool alternative is removed indicates that the ratio of the bus and rail probabilities is independent of the existence of carpool, but the ratio of the auto alone probability to either the bus or rail probability is not independent of the existence of the carpool alternative.

Table 4.1
Example of IIA holding within subsets of alternatives

Increase in probability of remaining alternatives, as % of original probability	Alternative removed			
	Auto alone	Carpool	Bus	Rail
Auto alone	—	5	7	7
Carpool	40	—	7	7
Bus	10	3	—	50
Rail	10	3	80	—

• With respect to removal of the bus alternative, the ratio of auto alone and carpool probabilities is independent, but not the ratio of the rail probability to either the auto alone or carpool probability.

• Finally, with respect to removal of the rail alternative, the ratio of auto alone and carpool probabilities is independent, but not the ratio of the rail probability to either the auto alone or carpool probability.

These facts suggest a partition of the set of alternatives into two subsets, with auto alone and carpool in one subset and bus and rail in the other subset. Under this partition, all relations among probabilities can be described succinctly: The ratio of probabilities of any two alternatives within the same subset is independent of the existence of other alternatives; however, the ratio of probabilities of two alternatives from different subsets is not independent of the existence of other alternatives. That is, IIA holds within subsets but not across subsets.

A convenient way to picture the choice situation is with a tree diagram. In such a tree, each branch denotes a subset of alternatives within which IIA holds, and every leaf on each branch denotes an alternative. For example, the tree diagram for the worker's choice of mode described above is given in figure 4.1. The (upside down) tree consists of two branches, labeled "auto" and "transit," for the two subsets of alternatives, and each of the branches contains two leaves for the two alternatives within the subset. Note that auto and transit are not themselves alternatives available to the worker, but rather are simply the names of groups of alternatives, designating the common feature among the alternatives within the group.

For any situation in which the alternatives can be partitioned in the manner described, or more graphically, depicted in a tree diagram with IIA

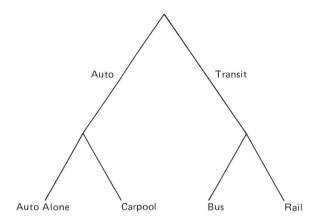

Figure 4.1
Tree diagram for mode choice.

holding for all leaves on each branch, a GEV model can be used to describe the choice situation.

Formally, the GEV model is specified as follows. Let the set of alternatives J_n be partitioned into K subsets denoted $B_n^1, \ldots, B_n^K$. The utility that person n obtains from alternative i in subset B_n^k is denoted, as usual, as $U_{in} = V_{in} + e_{in}$, where V_{in} is observed by the researcher and e_{in} is a random variable whose value is not observed by the researcher. The GEV model is obtained by assuming that e_{in}, for all elements i in J_n, are distributed in accordance with a generalized extreme value (GEV) distribution. That is, the joint cumulative distribution of the random variables e_{in}, for all i in J_n, is assumed to be

$$\exp\left\{ -\sum_{k=1}^K \alpha_k \left(\sum_{i \in B_n^k} e^{-e_{in}/\lambda_k} \right)^{\lambda_k} \right\}.$$

This distribution, as its name implies, is a generalization of the distribution that gives rise to the logit model. For logit, each e_{in} is independent with a univariate extreme value distribution. For GEV, the **marginal** distribution of each e_{in} is univariate extreme value, but all e_{in} with each subset are correlated with each other. The parameter λ_k is a measure of the correlation of unobserved utility within subset B_n^k. More precisely, $(1 - \lambda_k)$ is a measure of correlation since λ_k itself drops as the correlation rises.[1] For any i and j in different subsets (that is, i in B_n^k and j in B_n^h, where $k \neq h$), there is no correlation between e_{in} and e_{jn}.

McFadden (1978) has shown, using a proof that is complex and, since it is not heuristic, will not be reproduced here, that this distribution for the unobserved components of utility gives rise to the following choice probability for alternative i in subset B_n^k:

$$P_{in} = \frac{e^{V_{in}/\lambda_k}(\sum_{j \in B_n^k} e^{V_{jn}/\lambda_k})^{\lambda_k - 1}}{\sum_l (\sum_{j \in B_n^l} e^{V_{jn}/\lambda_l})^{\lambda_l}}. \tag{4.1}$$

Note that when $\lambda_k = 1$ for all k (and hence $1 - \lambda_k = 0$, indicating no correlation between the unobserved components of utility for alternatives within a subset), the choice probabilities become simply logit. Consequently, the GEV model is a generalization of logit that allows for particular patterns of correlation in unobserved utility.

Expression (4.1) is complex and, aside from the fact that it reduces to logit when all $\lambda_k = 1$, is not very illuminating. However, the choice probabilities can be expressed in an alternative fashion, as follows, that is quite simple and readily interpretable.

Without loss of generality, the observed component of utility can be decomposed into two parts: (1) a part that is constant for all alternatives within a subset, and (2) a part that is not constant within subsets. This can be denoted

$$U_{in} = W_n^k + \lambda_k Y_{in}^k + e_{in}, \qquad \text{for} \quad i \text{ in } B_n^k,$$

where

W_n^k is the mean of V_{in} over all alternatives in subset B_n^k;
Y_{in}^k is the deviation of V_{in} from the mean W_n^k; and
λ_k is a normalizing constant whose meaning will become evident.

Note that W_n^k varies over k (i.e., subsets) but not over i (i.e., alternatives within a subset), while Y_{in}^k varies over both k and i. Note that this decomposition is completely general, since Y_{in}^k is defined simply as $(V_{in} - W_n^k)/\lambda_k$.

Let the probability of choosing alternative i in subset B_n^k be expressed as the product of the probability that an alternative within subset B_n^k is chosen and the probability that alternative i is chosen (given that an alternative in B_n^k is chosen). This is denoted as

$$P_{in} = P_{in|B_n^k} \cdot P_{B_n^k},$$

where

$P_{in|B_n^k}$ is the conditional probability of choosing alternative i given that an alternative in the subset B_n^k is chosen, and

$P_{B_n^k}$ is the marginal probability of choosing an alternative in B_n^k (with the marginality being over all alternatives in B_n^k).

Note that this equality is exact since any probability can be written as the product of a marginal and a conditional probability.

The reason for decomposing P_{in} into a marginal and a conditional probability is that, with the GEV formula for P_{in}, the marginal and conditional probabilities take the form of logits. In particular, the marginal and conditional probabilities can be expressed as[2]

$$P_{in|B_n^k} = \frac{e^{Y_{in}^k}}{\sum_{j \in B_n^k} e^{Y_{jn}^k}},$$

$$P_{B_n^k} = \frac{e^{W_n^k + \lambda_k I_k}}{\sum_{l=1}^{K} e^{W_n^l + \lambda_l I_l}},$$

where

$$I_k = \ln \sum_{j \in B_n^k} e^{Y_{jn}^k}.$$

Stated in words, the conditional probability of choosing i, given that an alternative in B_n^k is chosen, is expressed as logit with variables that vary over alternatives within each subset entering representative utility in the logit formula. The marginal probability of choosing an alternative in B_n^k is also expressed as logit with the variables that vary over subsets of alternatives (but not over alternatives within each subset) entering representative utility. In addition, the representative utility in the marginal probability includes a term (i.e., I_k) that is the log of the denominator of the conditional probability. This term denotes the average utility that the person can expect from the alternatives within the subset. In recognition of this, the term I_k is called the "inclusive value" or "inclusive utility" of subset k.[3]

With this specification of the choice probabilities, it is clear that IIA holds within each subset but not across subsets. Consider two alternatives, i and m, both of which are in subset B_n^k.

$$P_{in}/P_{mn} = \frac{P_{in|B_n^k} \cdot P_{B_n^k}}{P_{mn|B_n^k} \cdot P_{B_n^k}} = \frac{P_{in|B_n^k}}{P_{mn|B_n^k}}$$

$$= \exp(Y_{in}^k)/\exp(Y_{mn}^k),$$

which is independent of alternatives other than m and i. However, for two alternatives in different subsets, say i in B_n^k and r in B_n^h,

$$P_{in}/P_{rn} = \frac{P_{in|B_n^k} \cdot P_{B_n^k}}{P_{rn|B_n^h} \cdot P_{B_n^h}},$$

which depends on the characteristics of all alternatives in B_n^k and B_n^h.

Example Because of the feature of the GEV model that IIA hold within subsets but not across subsets, it is particularly well-suited for describing situations like that of the worker's choice of mode, presented earlier. Suppose the only observed factors affecting each worker's choice are the total cost, c_{in}, and total time, t_{in}, of traveling on each mode. With linear utility, we have for worker n,

$$U_{in} = \alpha c_{in} + \beta t_{in} + e_{in},$$

where i denotes the mode. Similar unobserved factors enter the utility for auto alone and carpool (i.e., avoidance of strangers), making the e_{in} for these two alternatives correlated. The e_{in} for bus and rail are also correlated. However, there is, by assumption, no correlation between the unobserved utility of either transit mode with that of either auto mode.

An appropriate specification for this situation is a GEV model consisting of three "submodels": (1) a marginal probability submodel of the choice between auto and transit; (2) a conditional probability submodel for the choice of auto alone or carpool given that an auto mode is chosen; and (3) a conditional probability submodel for the choice of bus or rail given that a transit mode is chosen. This specification follows the tree diagram in figure 4.1, with a submodel for each of the three nodes in the tree.

To specify the variables entering each model, calculate the average time and cost of travel by transit and auto, that is, calculate

$$\bar{t}_n^t = (t_{bn} + t_{rn})/2;$$

$$\bar{t}_n^a = (t_{an} + t_{cn})/2;$$

$$\bar{c}_n^t = (c_{bn} + c_{rn})/2;$$

$$\bar{c}_n^a = (c_{an} + c_{cn})/2;$$

where subscripts a, c, b, and r denote auto alone, carpool, bus, and rail, respectively, and superscripts a and t denote auto and transit, respectively (or, more precisely, superscripts a and t denote the subsets of alternative labeled auto and transit). The time and cost of each mode is decomposed into the average for the mode's subset, just given, and a deviation from this average (denoted with a tilde over the letter):

$$t_{in} = \bar{t}_n^k + \tilde{t}_{in};$$

$$c_{in} = \bar{c}_n^k + \tilde{c}_{in};$$

for i = a, c, b, r and k = a or t as appropriate. Then utility for each mode can be decomposed into a portion that varies over subsets (i.e., over auto versus transit) but not modes within the subset and another component that varies over modes within a subset:

$$U_{in} = W_n^k + \lambda_k Y_{in}^k + e_{in},$$

where

$$W_n^k = \alpha \bar{c}_n^k + \beta \bar{t}_n^k;$$

$$Y_{in}^k = (\alpha \tilde{c}_{in} + \beta \tilde{t}_{in})/\lambda_k.$$

The three submodels can now be written explicitly. The submodel for the choice between auto alone and carpool, given that an auto mode is chosen, is logit with the conditional choice probabilities being

$$P_{in|a} = \frac{e^{Y_{in}^a}}{e^{Y_{an}^a} + e^{Y_{cn}^a}}, \qquad \text{for} \quad i = \text{a, c}.$$

Two explanatory variables enter the representative utility (Y_{in}^a) of each alternative. For the auto mode the variables are the cost of travel by auto alone expressed as a deviation from the average cost of travel by auto and carpool, and the time of travel by auto alone expressed as a deviation from the average time of travel by auto and carpool. For the carpool mode, similar variables enter. The coefficients of these two variables are α/λ_a and β/λ_a, respectively. (An estimate of λ_a is obtained from the marginal sub-model of auto versus transit, and so estimates of the coefficients of cost and time in this conditional submodel provide estimates of α and β.)

The submodel for the choice of bus or rail, given that a transit mode is chosen, is also logit with two explanatory variables entering the model: the deviation of cost and time of each mode from the average cost and time for both transit modes.[4]

The submodel for the choice between the auto and transit subsets is also logit with the marginal choice probabilities taking the form

$$P_n^k = \frac{e^{W_n^k + \lambda_k I_k}}{e^{W_n^a + \lambda_a I_a} + e^{W_n^t + \lambda_t I_t}}, \qquad \text{for} \quad k = \text{a or t.}$$

Three explanatory variables enter the "representative" utility of the auto and transit "modes" (quotation marks are used around these terms to indicate that auto and transit are not actually modes but groups of modes). For the auto "mode," the average cost and time of travel by auto enter (averaged over auto alone and carpool). In addition, the inclusive value of the auto modes (calculated as $I_a = \log(\exp(Y_{an}^a) + \exp(Y_{cn}^a))$ or, more simply, as the log of the denominator on the conditional submodel for auto versus carpool) enters as an explanatory variable. The coefficient of the cost and time variables are α and β, respectively, and the coefficient of the inclusive value term is λ_a. For the transit "mode," three similar variables enter, with averages being over the bus and rail modes. The coefficient of the inclusive value term for transit is λ_t.

Remark   A final note is required concerning terminology. Since, in GEV models, the subsets can be considered "nests" of alternatives, and since the choices of nests and alternatives within nests are described by logit formulas, the GEV model is often called "nested logit." Other commonly used terms for the GEV model are structured, or ordered, logit (to emphasize that the set of alternatives has a particular structure, or order, as represented by the partitioning) and sequential logit (since GEV probabilities are a sequence of marginal and conditional probabilities which are logit in form). Two of these terms, however, should be avoided. The term "ordered logit" has been used to denote models other than GEV and consequently can cause confusion. The term "sequential logit" can be misunderstood to suggest that the **decisionmaker** makes a sequence of choices, each of which is described by logit, whereas the GEV model is derived by assuming the decisionmaker makes one choice, namely, one alternative out of the available set. The sequence of probabilities in the GEV model is simply a method for the **researcher** to represent the lack of IIA among the choice probabilities.

4.2   More Complex GEV Models

The GEV model just described is called a two-level GEV model because there are, in a sense, two levels of modeling: the marginal probabilities and the conditional probabilities. In the case of the mode choice, the two levels are the marginal model of auto versus transit and the conditional model of **type** of auto or transit (auto alone or carpool given auto, and bus or rail given transit).

In some situations, however, three- or higher level GEV models are appropriate. Three-level GEV models are obtained by partitioning the set of alternatives into subsets and then partitioning the subsets into subsubsets. One logit model is used to describe the choice of subset; another logit model is used to describe the choice of subsubset; and a third describes the choice of alternative within the subsubset. The first of these models includes an inclusive value term that represents the average utility that the decision-maker can expect from the subsubsets with each subset. This is defined as the log of the denominator of the second model. Similarly, the second model includes an inclusive value term that represents the average utility that the decisionmaker can expect from the alternatives within each subsubset. It is defined as the log of the denominator of the third model.

As an example, a household's choice of housing unit can perhaps be described as a three-level GEV model. The household has a choice among all the available housing units in the household's area of residence. The housing units can be grouped according to neighborhood within the city, and then by the number of bedrooms in the unit. Using San Francisco, a tree diagram depicting this situation is given in figure 4.2. Following this tree diagram, the set of housing units are partitioned into subsets on the basis of neighborhood and into subsubsets on the basis of the number of bedrooms. A GEV model on this partitioning assumes that (1) the ratio of probabilities of two housing units in the same neighborhood **and** with the same number of bedrooms is independent of other alternatives, (2) the ratio of probabilities of two housing units in the same neighborhood but with different numbers of bedrooms is independent of the characteristics of housing in other neighborhoods but not independent of the characteristics of housing units in the same neighborhood, and (3) the ratio of probabilities of two housing units in different neighborhoods is not independent of the characteristics of any other housing units.

More complex GEV models, with, for example, overlapping "nests," can also be constructed (see Ben-Akiva and Lerman, 1985).

4.3   Estimation

The parameters of a GEV model can be estimated by standard maximum likelihood techniques. Substituting the choice probabilities of expression

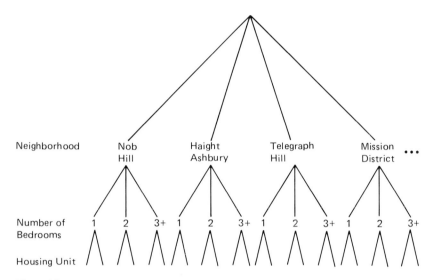

Figure 4.2
Tree diagram for choice of housing unit. (There are numerous housing units in each area
with each number of bedrooms; only two "leaves" are drawn for simplicity.)

(4.1) into the log likelihood function defined in section 2.6 gives the log
likelihood as an explicit function of the parameters of this GEV model. The
value of the parameters that maximizes this function is, under fairly general
conditions, consistent and efficient.

Since the GEV choice probabilities are fairly complex, estimation by this
standard maximum likelihood method is somewhat difficult. Computer
programs are now available for estimating GEV models in this way. However, they are not widely available, and the procedure tends to be relatively
expensive.

For these reasons, researchers often estimate GEV models in a sequential
fashion, exploiting the fact that the GEV choice probabilities can be decomposed into marginal and conditional probabilities that are logit. This
sequential estimation is performed "bottom up," in that the submodels for
the lower nodes of a tree diagram are estimated first, followed by the
submodels for the higher nodes.

For a simple two-level GEV model, the procedure is the following. First,
the logit models for the conditional probabilities are estimated using standard logit estimation routines. In the example of mode choice, described in
section 4.1, these are the models of auto alone versus carpool and bus versus

rail. Next, the inclusive value terms are calculated by taking the log of the denominator of the models estimated in the first step. Last, the logit model for the marginal probabilities is estimated with each of the inclusive value terms included as an explanatory variable. For the choice of mode, this is the model of auto versus transit with an inclusive value term from the model of auto alone versus carpool and another one from the model of bus versus rail included as explanatory variables. The estimated coefficients of the inclusive value terms are the estimates of the λ_k.

This all sounds very straightforward. There are, however two complications. First, in estimating the marginal submodel, an estimate of each I_k (based on the previously estimated conditional submodels) is entered rather than the "true" I_k. The estimate of I_k is consistent (since the conditional submodel is estimated consistently) and so the parameters of the marginal submodel are still estimated consistently. However, the standard errors of these parameters will be biased. In particular, the "true" standard errors will be larger than those estimated under the incorrect assumption that the inclusive value terms entering the submodel are without error. With downwardly biased standard errors, smaller confidence bounds and larger t-statistics are estimated for the parameters than are "true," and the submodel will appear to be better than it actually is.

Second, it is often the case that some parameters will be common to both the conditional and the marginal submodels. In the example of mode choice in section 4.1, the coefficients of the cost and time of travel (that is, α and β) appear in the conditional submodels of mode choice given auto or transit and the marginal submodel of auto versus transit. Estimating the conditional and marginal submodels sequentially results in two separate estimates of these parameters. It is always possible to specify a GEV model in such a way that different parameters enter each submodel (e.g., by letting the coefficients vary over alternatives, with the average coefficient estimated in the marginal submodel and the deviation from average for each alternative being estimated in the conditional submodel). However, the researcher might not think that such a specification truly describes the choice process being modeled.

These two complications are symptoms of a more general circumstance, namely, that sequential estimation of GEV models, while consistent, is not as efficient as simultaneous estimation (that is, standard maximum likelihood estimation of the complete GEV model). With simultaneous estimation, all information is utilized in the estimation of each parameter, and parameters that are common across submodels are necessarily constrained to be equal. Consequently, if a computer routine for maximum likelihood estimation of GEV models can be obtained, the addition expense[5] is probably warranted.

5 Continuous/Discrete Models

5.1 Motivation

Decisionmakers are often in the situation of making two interrelated choices. If in each choice the decisionmaker faces a finite and exhaustive set of mutually exclusive alternatives, then qualitative choice models can readily be applied to describe the two choices. All that is required is for the choice set facing the decisionmaker to be defined appropriately. For example, suppose a worker had a choice of how many cars to own and which mode of travel to use for the commute to work. To keep the example simple, assume that the alternative modes were auto and bus and that the worker cannot own more than two cars. The two choices that the decisionmaker has can be "collapsed" and considered one choice, with the decisionmaker facing a set of alternatives each of which denotes a particular number of cars **and** a particular mode. That is, the choice set that the decisionmaker faces consists of these alternatives: (1) own no cars and take a bus to work, (2) own one car and take an auto, (3) own one car and take a bus, (4) own two cars and take an auto, (5) own two cars and take a bus. (The alternative of owning no cars and taking an auto to work is not included under the presumption that it is logically impossible.) With alternatives defined in this way, any of the qualitative choice models can be applied. Perhaps the most appealing approach, for this example, is a GEV specification based on the tree diagram in figure 5.1.

In many situations, however, a decisionmaker makes two choices that are not both "qualitative." For example, a household chooses how many cars to own and how many miles to drive each car. The first choice is among a discrete set of alternatives (0, 1, 2, and so on up to some maximum) while the second is among a continuous set of alternatives (any number of miles, and fractions of miles, above zero and below some maximum). The choice of number of cars can be appropriately described by qualitative choice models, but not the number of miles.

Another example is a household's choice of whether or not to obtain air conditioning (with the alternatives being "yes" or "no") and the choice of how much to run the air conditioner each day if it is obtained (the alternatives are any number between 0 and 24 hours). The first choice is among a discrete set of alternatives and can be described by qualitative choice models, but the second choice is among a continuous set of alternatives and cannot appropriately be described by qualitative choice models.

Choice situations such as these are called "continuous/discrete" situations, reflecting the fact that the set of alternatives for one choice is

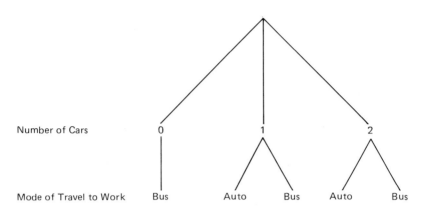

Number of Cars

Mode of Travel to Work

Figure 5.1
Tree diagram for choice of number of cars and mode of travel to work.

continuous while that for the other is discrete. Methods have recently been developed (Heckman, 1978, 1979; Dubin and McFadden, 1984) for specifying and estimating models that describe continuous/discrete choice situations. These methods are based on some relatively advanced concepts in microeconomic theory of utility maximization. Since these concepts are not widely known and are crucial to an understanding of continuous/discrete methodologies, they are now presented, prior to the discussion of the models themselves.

5.2   Relevant Background on Utility Maximization Theory

Assume (for simplicity) a two-good world and consider a consumer with fixed income y who has a choice of how much to consume of each of the two goods. The quantities of each good are denoted x_1 and x_2, respectively, and their prices, which are fixed from the consumer's perspective, are denoted p_1 and p_2, respectively. The consumer's utility function is denoted

$$U = U(x_1, x_2).$$

If the consumer is a utility maximizer, then he will purchase the quantities of the two goods that solves the constrained maximization problem

$$\max_{x_1, x_2} U(x_1, x_2)$$

such that $\quad y = p_1 x_1 + p_2 x_2.$

(5.1)

That is, he will choose the x_1 and x_2 that maximize utility subject to the budget constraint. Label the chosen quantities as x_1^* and x_2^*. These quantities will depend, of course, on the price of each good and the consumer's income, and hence can be written as functions of p_1, p_2, and y:

$$x_1^* = g_1(p_1, p_2, y),$$

$$x_2^* = g_2(p_1, p_2, y).$$

The functions g_1 and g_2 are the consumer's demand functions for x_1 and x_2.

All of this is standard material in microeconomic courses. These ideas can be extended, however, in the following way. We can substitute the **chosen** quantities of the two goods into the consumer's utility function to determine the utility that he would obtain at these chosen quantities; this gives the actual utility the consumer obtains after he has maximized his utility subject to the budget constraint:

$$U^* = U(x_1^*, x_2^*),$$

where U^* is the actual utility obtained with x_1^* and x_2^*. Since x_1^* and x_2^* are functions of p_1, p_2, and y, U^* is also a function of these variables:

$$U^* = U(x_1^*, x_2^*) = U(g_1(p_1, p_2, y), g_2(p_1, p_2, y))$$

$$= Y(p_1, p_2, y).$$

That is, the actual utility that the consumer obtains after he has chosen the quantities that maximize his utility depends on the prices of the goods and his income. The function denoting this relation, Y, is called the "indirect utility function."

We now have two utility functions:

1. $U(x_1, x_2)$, which gives the utility that the consumer obtains at given quantities of each good and is called the "direct utility function," and
2. $Y(p_1, p_2, y)$, which gives the utility that the consumer obtains at given prices and income once he has chosen the quantities that maximize his (direct) utility subject to the budget constraint for the given prices and income.

It can be shown (see Varian, 1978) that a consumer's preferences can be equivalently represented by either a direct utility function or an indirect utility function. That is, given a direct utility function that represents the consumer's preferences, a particular indirect utility function can be derived; and, given a appropriate indirect utility function, the consumer's direct utility function can be derived. Consequently, a researcher can specify an indirect utility function to represent a consumer's preferences[1] and know that a direct utility function is implicit.

Why is this important? A researcher usually examines a consumer's utility function for the purpose of determining the functional form of the consumer's demand function for goods; it is rare that a researcher is interested in the shape of the utility function for its own sake. For deriving demand functions, it is much easier, as will be shown, to work with a consumer's indirect utility function rather than with his direct utility function.

Under the standard analysis of consumer behavior, demand curves are derived from the direct utility function by solving the constrained maximization problem given in (5.1). This involves specifying the Lagrangian, taking derivatives of the Lagrangian with respect to each good and the Lagrangian multiplier, setting these derivatives to zero, and solving for the quantities of each good. Except for every simple direct utility functions, this procedure becomes very complex, and often intractable, so that specific demand functions cannot be derived.

Deriving demand functions from indirect utility functions is much easier, thanks to a result called "Roy's identity." Roy's identity states that the demand for a good is equal to (the negative of) the derivative of the indirect utility function with respect to the good's price divided by the derivative of the indirect utility function with respect to income. That is, using the previous notation,

$$x_1^* = -(\partial Y/\partial p_1)/(\partial Y/\partial y) = g_1(p_1, p_2, y),$$

$$x_2^* = -(\partial Y/\partial p_2)/(\partial Y/\partial y) = g_2(p_1, p_2, y).$$

Proof of Roy's Identity   The maximum utility the consumer obtains from prices p_1, p_2 and income y is given by indirect utility function

$$U^* = Y(p_1, p_2, y).$$

By definition

$$Y(p_1, p_2, y) = U(x_1^*, x_2^*), \tag{5.2}$$

where x_1^* and x_2^* are the utility maximizing values of x_1 and x_2 and are themselves functions of p_1, y_2, and y. When utility is maximized, two things occur. First, all income is spent:

$$y = p_1 x_1^* + p_2 x_2^*.$$

Consequently, given the utility maximizing amount of good one, we know the utility maximizing amount of good two:

$$x_2^* = (y - p_1 x_1^*)/p_2.$$

Substituting into (5.2) we have

$$Y(p_1, p_2, y) = U(x_1^*, (y - p_1 x_1^*)/p_2).$$

Second, at the utility maximizing quantities x_1^* and x_2^*, the ratio of marginal utilities is equal to the ratio of prices:[2]

$$MU_1/MU_2 = p_1/p_2,$$

where MU_1 and MU_2 are the marginal utility of goods 1 and 2, respectively. This can be rewritten as $MU_1 - (p_1/p_2) MU_2 = 0$. Therefore, indirect utility can be written as

$$Y(p_1, p_2, y) = U(x_1, (y - p_1 x_1)/p_2) \quad \text{(evaluated at the point at which} \\ (MU_1 - (p_1/p_2) MU_2) = 0).$$

We can now determine the derivatives of Y;

$$\partial Y/\partial p_1 = (\partial U(x_1, (y - p_1 x_1)/p_2)/\partial p_1) \quad \text{(evaulated at the point at which} \\ (MU_1 - (p_1/p_2) MU_2) = 0)$$

$$= (\partial x_1/\partial p_1) MU_1 + (-x_1/p_2 - (p_1/p_2)(\partial x_1/\partial p_1)) MU_2$$

$$= -(x_1/p_2) MU_2 + (\partial x_1/\partial p_1)(MU_1 - (p_1/p_2) MU_2)$$

$$= -(x_1/p_2) MU_2$$

and

$$\partial Y/\partial y = (\partial U(x_1, (y - p_1 x_1)/p_2)/\partial y) \quad \text{(evaluated at the point at which} \\ (MU_1 - (p_1/p_2) MU_2) = 0)$$

$$= (\partial x_1/\partial y) MU_1 + ((1/p_2) - (p_1/p_2)(\partial x_1/\partial y)) MU_2$$

$$= (1/p_2) MU_2 + (\partial x_1/\partial y)(MU_1 - (p_1/p_2) MU_2)$$

$$= (1/p_2) MU_2.$$

Therefore,

$(\partial Y/p_1)/(\partial Y/\partial y) = -x_1,$ as required.

The result for good two is obtained analogously. □

In short, a researcher can derive the functional form of demand equations from either direct or indirect utility functions. Since consumers' preferences can be equivalently expressed with either type of utility function, demand curves derived from either are necessarily the same. However, it is much easier to derive demand equations from the indirect utility function (using Roy's identity) than from the direct utility function (which requires solving a constrained maximization problem).

5.3   Specification of Continuous /Discrete Models

Consider a person who faces two choices: (1) which alternative to choose from a finite and exhaustive set of mutually exclusive alternatives; and (2) how much of a particular good to obtain, where the amount of the good can be represented by a continuous variable. In general these choices will depend, at least partially, on the same underlying factors, so that the two choices are interrelated.[3] The researcher wishes to describe the situation by specifying both (1) the probability that the person will choose each alternative and (2) the demand function for the continuous good. Label the set of alternatives as J, observed characteristics of each alternative i in J as z_i, the quantity of the good as x, the person's income as y, other observed characteristics of the person as s, and all unobserved factors as w_i. The price of the good can, in the general case, vary depending on which alternative is chosen,[4] and so the price is denoted p_i, that is, the price per unit of x given that alternative i is chosen.

Suppose, for the moment, that the person chose alternative i in set J but has not decided how much of the good x to consume. The maximum utility that the person can obtain, given that he has chosen alternative i, depends on the price of the good and the person's income (as well as, of course, the characteristics of the person and alternative i). This maximum-attainable utility, given alternative i, can be written

$Y_i = Y_i(p_i, y, z_i, s, w_i).$

This function is an indirect utility function, giving the maximum utility attainable at given price and income. More precisely, it is the indirect utility function that the person faces **given** that he has chosen alternative i. Since it is conditional on the choice of alternative i, it is called the "conditional indirect utility function" for alternative i. Conditional indirect utility functions can be constructed for each alternative in the set J; each of these gives the maximum utility that the person can obtain if he chooses a particular alternative.

We can now specify the demand equation for the good and the choice probabilities for the alternatives. The person will choose alternative i if and only if the conditional indirect utility is higher for alternative i than for any other alternative:

$$Y_i(p_i, y, z_i, s, w_i) > Y_j(p_j, y, z_j, s, w_j) \qquad \text{for all} \quad j \text{ in } J, \quad j \neq i.$$

Consequently, the probability of alternative i being chosen is

$$P_i = \text{Prob}(Y_i(p_i, y, z_i, s, w_i) > Y_i(p_j, y, z_j, s, w_j) \text{ for all } j \text{ in } J, j \neq i). \qquad (5.3)$$

To specify these probabilities, recall that factors w_i entering indirect utility are not observed by the researcher. Therefore, we decompose indirect utility into observed and unobserved parts,

$$Y_i(p_i, y, z_i, s, w_i) = V_i(p_i, y, z_i, s) + e_i,$$

where e_i is a function of unobserved variables w_i and V_i is simply the difference between e_i and Y_i. By specifying a distribution for e_i and substituting into (5.3), explicit formulas for the choice probabilities are derived exactly the same as for any qualitative choice model. For example, if each e_i is assumed to be distributed independently, identically extreme value, then the choice probabilities are logit with V_i as representative utility:

$$P_i = \exp(V_i(p_i, y, z_i, s)) / \sum_{i \in J} \exp(V_j(p_j, y, z_j, s)).$$

It is important to note that representative utility in the choice probabilities includes as an explanatory variable the price of the good whose quantity is being chosen simultaneously with the choice of alternative.

The demand for good x is determined from the conditional indirect utility functions using Roy's identity. That is, the demand for x, given that alternative i is chosen, is

$$x_i = (\partial Y_i(p_i, y, z_i, s, w_i)/\partial p)/(\partial Y_i(p_i, y, z_i, s, w_i)/\partial y) = g_i(p_i, y, z_i, s, w_i).$$

This is the conditional demand for x (conditional on alternative i being chosen). The marginal demand for x, marginal over all alternatives, is the weighted average of conditional demands with the choice probabilities being weights:

$$x = \sum_{i \in J} P_i g_i(p_i, y, z_i, s, w_i).$$

Note that both the conditional and marginal demands for x depend on unobserved as well as observed factors; the error structure for these equations will depend on how w_i enters g_i.

Example A simple example will demonstrate how functional forms for choice probabilities and demand functions are derived from indirect utility functions, using the ideas just expressed. Suppose the conditional indirect utility function is of the form

$$Y_i = \ln((\alpha^i + \beta^i p + \theta y + \psi f(z_i, s) + e_i) \cdot e^{-\theta p}),$$

where f is a vector-valued function of observed characteristics of alternative i and the person, e_i is a function of unobserved factors, α^i, β^i, and θ are scalar parameters, and ψ is a vector of parameters. Note that in this example, the price of good x does not depend on the alternative chosen, and so p is not subscripted by i. The demand for x is obtained with Roy's identity. First, take the derivatives of Y_i with respect to p and y:

$$\partial Y_i / \partial p = (1/A)(\beta^i e^{-\theta p} - \theta B e^{-\theta p}) = (1/A)(e^{-\theta p}(\beta^i - \theta B)),$$

$$\partial Y_i / \partial y = (1/A)(\theta e^{-\theta p}),$$

where

$$A = (\alpha^i + \beta^i p + \theta y + \psi f(z_i, s) + e_i)e^{-\theta p}$$

and

$$B = \alpha^i + \beta^i p + \theta y + \psi f(z_i, s) + e_i.$$

The conditional demand for x is the negative of the ratio of these two derivatives:

$$x_i = -(\partial Y_i / \partial p)/(\partial Y_i / \partial y) = -(\beta^i - \theta B)/\theta = B - (\beta^i/\theta)$$

$$= (\alpha^i - (\beta^i/\theta)) + \beta^i p + \theta y + \psi f(z_i, s) + e_i. \tag{5.4}$$

That is, the conditional demand equation for good x is linear in price, income, and other explanatory variables, with an intercept term $(\alpha^i - (\beta^i/\theta))$ and an additive error.

The choice probabilities are also simple in form. The conditional indirect utility functions can be rewritten

$$Y_i = \ln(\alpha^i + \beta^i p + \theta y + \psi f(z_i, s) + e_i) - \theta p.$$

Since θp does not vary over i, the decisionmaker ignores its value in comparing Y_i and Y_j and considers only

$$\tilde{Y}_i = \ln(\alpha^i + \beta^i p + \theta y + \psi f(z_i, s) + e_i).$$

Furthermore, since $\tilde{Y}_i > \tilde{Y}_j$ if and only if $\exp(\tilde{Y}_i) > \exp(\tilde{Y}_j)$, the decisionmaker effectively chooses an alternative on the basis of comparison among

$$\exp(\tilde{Y}_i) = \alpha^i + \beta^i p + \theta y + \psi f(z_i, s) + e_i.$$

Therefore, the probability of choosing alternative i is

$$P_i = \text{Prob}(V_i + e_i > V_j + e_j \text{ for all } j \text{ in } J, j \neq i),$$

where

$$V_i = \alpha^i + \beta^i p + \theta y + \psi f(z_i, s).$$

Specification of the distribution of e_i (e.g., extreme value) provides a functional form (e.g., logit) for the choice probabilities, with representative utility being V_i. Note that this representative utility function is linear in price, income, and other explanatory variables, with an alternative-specific constant and an alternative-specific coefficient for price. Other examples of simple continuous/discrete model specifications based on utility theory are given by Dubin and McFadden (1984).

Remark A final note is required regarding terminology. It was stated at the beginning of this section that the discrete and continuous choices described by these models are assumed in general to be interrelated, but the form of this interrelation was not described. It is now possible to clarify this point. In the previous specification, the decisionmaker is assumed to choose the discrete alternative and the amount of the continuous good that, in combination, provide the greatest utility. Since the choices are simultaneous, it is not possible for one choice to cause the other, in a strict sense of causation. However, the two choices are caused, or determined, by the same underlying factors, and so there is an observable association between the two. That is, the decisionmaker would (in general) choose a different alternative if, due to a change in an underlying factor, the chosen amount of the continuous good changed; and the person would consume a different amount of the continuous good if, due to a change in an underlying factor, the person were to choose a different alternative. In these statements, the phrase "due to a change in an underlying factor" is important since the reason each choice changes when the other does is not because of direct causation between the choices but rather because both choices are determined by the same underlying factors.

5.4 Estimation

The parameters of both the choice probabilities and the demand equations for the continuous good can conceivably be estimated simultaneously with full information maximum likelihood methods. To do so, it is necessary to (1) specify the probability of each sampled observation (i.e., the probability of observing the alternative that was actually chosen and the amount of the continuous good that was actually consumed), (2) substitute the probability of each observation into the log likelihood function, and (3) maximize the function with respect to the parameters. While feasible, this procedure is difficult, and, to date, no special purpose computer routines have been developed for such estimation.

It is usually the case that researchers estimate the choice probabilities and demand equation sequentially, starting with the choice probabilities. Recall that the choice probabilities in continuous/discrete situations are a function of representative utility ($V_i(p_i, y, z_i, s)$) for all i, with the form of the function determined by the distributional assumptions regarding unobserved utility. Since each of the variables entering V_i is exogenous,[5] the parameters of choice probabilities can be estimated the same as if no continuous good were involved. These estimates are consistent, but since (1) some parameters might be common to both the choice probabilities and the demand equation for the continuous good and (2) the unobserved component of utility and the error in the demand equation generally contain some common unobserved factors, the estimates are not as efficient as full information maximum likelihood.

Estimation of the demand equation for the continuous good is considerably less straightforward. The basic difficulty is that some of the explanatory variables in the demand function are, in general, correlated with the error term, causing ordinary least squares estimation to be biased. The precise source of the bias and the methods that are available for eliminating it are most easily discussed in terms of a specific and simple example. Generalization to more complicated cases is fairly obvious.

Consider a situation in which a household has a choice between a room air conditioner and a central air conditioning system and also chooses how long each day to run the air conditioner. Suppose the conditional demand equations are linear in price and income similar to (5.4). However, in this example, price varies over alternatives since the cost of operating a room air conditioner for a minute is different from that for a central system. In particular, let the conditional demand equations be

$$x_c = \alpha + \beta p_c + \theta y + e_c, \tag{5.5}$$

$$x_q = \beta p_q + \theta y + e_q, \tag{5.6}$$

where x_c is use given that a central air conditioner is chosen and the household faces price p_c per minute of use, and x_q is defined analogously for a room system.

These equations can be estimated simultaneously on the entire (i.e., pooled) sample, or separately on the subsample of households that chose each alternative (i.e., estimate (5.5) on those households that chose a central system and (5.6) on those that chose a room system). In either case, ordinary least squares is biased and alternative estimation methods are required. The source of the bias and methods for eliminating it are now described.

Two Stage Estimation on Pooled Sample

Since the parameters β and θ are common to both equations, estimation of (5.5) and (5.6) on the pooled sample is equivalent to estimating the single equation

$$x = \alpha d^c + \beta p + \theta y + e,$$

where x is the observed use level of the household, d^c is a dummy variable that equals one if the household chose a central system and zero otherwise, p is the price that the household is observed to face given its chosen system (i.e., p is the price of using a room system if the household chose a room system and the price associated with a central system if it chose a central system), y is income, and e is an error term. Note that this equation is simply a more concise way of writing (5.5) and (5.6) and does not entail any change in specification.

The basic difficulty in estimating this equation is that the dummy variable d^c and the price p are, in general, correlated with the error term.

Consider first the dummy variable. A household whose dwelling, for some unobserved reasons (e.g., poor insulation, large picture windows in unshaded areas), tends to become unusually hot, will tend to purchase a central system since it provides greater cooling capacity than a room system. Thus, for this household, d^c would probably be one, indicating a central system. This household would also, for the very same unobserved reasons, tend to use the air conditioner more than average: since the dwelling becomes unusually hot, the household would run the system for an unusually long time to reduce the heat. That is, e would be high for this household. In this case, d^c is one when e is high. In other cases (e.g., little need for air conditioning because all the household members are away from the house during the hot part of the day), a low e would be associated with a d^c of zero.

Similarly, the price variable is correlated with e. The cost per minute of operation is generally higher for a central system than for a room system. Households that, due to unobserved factors such as poor insulation, tend to choose a central system will also tend to have above average use of the system; consequently, p will tend to be high when e is high. For similar, but reversed reasons, a low p will be associated with a low e.

The basic problem here is one of endogeneity. The household determines the values of d^c and p in choosing which air conditioner to purchase. Since the choice of air conditioner is endogenous with the use of the air conditioner, d^c and p are necessarily endogenous. Treating them as exogenous in the estimation of the demand equation results in standard endogeneity bias.

The bias is shown visually in figure 5.2. The true relation between price p and use x is depicted by the solid line. The observed data points are the asterisks. Recall that p is correlated with e, so that use tends to be below average when p is low and above average when p is high. This correlation is represented in the placement of the asterisks: for low p, most of the observed data points are below the true line (i.e., below the true average), while for high p, most are above the true line. As can be seen from this graph, the line that best fits these data is the dashed line. This estimated relation is necessarily less steep than the true line, indicating that the estimated effect of price on use is biased toward zero when price is correlated with the error term.

The solution to this problem is a two stage procedure, analogous to that for eliminating endogeneity bias in standard simultaneous equation sys-

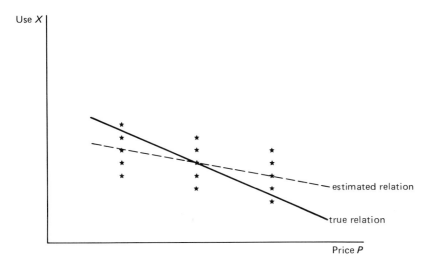

Figure 5.2
Bias due to endogeneity.

tems. In particular, the solution is to replace the endogenous explanatory variables by consistently estimated functions of exogenous variables. In the context of our example, the following two steps are required. First, an equation is estimated for each of the two variables d^c and p with only exogenous variables entering on the right-hand side:

$$d^c = f(w);$$

$$p = g(w);$$

where w is a vector of exogenous variables and f and g are parametric functions whose parameters are estimated. Using the estimated parameters in f and g, predicted values of d^c and p are obtained denoted $\hat{d}^c$ and $\hat{p}$, respectively. Second, the demand equation for air conditioner use is estimated with the estimated values of d^c and p replacing the observed values:

$$x_i = \alpha\hat{d}^c + \beta\hat{p} + \theta y + e_i.$$

Ordinary least squares is a consistent estimator for this equation; since $\hat{d}^c$ and $\hat{p}$ are functions of exogenous variables, they are necessarily uncorrelated with e.

The only question with this approach is what functions f and g to use in replacing d^c and p. Any function of exogenous variables will allow consistency; three particular functions have traditionally been used.

METHOD I   The most obvious and, in some sense, straightforward method is to specify f and g as regression equations of all observed exogenous variables: $d^c = \omega w + u_1$ and $p = \phi w + u_2$, where w is a vector of observed exogenous variables, ω and ϕ are vectors of parameters, and u_1 and u_2 are error terms. Ordinary least squares applied to these equations provides consistent estimates of ω and ϕ.

METHOD II   The choice probabilities are functions of exogenous variables. Since these have previously been estimated, d^c and p can be expressed in terms of the choice probabilities, thus avoiding the estimation of additional regression equations. That is, let the function replacing d^c be the estimated probability of choosing a central system, and let the function replacing p be the expected price given that either of the two systems could be chosen:

$$\hat{d}^c = \hat{P}_c,$$

$$\hat{p} = p_c \hat{P}_c + p_q \hat{P}_q,$$

where $\hat{P}_c$ and $\hat{P}_q$ are the estimated probabilities of choosing a central and a room system, respectively.

METHOD III   Methods I and II can be combined for greater efficiency. Let f and g be regression equations, but include the estimated choice probabilities as explanatory variables in addition to exogenous variables. That is, estimate by ordinary least squares:

$$d^c = \alpha_1 \hat{P}_c + \omega w + u_1,$$

$$p = \alpha_2 (\hat{P}_c p_c + \hat{P}_q p_q) + \phi w + u_2,$$

where α_1 and α_2 are scalar parameters. Since method I is obtained when $\alpha_1 = \alpha_2 = 0$ and method II results from $\alpha_1 = \alpha_2 = 1$ and $\omega = \phi = 0$, this third method is a generalization of the other two and is consequently more efficient.

It is important to note that methods I and III are equivalent to instrumental variables estimation. For method I, the instruments are all exogenous variables available prior to estimation of the choice probabilities, while for method III the instruments are all of these exogenous variables plus the estimated choice probabilities and variables created from these choice probabilities. Furthermore, just as two stage least squares can be equivalently performed in one stage as instrumental variables estimation, methods I and III can also be estimated in only one stage using instrumental variables routines.

Parameters Varying over Equations In the previous example, there are parameters common to both conditional demand equations. While this specification simplifies the notation, it is important to realize that the two stage estimation procedure is not restricted to cases with common parameters. To show this fact, suppose that all the parameters in the air conditioner use equations are different for room and central systems:

$$x_c = \alpha + \beta^c p_c + \theta^c y + e_c,$$

$$x_q = \beta^q p_q + \theta^q y + e_q.$$

This specification is actually quite reasonable. A central air system produces much more cooling within a given period of time than does a room system. A household would consequently be more willing to use a central system than it would a room system if the household (somehow) faced the same price per minute of operation for each type of system. That is, β^c is less negative than β^q. For similar reasons, income might have a larger effect on the use of a room system than on a central one, implying that θ^q is larger than θ^c.

With parameters varying over alternatives, the approach just described is applied by rewriting the two use equations as one:

$$x = \alpha d^c + \beta^c p_c d^c + \beta^q p_q d^q + \theta^c y d^c + \theta^q y d^q + e,$$

where d^c and d^q are dummies indicating that central and room systems were chosen, respectively. The parameters are estimated by first replacing d^c and d^q by their predicted values based on estimated functions of exogenous variables (using any of the three methods described), and then applying ordinary least squares.

Selectivity Correction Approach

It is most natural to discuss this approach in the context of parameters that are not equal over equations, since the additional complication of incorporating this equality is avoided. Therefore, consider for now the specification

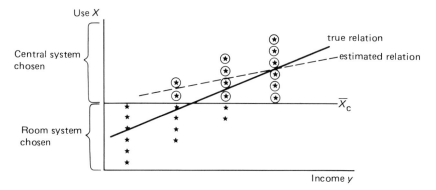

Figure 5.3
Bias due to self-selection.

$$x_c = \alpha + \beta^c p_c + \theta^c y + e_c, \tag{5.7}$$

$$x_q = \beta^q p_q + \theta^q y + e_q, \tag{5.8}$$

where $\beta^c \neq \beta^q$ and $\theta^c \neq \theta^q$ for the reasons discussed.

Suppose the researcher segmented the sample on the basis of the type of air conditioner chosen, and estimated (5.7) on the subsample that chose central air and (5.8) on the subsample that chose room air conditioner. Both equations would be estimated with bias. Consider income y in (5.7). A household that had low income would have a low probability of choosing a central system since it costs more than a room system. As a result, if a low income household chose a central system, then there must be unobserved factors (such as poor insulation in the house necessitating a powerful air conditioner) that induced the household to do so. These same factors would also tend to induce the household to use the system more than expected. Thus, when y is low for a household that chose a central system, we would expect e_c to be high; the household must have higher than expected use to induce it to purchase the central air system.

The bias is shown graphically in figure 5.3. Suppose the household chooses a central system if its use will exceed $\bar{x}_c$ but will choose a room air conditioner if its use of a central system will be below $\bar{x}_c$. Suppose further that use increases with income. If the amount that a household would use a central air system were somehow observed for all households, whether or not they actually chose a central system, then the data points indicated by asterisks would be obtained; for any given income level, there would be a distribution of use around the "true" line. However, if the equation is estimated **only** on those people who actually chose a central system, then the only data points used in the regression are those above $\bar{x}_c$, that is, the circled asterisks. As this graph shows, the line that best fits the data points used in the regression has a downwardly biased slope. This bias is called "selectivity bias," or "self-selection bias," because the estimation is performed on a subsample of households that, through their choice of alternative, essentially selected themselves to be included in estimation.

The correlation between income and the error term in the demand equation can also be seen in figure 5.3. For low levels of income, the only observed data points are those above the true line, i.e., those with positive errors; however, as income rises, negative errors become likely and larger in magnitude. Hence the negative correlation between y and e_c.

The bias is not limited to income. The choice probabilities are really the underlying issue; when the probability of choosing a central air system is low and it is purchased anyway, we expect use to be higher than average. Thus, any variable that affects the choice probability P_c is correlated, in that portion of the sample that chose central air, with the error term e_c in the use equation.

Stated more formally, the problem is that the expectation of e_c is not zero for each observation as required for ordinary least squares, but rather a function of the choice probability P_c. Therefore, to solve this problem, we decompose e_c into its expectation and a deviation from its expectation:

$$e_c = E(e_c) + \eta,$$

where $E(e_c)$ is a function of the probability of choosing a central system. The deviation η is due to factors that are unrelated to the choice between central and room systems and so is independent of P_c. The use equation for a central system becomes

$$x_c = \alpha + \beta^c p_c + \theta^c y + E(e_c) + \eta. \tag{5.9}$$

Since $E(\eta) = 0$ and p_c, y, and $E(e_c)$ are independent of η, this equation can be estimated by ordinary least squares if a consistent estimate for $E(e_c)$ can be obtained. The term $E(e_c)$ is called the "selectivity correction" since its inclusion corrects for selectivity bias.

Heckman (1978, 1979) has derived expressions for $E(e_c)$ under various sets of distributional assumptions. Using these techniques, Dubin and McFadden have shown that, if the choice probabilities are logit and e_c and e_q are normally distributed, then the selectivity correction is

$$E(e_c) = (\sqrt{6\sigma^2}/\pi)[(\rho_q P_q \ln P_q/(1 - P_q)) - \rho_c \ln P_c], \tag{5.10}$$

where σ^2 is the variance in e in the entire population (not conditional on the choice of system) and ρ_q and ρ_c are the correlation of e with the unobserved utility associated with room and central air systems, respectively.[6]

Generally σ^2, ρ_q, and ρ_c are unknown to the researcher. Furthermore, ρ_q and ρ_c are not independent; in fact, ρ_c necessarily equals the negative of ρ_q. This fact is explained as follows. Recall that only differences in utility matter, not the absolute level (see section 2.3). Therefore, any factor either (1) increases the utility of a central system relative to a room system (and thereby decreases the relative utility of a room system) or (2) decreases the relative utility of a central system (and increases that of a room system). A factor cannot increase or decrease the relative utility of **both** alternatives. (If the utility of a central system increased by u_c and that of a room system increased by u_q, then the relative utility of a central system increases and the relative utility of a room system decreases if $u_c - u_q$ exceeds zero, and vice versa if $u_c - u_q$ is less than zero.) Consider now an unobserved factor that increases a household's use of an air conditioner (for example, poor insultation). If this factor increases the relative utility of a central system, then it necessarily decreases the relative utility of a room system by the same amount. Thus, if ρ_c is positive, then ρ_q is necessarily negative by the same amount.

Since $\rho_c = -\rho_q$, equation (5.10) can be expressed in a form that does not require the researcher to know σ^2, ρ_q, or ρ_c. In particular, substituting $-\rho_c$ for ρ_q in (5.10), we have

$$E(e_c) = -(\sqrt{6\sigma^2}/\pi) \cdot \rho_c \left[\frac{P_q \ln P_q}{1 - P_q} + \ln P_c \right]. \tag{5.11}$$

With estimated choice probabilities P_q and P_c, the researcher can calculate the term in brackets. Entering this into the use equation gives

$$X_c = \alpha + \beta^c p_c + \theta^c y + \gamma^c C_c + \eta, \tag{5.12}$$

where C_c is the "selectivity correction term," calculated as $((P_q \ln P_q/(1 - P_q)) + \ln P_c)$ and γ^c is the coefficient of the selectivity correction term, which equals $(-\sqrt{6\sigma^2}/\pi)\rho_c$. Estimation of (5.12) provides a consistent estimate of each coefficient, including γ^c. Note that if the researcher expects ρ_c to be positive (e.g., unobserved factors that cause high use also increase the utility of a central system), then the coefficient of the selectivity correction term is expected to be negative.[7]

By the same arguments, we can show that the conditional demand equation for use of room air conditioners can be estimated by ordinary least squares on the subsample of households that chose a room system, provided a selectivity correction term is added. The estimation equation is

$$x_q = \beta^a p_q + \theta^a y + \gamma^a C_q + \eta,$$

where C_q equals $(P_c \ln P_c/(1 - P_c) + \ln P_q)$ and γ^q equals $(-\sqrt{6\sigma^2/\pi})\rho_q$, which can be estimated by ordinary least squares on the subsample of households that chose a room system.

The Selectivity Approach with Common Parameters   In the specification used thus far in describing the selectivity correction approach (i.e., equations (5.7) and (5.8)), there are no parameters that are equal across the use equations.[8] However, in the original specification of the example (equations (5.5) and (5.6)), common parameters appeared in the two equations. In fact, in many real world situations, particularly if the number of choice alternatives is large compared with the sample size, the researcher will choose to specify the conditional demand equations with parameters equal over equations.

Common parameters can be handled in two ways with the selectivity correction approach. The demand equations can be estimated as a system of simultaneous equations with each equation estimated on its own subsample (i.e., the subsample that chose that alternative) and with parameters explicitly restricted in the estimation procedure to be equal across equations. Alternatively, and usually more simply, the separate demand equations can be written as one and estimated on the pooled sample. In the example of air conditioner use, equations (5.5) and (5.6) would be rewritten as

$$x = \alpha d^c + \beta(p_c d^c + p_q d^q) + \theta y + \gamma_c(C_c d^c - C_q d^q) + \eta \qquad (5.13)$$

(since $\gamma_c = -\gamma_d$). With the selectivity correction term, the explanatory variables are not correlated with η and so ordinary least squares is consistent.

Equation (5.13) points out that the selectivity correction approach can be applied on either a pooled sample or choice based subsamples. When applied on a pooled sample, it is an alternative to two stage estimation, while on choice based samples it is the only option (since two stage estimation requires a pooled sample). In fact, even if there are no common parameters, the selectivity correction approach can be applied on a pooled sample. In the air conditioning example, instead of estimation of

$$x_c = \alpha + \beta^c p_c + \theta^c y + \gamma^c C_c + \eta$$

and

$$x_q = \beta^q p_q + \theta^q y + \gamma_q C_q + \eta$$

separately on the subsample of households that chose room and central systems, respectively, the researcher can estimate

$$x = \alpha d^c + \beta^c p_c d^c + \beta^q p_q d^q + \theta^c y d^c + \theta^q y d^q + \gamma_c (C_c d^c - C_q d^q) + \eta$$

on the pooled sample. In short, the selectivity correction approach is not restricted to the use of choice based subsamples, but is also applicable on pooled samples as an alternative to the two step estimation procedures described.

The Selectivity Correction Approach When Conditional Demand Is Observed Only for a Subsample   The selectivity correction approach is applicable in situations that cannot be handled with the two stage estimation procedures, namely, when conditional demand is observed only for those sampled decisionmakers that chose a particular alternative. For example, suppose an electric utility has a conservation program that customers are invited to join. The utility records the savings in electricity that each program participant obtained as a result of the program, and wants to relate these savings to characteristics of the customer as well as the price of electricity faced by the customer. The situation is a continuous/discrete one, with the choice of whether to join the program being discrete and the savings from the program being continuous. However, savings are observed only for those customers who joined the program. The savings that **would have** been obtained from participating in the program by those who did not join are not observed, and savings resulting from nonparticipation are necessarily zero. The savings equations in this case are

$$x_p = \theta s + e,$$

$$x_n = 0,$$

where x_p is the savings conditional upon being a participant, x_n is the savings conditional upon choosing not to be a participant, and s is a vector of characteristics of the customer and other explanatory variables.

The selectivity correction approach is perfectly appropriate for this situation (and was in fact developed for this type of situation rather than for ones in which two stage estimation could be used as an alternative). The researcher estimates a qualitative choice model on a sample of participants and nonparticipants; this model allows calculation of the probability of participating as a function of exogenous variables. The researcher then estimates the equation

$$x_p = \theta s + \hat{E}(e/p) + \eta, \tag{5.14}$$

on the subsample of customers that chose to participate in the program. In this equation, $\hat{E}(e/p)$ is a consistent estimate of the expectation of the error given that the customer participated in the program and is calculated as a function of the estimated probability of choosing to be a participant. If the choice model is logit, then $\hat{E}(e/p)$ takes the form of equation (5.11) with an appropriate change in terms. With this value of $\hat{E}(e/p)$, ordinary least squares applied to (5.14) is consistent.

6 Simulation with Qualitative Choice Models

Qualitative choice models operate at the level of individual decisionmakers. However, economists and policy analysts are usually interested in aggregate variables, such as national demand or demand within a state or metropolitan area. Issues concerning the estimation of aggregate variables from qualitative choice models are described in this chapter.

6.1 Aggregation

Introduction

In standard regression models, estimates of aggregate values of the dependent variable are obtained by inserting aggregate values of the explanatory variables. For example, suppose h_n is housing expenditures of person n, y_n is income of person n, and the model relating them is $h_n = \alpha + \beta y_n$. Since this model is linear, the average expenditure on housing is simply calculated as $\alpha + \beta \bar{y}$, where $\bar{y}$ is average income. Similarly, total expenditures on housing within an area (e.g., state) is $\alpha + \beta Y$, where Y is the total income in the area.

Qualitative choice models are not linear in explanatory variables, and, consequently, inserting aggregate values of the explanatory variables into the models will not provide an unbiased estimate of the aggregate value of the dependent variable. Consider a simple binary choice situation in which each household either rents or owns its dwelling. The probability of owning depends only on the household income; assume for convenience that the probability is logit:

$$P_{in} = \exp(\beta y_n)/(1 + \exp(\beta y_n)), \qquad i = \text{owning.}$$

Given this nonlinear model, the average probability of owning, $\bar{P}_i$, is not equal to the logit formula evaluated at average income, $\exp(\beta \bar{y})/(1 + \exp(\beta \bar{y}))$. This inequality is shown graphically in figure 6.1. Households one and two have incomes y_1 and y_2 and ownership probabilities of P_{i1} and P_{i2}, respectively. Their average income is $\bar{y}$. At this average income, the ownership probability given by the logit curve (that is, $\exp(\beta \bar{y})/(1 + \exp(\beta \bar{y}))$) is the value $P(\bar{y})$. This probability is higher (in this example) than the average probability, $\bar{P}_i$, which is the midpoint between P_{i1} and P_{i2}.

Aggregate estimates can be obtained from qualitative choice models in any of several ways. Three of these methods are now described.

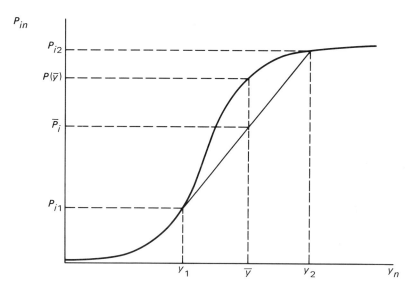

Figure 6.1
Demonstration that $\bar{P}_i \neq \exp(\beta\bar{y})/(1 + \exp(\beta\bar{y}))$, where $\bar{P}_i = (P_{i1} + P_{i2})/2$ and $\bar{y} = (y_1 + y_2)/2$.

Sample Enumeration of Choice Probabilities

The most straightforward, and by far the most popular, approach is sample enumeration, by which the choice probabilities of each decisionmaker in a sample are summed, or averaged, over decisionmakers. Consider a qualitative choice model that gives the probability, P_{in}, that decisionmaker n will choose alternative i from a set of alternatives. Suppose a sample of N decisionmakers, labeled $n = 1, \ldots, N$, was drawn from the population for which aggregate estimates are required. Each sampled decisionmaker has some weight associated with it, representing the number of decisionmakers similar to it in the population (this weight, for samples based on exogenous factors, is the inverse of the probability that the decisionmaker was selected for the sample). Label the weight for decisionmaker n as w_n. Note that if the sample is purely random, then w_n is the same for all n; if the sample is stratified random, then w_n is the same for all n within a stratum.

A consistent estimate of the total number of decisionmakers in the population that choose alternative i (labeled $\hat{N}_i$) is simply the weighted sum of the individual probabilities:

$$\hat{N}_i = \sum_n w_n P_{in}.$$

The average probability for alternative i is

$$\bar{P}_i = \hat{N}_i/N = (1/N)\sum_n w_n P_{in}.$$

Obviously, the average probability is the estimated share of decisionmakers that choose alternative i.

Sample Enumeration of Randomly Generated Choices

Recall from chapter 1 that for qualitative choice models the decisionmaker is assumed to choose the alternative that provides the greatest utility. Utility is composed of an observed and an unobserved part, and assumptions about the distribution of the unobserved component give rise to the choice probabilities. These facts can be utilized in an alternative method of estimating aggregate variables.

Assume each decisionmaker faces a choice among a set J of alternatives, with utility $V_{in} + e_{in}$ associated with each i in J. Representative utility is calculated from observed data and estimated parameters. In the straight-forward procedure just described, choice probabilities are calculated from the values of representative utility. Alternatively, the choice of the decision-maker can be "mimicked" by selecting a value of e_{in} for each i in J from its assumed distribution and observing for which alternative the quantity $V_{in} + e_{in}$ is greatest. That is, for each decisionmaker, a random number generator assigns a value to each e_{in}, for all i in J. The assumed distribution of e is used as the basis of the random number generator (e.g., if the model is logit, then random numbers are generated from the extreme value distribution; if probit, then from the normal). The value of each e_{in} generated in this way is then added to the representative utility for the alternative, and the decisionmaker is considered to choose the alternative with the highest utility.

The total number of decisionmakers in the population who choose a particular alternative is estimated as the weighted sum of sampled decision-makers who "chose" that alternative:

$$\hat{N}_i = \sum_i w_n D_{in},$$

where $D_{in} =$ one if $V_{in} + e_{in}$ is greater than $V_{jn} + e_{jn}$ for all $j \neq i$, given the calculated values of V_{in} and generated values of e_{in}, and is zero otherwise.

If each sampled decisionmaker's choice is mimicked numerous times, with the random number generator assigning new values of e_{in} each time, then the proportion of times the decisionmaker "chooses" each alternative will approach the choice probability for that alternative. Alternatively, if the sample size is expanded, then the proportion of the decisionmakers with the same values of observed variables who choose a particular alternative will approach the choice probability for that alternative. Therefore, $\hat{N}_i$ is a consistent estimate of the actual number of decisionmakers in the population that choose alternative i.

For a given sample size, sample enumeration on choice probabilities produces more accurate estimates of aggregate variables than sample enumeration with randomly generated choices. However, if the choice probability is complex (e.g., with probit or a complicated GEV structure), then the computer time required to generate random numbers for each alternative might be considerably less than that required to calculate choice probabilities. For given computer costs, therefore, a larger sample is possible if randomly generated choices are used rather than choice probabilities.

Segmentation

When the number of explanatory variables in a qualitative choice model is low, and those variables take only a few values, it is possible to estimate aggregate variables without utilizing a sample of decisionmakers. Consider, for example, a model with only two variables entering the representative utility of each alternative: education level and sex of the decisionmaker. Suppose the education variable consists of four categories: did not complete high school (A), completed high school, but had no college (B), had some college, but did not receive a degree (C), and received a college degree (D). Then the total number of different types of decisionmakers is eight; these eight segments are depicted in figure 6.2 and are labeled $s = 1, \ldots, 8$.

If the researcher has data on the number of people in each segment of the population (i.e., the number of decisionmakers in each cell in figure 6.2), then aggregate variables can be estimated by calculating choice probabilities for each of the eight types of decisionmakers and taking the weighted sum of these choice probabilities. That is, an estimate of the number of decisionmakers in the population who choose alternative i is

$$N_i = \sum_{s=1}^{8} w_s P_{is},$$

	Male	Female
(A) Did not complete high school	1	2
(B) Completed high school, but had no college	3	4
(C) Had some college, but did not receive a degree	5	6
(D) Received a college degree	7	8

Figure 6.2
Segmentation of population.

where P_{is} is the probability that a decisionmaker in segment s (i.e., with a given education level and sex) chooses alternative i, and w_s is the number of decisionmakers in the population who are in segment s.

Note that this procedure is entirely dependent on the researcher knowing the number of decisionmakers in the population who are in each segment. Sometimes this information can be obtained from published population statistics, such as census summaries. Often, however, the information can only be estimated from a sample drawn from the population. In these cases, the procedure does not allow the researcher to avoid taking a sample. However, if the number of segments is smaller than the sample size, then the procedure can reduce computer costs; choice probabilities are calculated for each segment rather than each sampled decisionmaker, and the sample is used simply to estimate the number of decisionmakers in each segment.

6.2 Forecasting

For forecasting into some future year, the same basic procedures described are applied. However, the exogenous variables and/or the weights are adjusted to reflect changes that are anticipated over time. For the sample enumeration procedures, the sample is adjusted in either of these two ways so that it **looks like** a sample that would be drawn in the future year. For example, to forecast the number of people who will choose a given alternative five years in the future, a sample drawn in the current year is adjusted to reflect changes in socioeconomic and other factors that are expected to occur over the next five years. The sample is adjusted in either or both of two ways, (1) by changing the values of the variables relating to each sampled decisionmaker (e.g., increasing each decisionmaker's income to represent real income growth over time) and/or (2) by changing the weight, w_n, attached to each decisionmaker to reflect changes over time in the number of decisionmakers in the population that are similar to the sampled decisionmaker (e.g., increasing the weights for one-person households and decreasing the weights for six-person households to represent expected decreases in household size over time).

For the segmentation approach, changes in explanatory variables over time are represented by changes in the number of decisionmakers in each segment. The explanatory variables themselves cannot logically be adjusted since the distinct values of the explanatory variables define the segments. Changing the variables associated with a decisionmaker in one segment simply shifts the decisionmaker to another segment.

Changing the weights associated with each sampled decisionmaker in the sample enumeration procedure, and adjusting the number of decision-makers in each segment for the segmentation approach, are essentially the same process. Consider a choice model with one explanatory variable, a dummy indicating whether the decisionmaker is over 30 years old or under 30. Label the number of decisionmakers over and under 30 in the base year as $O30_b$ and $U30_b$, respectively, where b denotes the base year (i.e., the year in which the sample used for forecasting was drawn). Suppose that the researcher predicts (or assumes) that in the forecast year the number of decisionmakers over and under 30 will be $O30_f$ and $U30_f$, where f denotes the forecast year. For sample enumeration, the appropriate adjustment in weights in this case is the following. For each sampled decisionmaker under 30 in the base year, the weight for the forecast year is calculated as $(U30_f/U30_b)$ times the decisionmaker's original weight in the base year. Similarly, the forecast year weight for a decisionmaker over 30 is $(O30_f/O30_b)$ times the base year weight. For the segmentation approach, the number of people in the under 30 segment is considered to be $U30_f$ instead of $U30_b$; and similarly for the over 30 segment.

This concept can be generalized to any number of segments. Suppose the explanatory variables in a particular model can take K distinct combinations of values, labeled $k = 1, \ldots, K$, and called segments. Assume the number of decisionmakers in segment k in the base and forecast years is M_b^k and M_f^k, respectively. With sample enumeration, the weight for any sampled decisionmaker who is in segment k in the base year is adjusted by M_f^k/M_b^k for

the forecast year. For estimation of aggregates by the segmentation procedure, the choice probabilities for segment k are weighted by M_f^k in the
forecast year rather than M_b^k.[1]

6.3   Recalibration of Alternative-Specific Constants

Often the representative utility for each alternative in a qualitative choice
model includes a constant term, for example,

$$V_{in} = \beta z_{in} + \alpha_i,$$

where z_{in} is a vector of variables relating to decisionmaker n's utility for
alternative i, β is a vector of parameters, and α_i is a scalar parameter. The
true value of α_i is the mean of all factors that affect the utility of alternative i
but are not included in the vector z_i (see section 2.3).

The value of α_i for each i is estimated along with β on the sample used for
estimation. However, if, in simulation, the model is run on a sample from a
different area or different time than the sampled used for estimation (e.g., if
the forecasting sample is drawn from one state while the estimation sample
was nationwide, or the forecast sample is drawn in 1984 while the estimation sample was drawn in 1980), then the value of α_i for each i will need to
be reestimated to reflect the fact that the mean of unincluded variables in
the area for which forecasts are made is not the same as those in the area
from which the estimation sample was drawn.[2]

The α_i for all i are recalibrated with an iterative procedure that utilizes
information on the number of decisionmakers that actually chose alternative i in the forecast area in some base year. The procedure can be described
as follows. Let S_i denote the number of decisionmakers that chose alternative i in the forecast area in the base year. Run the model with its original
values of α_i for all i on the sample of decisionmakers for the forecast area
and estimate the number of decisionmakers to choose alternative i; label the
predicted number for alternative i as N_i^o, where the superscript o denotes
that these predictions are based on the original values of the α_i.

The next step is to compare the proportion of decisionmakers predicted
to choose each alternative with the proportion who actually did. That is, let
the predicted and actual proportions be denoted

$$n_i^o = N_i^o / \sum_j N_j^o; \qquad s_i = S_i / \sum_j S_j.$$

The model with its original values of the α_i is overpredicting alternative i if n_i^o is larger than s_i, and underpredicting if s_i is larger than n_i^o. This misprediction can be attributed to the fact that the original α_i for all i represent the mean of unincluded variables in the estimation area rather than in the forecast area. Consequently, each α_i should be corrected. In particular, each α_i is adjusted to new values using the formula

$$\alpha_i^1 = \alpha_i^o + \ln(s_i/n_i^o),$$

where α_i^o is the original value of α_i and α_i^1 is the first adjusted value. Note that if s_i is larger than n_i^o, and the model is underpredicting alternative i, then the adjustment increases the value of α_i, thereby increasing its desirability as measured by V_i. Conversely, if n_i^o is greater than s_i, the model is overpredicting alternative i, and the adjustment decreases α_i and hence the representative utility of alternative i.

The adjustment just described completes the first iteration of the recalibration procedure. For the second iteration, the model is run with the new values of α_i (that is, the α_i^1) and new predictions are obtained. Label the proportion of decisionmakers that are predicted to choose alternative i with these new α_i^1 as n_i^1. Compare n_i^1 with s_i for all i. If these values are close, then use the α_i^1 as the final recalibrated values. If n_i^1 and s_i are not close for all i, then adjust each α_i by the formula

$$\alpha_i^2 = \alpha_i^1 + \ln(s_i/n_i^1),$$

where α_i^2 is the twice-adjusted value of α_i. Continue this process, obtaining new values of the α_i with each iteration, until the predicted proportion for each alternative is close to the actual proportion.

6.4   Pivot Point Analysis with Logit Models

The standard way to analyze policies and "what if" situations with a qualitative choice model is to simulate demand with the model twice, once with "base case" values for explanatory variables (i.e., observed values for the base year and assumed values for the forecast years) and a second time with one or more of the explanatory variables changed to represent the policy or situation being examined. For example, the effect of a gas tax on automobile demand is usually assessed by simulating aggregate demand for each class of vehicle using expected gas prices, and then estimating demand again with higher gas prices (representing the tax) entering the model. The difference in the two simulation results is the estimated impact of the gasoline tax.

This standard procedure is the most accurate and is applicable for all qualitative choice models. If the model is logit, however, an approach called "pivot point analysis" is sometimes used instead. It is much easier and less expensive than the standard approach. And, for small changes in explanatory variables, it is perhaps not too inaccurate.

The method is based on the derivatives of the logit formula. Suppose a researcher is interested in examining the impact of a change in a particular explanatory variable affecting the utility of alternative i for all decisionmakers. For decisionmaker n, this variable is labeled X_{in}. If the choice probabilities are logit, the change in the probability that decisionmaker n will choose alternative i (see section 2.4) is

$$\partial P_{in}/\partial X_{in} = (\partial V_{in}/\partial X_{in})P_{in}(1 - P_{in}).$$

That is, the researcher can estimate the effect of the change in X_{in} by running the model only once, to obtain the choice probabilities prior to the change. By knowing the derivative of representative utility with respect to X_{in} (e.g., if V_{in} is linear in X_{in}, then $\partial V_{in}/\partial X_{in}$ is simply the estimated coefficient of X_{in}), the researcher calculates the impact on decisionmaker n by the formula just given. The impact at the aggregate level is similarly determined:

$$\partial \hat{N}_i/\partial X_{in \text{ for all } n} = \sum_n w_n(\partial V_{in}/\partial X_{in})P_{in}(1 - P_{in}),$$

where $\hat{N}_i$ is the estimated number of decisionmakers who choose alternative i.

When a sample of decisionmakers is unavailable for the area for which policy analysis is being performed, a common practice has been to estimate the impact of changes in explanatory variables by applying pivot point analysis to the average probabilities. That is, the change in the proportion of decisionmakers choosing alternative i is estimated as

$$((\partial \bar{V}_i/\partial \bar{X}_i)\bar{P}_i(1 - \bar{P}_i)),$$

where $\bar{X}_i$, $\bar{V}_i$, and $\bar{P}_i$ are the averages of X_{in}, V_{in}, and P_{in}, respectively, over all n. $\bar{P}_i$ can be observed from aggregate data. It is simply the proportion of decisionmakers who actually chose alternative i. The quantity $\partial \bar{V}_i/\partial \bar{X}_i$ can also be known in many cases without sample information; for example, if V_{in}

is linear in X_{in}, then $\partial \bar{V}_i / \partial \bar{X}_i$ is simply the coefficient of X_{in}. Thus, the change in average probabilities is estimated without a sample.

This procedure does not produce a consistent estimate of the impact of changes in explanatory variables. It misses the fundamental point that the average probability is not the probability calculated at the average of the explanatory variables and similarly that the derivative of the average probability is not the derivative of the probability calculated at the average explanatory variables.

II AN APPLICATION TO AUTOMOBILE DEMAND

7 Previous Research on Automobile Demand[1]

7.1 Introduction

Forecasts of auto demand and use play a central role in the planning and decisionmaking of numerous public agencies and private organizations. For example:

• The U.S. Department of Energy, and the equivalent agencies for various states, are responsible for anticipating gas shortages and establishing policies and programs to reduce gas consumption to prevent future shortages and reduce U.S. dependence on foreign oil. Projections of future gas consumption, and the impact on gas consumption of various possible forms of government intervention, are routinely based on forecasts of auto demand and use.

• State Departments of Transportation depend on revenues from gas taxes to finance the construction and maintenance of highways. The size of these revenues depends on the demand and use of autos, so that the prediction of this demand and use is critical to these departments' planning of capital programs.

• Air quality boards at the local, state, and federal levels are mandated to monitor air quality and recommend policies to reduce air pollution. Since auto emissions are a large component of pollution, air quality standards and policies are largely based upon projected auto use.

• The health of the auto industry in general depends on consumers' demand for autos, and consumers' choices among the various makes and models determine the relative well-being of individual firms within the industry. Auto manufacturers use demand forecasts in their financial planning and in decisions regarding expansions and contractions of plant capacity.

• Local transit agencies employ models of transit patronage in assessing carrier requirements (e.g., how many buses are needed) and in planning for service changes. In most of the more recent patronage forecasting models, the number of autos owned in the area is an important input. Consequently, transit agencies utilize projections of auto ownership levels as a step toward obtaining accurate projections of transit patronage.

• Recently, electric utilities have been interested in assessing the potential impact that electric autos would have on total electricity demand and time-of-day use patterns for electricity. These investigations have been based on various forecasts of the potential demand for electric cars over the next twenty years (see, for example, the analysis by Beggs, Cardell, and Hausman, 1979, for the Electric Power Research Institute).

Given the important role that auto forecasts play in a wide variety of settings, it is no surprise that auto demand and use has been a lively area of research. Numerous models have been constructed to forecast auto demand, and the accuracy and usefulness of these models in forecasting and policy analysis has, in general, increased steadily over time. A review of these models is the topic of this chapter.

The purpose of this review is twofold. The first is to identify factors that have been found consistently in previous research to affect auto demand. The emphasis here is on consistency across studies. Any one study can identify factors that, with its data and methodology, seem to affect auto demand; the value of a review of numerous studies is the ability to compare results across data sets and methodologies to find factors that arise persistently and, hence, cannot be thought to be data- or methodology-dependent. The second purpose is to identify limitations that are consistently encountered in previous models. Knowing these limitations allows for more accurate forecasting and policy analysis since the effects of the limitations on the models' forecasts can be understood and, if necessary, compensated for. Furthermore, limitations that are common to all previous models define the frontier in the field and, as such, guide the way for future research.

Both of these purposes serve the ultimate aim of the literature review, which is to motivate and place in perspective the new model of automobile demand presented in the following chapter. The set of factors found in previous research to influence auto demand becomes, in considering the new model, a list of variables that the model should incorporate; and the new model's findings regarding what factors significantly affect demand are verified, or validated, by comparison with the previous findings. In addition, for the new model to be considered an advance toward more complete and more accurate assessment of auto demand, it should overcome some of the limitations found in previous research. That is, the limitations of previous research become the benchmark for evaluating new research.

This chapter is organized along methodological lines. That is, the previous research is divided into groups on the basis of the methods employed for addressing the issue of auto ownership, and studies within each of the groups are discussed together. This organizational scheme serves three functions. First, it saves space since the method used in a given group is

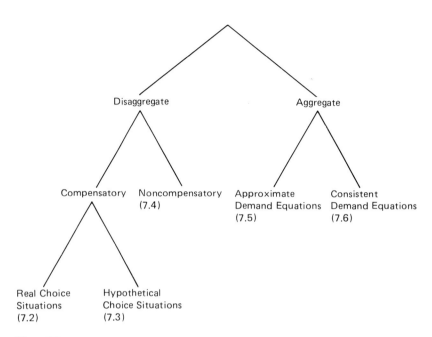

Figure 7.1
Categorization of previous research on auto ownership decisions. Note: The numbers in parentheses denote the sections in which the categories of research are discussed.

discussed only once and then applied to each of the studies in the group. Second, the scheme facilitates an understanding of the kind of information that can be obtained with each method, and consequently aids in the planning of future research. Third, the relation of the new demand model presented in chapter 8 to previous studies, and, in particular, the methodological tradition in which this new model was bred, is more easily discernible.

The categories of research are depicted in figure 7.1, with the numbers in parentheses designating the chapter sections in which each group is discussed. The terms, and the relevant distinctions that motivate this categorization, are defined and delineated in the appropriate sections.

7.2 Disaggregate, Compensatory Models Based on Real Choice Situations

Studies within this group apply the qualitative choice methods discussed in part I to households' auto ownership decisions. The approach, in this context, consists of the following set of assumptions. Each household decides how many autos and which autos to own. These decisions entail a choice among several alternatives. In deciding how many autos to own, the consumer has a choice of zero, one, two, and so on. In deciding which autos to own, the choice is among all the available makes, models, and vintages of automobiles. Each alternative that is available to the household is seen by the household as consisting of a set of characteristics. In the choice of which autos to own the household characterizes each make, model, and vintage of auto by its purchase price, fuel economy, number of seats, luggage-carrying capacity, and so on. In the choice of how many autos to own, the relevant characteristics include the cost of owning the number of autos designated by the alternative (e.g., the cost of owning two autos) and the usefulness to the household of having the number of autos designated by the alternative (as reflected in such factors as the number of people in a household, the number of household members who need to drive an auto to work, and so on).

The household would derive some happiness or "utility" from each alternative if it were to choose that alternative. This utility depends on the characteristics of the alternative; in particular, the consumer places some value on each of the characteristics of the alternative, and the utility derived from the alternative is the aggregate of the utility from each of the characteristics of the alternative. The household chooses the alternative that provides it higher utility than any of the other alternatives. In the choice of how many autos to own, the household chooses one auto if it obtains more utility from having one auto (considering both the cost of owning autos and their usefulness) than from having no autos or more than one auto. In the choice of which auto to own, the household chooses the particular make, model, and vintage of auto that it sees as having the most desirable set of characteristics, including price, operating cost, seating, and so on.

The researcher observes the actual choices that a sample of households makes (that is, the researcher observes how many and which autos each household in a given sample owns). The researcher also observes the characteristics of the alternatives that were available to the household. With this information, the researcher statistically infers the value that households place on each characteristic. The inferred values are those that would result in the households' choosing the alternatives that they actually chose.

Studies that use this method are labeled "disaggregate compensatory models based on real choice situations" because

1. the unit of analysis is the individual consumer (or household), and hence the term "disaggregate";
2. the household is assumed to trade off characteristics in the sense that a high value of one characteristic can compensate for a low value of another characteristic (for example, the household would choose an auto that is smaller than it wants if the price is sufficiently low)—therefore the models are "compensatory"; and
3. the researcher observes the household's actual choice in a real choice situation, rather than asking the household what it would do in a hypothetical situation.

Numerous studies of this type have examined consumers' choices of **how many** autos to own: Farrell (1954), Janosi (1959), Kreinin (1959), Huang (1964, 1966), Burns and Golob (1975), Johnson (1975, 1978), Lerman and Ben-Akiva (1976), Kain and Fauth (1977), Mogridge (1978), Train (1980a), Hocherman, Prashker, and Ben-Akiva (1982),[2] Booz, Allen, and Hamilton, Inc. (1983), Hensher and Le Plastrier (1983), and Mannering and Winston (1983).

There is a fair degree of consistency among the findings of these studies. First, each of the studies included income as an explanatory variable, and it entered significantly in all but two. Second, Farrell; Huang; Kreinin; Lerman and Ben-Akiva; Mogridge; Train; Hocherman, Prashker, and Ben-Akiva; Booz, Allen, and Hamilton, Inc.; Hensher and Le Plastrier; and Mannering and Winston included a variable, which in each case entered significantly, reflecting the cost of owning an auto, either purchase price or an annualized user cost.[3] Third, the availability and ease of travel on public transit entered as an explanatory variable (in different forms in different studies) in the models of Burns and Golob; Lerman and Ben-Akiva; Train; Hocherman, Prashker, and Ben-Akiva; and Hensher and Le Plastrier. This variable had a strong influence in all of these models; furthermore, its omission in the other studies is due to the fact that the other researchers did not construct such a variable, rather than that they attempted to do so and found that the variables did not enter significantly. Finally, the number of workers in the household significantly affects the household's choice of how many autos to own in the models of Lerman and Ben-Akiva; Train; Booz, Allen, and Hamilton, Inc.; Hensher and Le Plastrier; and Mannering and Winston. This reflects, of course, the high probability of a worker needing to use an auto for the commute to work.

The studies do not exhibit consistency with respect to any other variables; that is, no other variable enters significantly in several of the studies. It seems, therefore, that these studies demonstrate that (at least) four factors affect consumers' decisions as to how many autos to own, namely, the cost of auto ownership, the availability/ease of public transit, the income of the household, and the number of workers in the household.

Recently, research has focused on the choice of which vehicle to own. Such studies have been conducted by Lave and Train (1979), Cambridge Systematics, Inc. (as reported by Cambridge Systematics, Inc., 1980a and 1980b, and Manski and Sherman, 1980), Charles River Associates (as reported by Beggs and Cardell, 1980, and Charles River Associates, 1980), Lave and Bradley (1980), Hocherman, Prashker, and Ben-Akiva (1982), Booz, Allen, and Hamilton, Inc. (1983), Hensher and Le Plastrier (1983), Mannering and Winston (1983), Winston and Mannering (1984), and Berkovec and Rust (1985).

While these studies used a common methodology, they are not completely comparable because each study examined a somewhat different aspect of consumers' choice of auto type. Lave and Train, and Winston and Mannering, focused on new car purchases, with Winston and Mannering examining the household's choices among each make and model of new vehicle and Lave and Train examining which class of new auto was chosen (with all makes and models of new autos aggregated into ten classes). The other studies included both new and used vehicles in their analyses, but did so in quite different ways. The model of Hocherman, Prashker, and Ben-Akiva described households' purchases (i.e., make, model, and vintage choice conditioned upon a purchase being made), while the remaining studies examined vehicle holdings (i.e., the types of vehicles held by a household at a given point in time). Among the latter studies, Berkovec and Rust restricted their analysis to one-vehicle households, and Charles River Associates to households with two or more vehicles. Furthermore, Cambridge Systematics, Inc.; Booz, Allen, and Hamilton, Inc.; Berkovec and Rust; and Mannering and Winston examined the choice among each available make and model of vehicle, while Lave and Bradley examined only the choice between domestic and foreign vehicles and Hensher and Le Plastrier examined the choice among the three makes and models that the houehold stated it considered most closely. As a final anomaly, Charles River Associates examined the choice of class and vintage for the **smallest** vehicles owned by multivehicle households.

Given the differences among the studies, there is a surprising consistency among the results. Table 7.1 presents the explanatory variables that entered

Table 7.1
Explanatory variables entering models of auto type choice

	Lave and Train	Cambridge Systematics, Inc.		Charles River Associates	Lave and Bradley
		One-auto household	Two-auto household		
Choices examined	Class of new car to purchase (ten size classes)	Make, model, and vintage of vehicle held	Make, model, and vintage of pair of vehicles held	Class and vintage of the smallest vehicle held by multivehicle households, with five size classes and four vintage categories	Foreign or domestic cars held
Vehicle characteristics	Purchase price Operating cost Number of seats Weight Horsepower to weight ratio	Purchase price Operating cost Number of seats Weight Acceleration time Turning radius Braking distance Luggage space Scrappage probability	Purchase price Operating cost Number of seats Weight Acceleration time Luggage space Scrappage probability	Purchase price Operating cost Wheelbase "Depreciated luxury" Age of vehicle	
Characteristics of consumers (households)	Income Number of people in household Age Education Number of autos owned Vehicle miles traveled per month	Income Number of people in household Age Education Whether households lives in a city or rural area	Income Number of people in household Age Education Whether household lives in a city or rural area	Income Number of people in household Distance to parking	Education Number of autos owned Whether household lives near coast or not Percent of U.S. built cars assembled in state in which household lives

Table 7.1 (continued)

	Hocherman, Prashker, and Ben-Akiva	Booz, Allen, and Hamilton, Inc.		Hensher and Le Plastrier
		One-auto household	Two-auto household	
Choices examined	Make, model, and vintage of vehicle to purchase	Make, model, and vintage of vehicle held	Make, model, and vintage of pair of vehicles held	Make, model, and vintage of each vehicle held from among three most closely considered
Vehicle characteristics	Purchase price Fuel efficiency Length and width Horsepower to weight ratio Luggage space Engine size Age of vehicle	Purchase price Operating cost Number of seats Horsepower to weight ratio Reliability (*Consumer Reports*) Age of vehicle	Purchase price Operating cost Number of seats Horsepower to weight ratio Age of vehicle	Registration charge Service and repair expense Sales tax on purchase price Number of seats Fuel efficiency Weight Luggage space Age of vehicle
Characteristics of consumers (households)	Income Number of people in household Age Whether car is used for work Whether driver is disabled and hence exempt from sales tax[a] Whether household is reimbursed for operating expenses by employer or business	Income Number of people in household Age Education Whether household lives in a city or rural area Region of country in which household resides Number of miles the household drives annually	Income Number of people in household Age Education Region of country in which household resides Number of miles the household drives annually	Age Number of passengers normally carried Whether vehicle is driven over 600 miles per month Whether auto is used for paid work

	Mannering and Winston		Winston and Mannering	Berkovec and Rust
	One-auto household	Two-auto household		
Choices examined	Make, model, and vintage of vehicle held	Make, model, and vintage of pair of vehicles held	Make and model of new vehicle to purchase	Make and model of vehicle held, for one-auto household
Vehicle characteristics	Purchase price Operating cost Shoulder room Horsepower to engine displacement ratio Luggage space Age of vehicle	Purchase price Operating cost Shoulder room Age of vehicle	Purchase price Fuel efficiency Weight Horsepower Expected collision costs Probability of injury over $1,000 given an injury occurs	Purchase price Operating cost Number of seats Horsepower to weight ratio Turning radius Age of vehicle
Characteristics of consumers (households)	Income Number of people in household Age Number of miles driven in previous year	Income Number of people in household Number of miles driven in previous year	Income Number of vehicles owned Number of miles driven in previous year	Income Number of people in household Age Whether household lives in a city with over one million people, smaller city, or rural area

a. Study conducted in Israel.

each model. Excluding the Lave and Bradley study (which did not attempt to enter vehicle characteristics), each of the studies found that consumers consider price,[4] operating cost (or fuel efficiency), and some measure of size (e.g., number of seats, weight, and/or wheelbase) when deciding which auto to buy or own. In addition, the age of the auto appears as a factor affecting consumers' decisions in all of the models except those of Lave and Train, and Winston and Mannering, which examined new car purchases only and hence cannot logically include a vehicle age variable.[5]

The power of the vehicle (as measured by horsepower, horsepower to weight ratio, or acceleration time) enters seven of the models. However, the studies were consistently unable to find a significant and general relation of vehicle power to households' choices. Power variables enter with an incorrect sign in one study (Cambridge Systematics, Inc.) and with inconsistent results in each of two others (Booz, Allen, and Hamilton, Inc., and Berkovec and Rust). In Lave and Train, and in Mannering and Winston, the sign is correct, but the variable does not enter significantly. In the two studies in which vehicle power entered significantly and with the correct sign, it does so for only a part of the population (drivers 30 to 45 years of age) in one (Hocherman, Prashker, and Ben-Akiva) and with regard only to new car purchases in the other (Winston and Mannering). Furthermore, the researchers at Charles River Associates, who decided not to enter a power variable, apparently did not do so because of problems in estimating a sensible coefficient for the variable (see the discussion of model C in Beggs and Cardell, 1980). It seems reasonable to conclude, therefore, that vehicle power plays little or no role in consumers' choices of vehicle. On this point, the studies are quire consistent in their lack of positive results.

There is also a fair degree of consistency regarding the characteristics of households that most affect the choice of auto type. Eight of the ten studies found income to be important. (Lave and Bradley, and Hensher and Le Plastrier, are the exceptions; they did not enter an income variable and consequently could not determine whether income was important.) The number of people in the household and variables denoting the age of the household head or primary driver entered seven models. The number of autos owned by the household was found to affect the choice of auto type in six of the studies.[6] However, of the four studies that did not include the number of autos, one study could not logically do so (Berkovec and Rust analyzed one-vehicle households only) and another could do so only if the effect of owning three vehicles is different from that of owning two (Charles

River Associates examined only households with more than one vehicle). Therefore, the number of autos was found to be important in six of the eight studies in which its effect could be examined.

In summary, it seems that previous research indicates that the following factors affect consumers' choices of which type of auto to own: the price, operating cost, size, and age of the auto, and the income, size, and age of the household, as well as the number of autos that is owns.

Despite the consistency among these studies in their appraisal of the factors that affect consumers' choices, all of the models have serious limitations that inhibit their accuracy and usefulness in forecasting and policy analysis. The first and perhaps most serious limitation is that previous models examine only a few of the many interrelated choices that determine a household's demand for vehicles. For example, most of the models examine either the household's choice of how many vehicles to own or its choice of vehicle class or make/model, but not both.[7] Insofar as these two choices are interrelated, ignoring one in the analysis of the other could, in addition to rendering the analysis less complete, produce bias in the estimated parameters.

Similarly, the interrelation of vehicle choice and vehicle use is not usually incorporated in a consistent fashion. Only one of the studies (Mannering and Winston) has modeled the household's choice of how much to drive each vehicle and the interrelation of this choice with the choice of how many and what class or make/model of vehicles to own. Most of the studies ignore the amount the household drives in the analysis of how many or what class or make/model of vehicle the household owns, implicitly assuming that there is no relation among the choices. A few of the studies have included the household's annual vehicle miles traveled as an explanatory variable, reflecting the idea that households that drive a lot have an incentive to buy vehicles with low operating costs.[8] However, in reality, the amount that a household drives is itself affected by the cost per mile of the household's vehicles; that is, the number of miles a household drives both affects and is affected by its choice of vehicle class and make/model, since the operating cost that the household faces is determined when the household chooses a particular class and make/model of vehicle. Consequently, including vehicle miles traveled, which is an endogenous variable, in a model of the choice of class or make/model, and estimating the model as if the variable were exogenous, produces classic simultaneity bias in the estimated parameters.

As stated, only Mannering and Winston have specified, and determined an appropriate estimation procedure to account for, the interrelated choice of how many vehicles to own, and what class and make/model of vehicles to own, and how much to drive. Unfortunately, their model examines only the choices of households that own at least one vehicle and ignores the household's choice of whether or not to own any vehicle. This means that no model currently exists that describes, in a consistent manner, the inter-related decisions of how many vehicles to own (including none), what types of vehicles to own, and how much to drive each vehicle. Such a model is needed for accurate assessment of the impact of policies and changes in demographics, fuel prices, and vehicle characteristics on the demand for automobiles and consumption of gasoline.

The second problem, or unsolved dilemma, in previously estimated models concerns their handling of individual makes and models of vehicles. Lave and Train; Charles River Associates; and Lave and Bradley grouped makes and models of vehicles into classes, calculated the average character-istics (e.g., average price) for each class,[9] and described the household's choice among these classes. Any two classes that have the same average characteristics are predicted by these models to have the same demand. However, in reality, the demand for two classes will be very different if one class has a wider variety of vehicles within it than another class, even if average characteristics of makes/models within the two classes are the same.

The other seven studies of vehicle type choice avoided this problem by describing the demand for each individual make and model of vehicle. However, their approaches to doing so entailed different problems. First, each of the studies used a logit model to describe the choice among each make and model of vehicle. While simple computationally, the indepen-dence from irrelevant alternatives property of the logit model is most definitely violated in this application.[10] Unobserved factors that affect the utility that households obtain from a particular vehicle are related to those for a similar vehicle; consequently, the unobserved component of utility is correlated over similar alternatives, in contradiction to the assumptions of the logit model. For example, Toyotas and Nissans are similar to each other and different from Cadillacs and Oldsmobiles in ways that are not mea-sured by the researcher, just as Cadillacs and Oldsmobiles are similar to each other and different from Toyotas and Nissans in characteristics that are not entered by the researcher into the models. Treating the choice situation as if unobserved factors were uncorrelated across vehicles results in inconsistent estimates of model parameters.[11]

In forecasting, the specification of the model in terms of makes and models of vehicles presents difficulties at a practical level. First, the models require an unwieldy amount of input data when forecasting (namely, projections of the characteristics of each future make and model). Second, some ad hoc procedures are required in forecasting to reduce the enormous number of calculations that are necessary. For example, the standard way to predict market demand is to calculate, for each sampled household, the probability of choosing each make and model of vehicle, and to sum these probabilities over the sampled household (i.e., the market demand for any make/model is the sum over households of the probability of the household choosing that make/model). However, this procedure is very expensive since the number of makes and models is so large. To reduce costs, Cambridge Systematics, Inc., for example, assigned to each household a particular make/model on the basis of a random number generator that reflects the probability of choosing each make and model; market demand for a make/model is obtained by counting the number of households that are assigned that make/model. This procedure, which is equivalent to raising the probability of the assigned make/model to one and lowering all the other probabilities to zero, requires less calculation but necessarily reduces the forecasting accuracy. If the sample size is small compared with the number of makes and models (as it is likely to be), this reduction in accuracy can be substantial.[12]

A final limitation in the previous research is that most of the models that contain a sufficient number of explanatory variables to be potentially useful in policy analysis also contain estimated parameters that have unreasonable implications. For example, the Lave and Train model contains squared terms that can dominate nonsquared terms and thereby give nonsensical results. Specifically, the model includes two terms for vehicle price: price divided by the household's income, and this quantity squared. As expected, the nonsquared term enters with a negative coefficient, and the squared term with a positive coefficient. However, for low income households and high-priced vehicles the squared term dominates, implying that an increase in the vehicle's price will increase the probability that the household will choose it. Similar results are also obtained for the terms representing the interaction of vehicle weight and the age of the household head and for the terms representing the interaction of vehicle performance and education level of the household. Other models also contain unreasonable implications. These anomalies are often minor and would not interfere with most uses of the models; they do, however, limit the usefulness of the models.

In summary, three limitations are evident in previous research using disaggregate compensatory models on real choice situations: (1) the interrelated set of decisions that affect auto demand are not fully incorporated; (2) the handling of makes and models of vehicles in describing household's vehicle type choices is not completely satisfactory; and (3) the models often contain unreasonable implications. Despite these limitations, each of the models can and has been very useful in policy analysis (see, for example, Train, 1980b, and Millar et al., 1982). In fact, delineation of the limitations allows for more accurate analysis, since the effect of the limitations on analysis thereby can be understood and compensated for. It would be desirable, of course, to have a model with fewer limitations; this was the goal in developing the model presented in chapter 8.

7.3   Disaggregate, Compensatory Models Based on Hypothetical Choice Situations

For some types of analysis, the real world does not provide sufficient information to the researcher on factors that are perhaps quite important. For example, from examining real choice situations, it is impossible to infer the value of a vehicle characteristic if no autos currently exhibit this characteristic. This problem is particularly relevant in forecasting the demand for new types of vehicles, such as electric vehicles. The limited range of electric vehicles, that is, the fact that they can only be driven a certain number of miles before a lengthy recharging is required, is a characteristic of electric vehicles that no currently (or widely) available autos exhibit. Therefore, by observing consumers' choices in the real world, consumers' value of the range of an auto cannot be determined.

A less extreme version of this limitation arises when in the real world vehicle characteristics are highly correlated, so that there is little independent variation in each characteristic. For example, it is probably the case that consumers are affected by both a vehicle's interior size and its weight.[13] However, these two characteristics are highly correlated in the real world; autos with large interiors generally weigh more than those with smaller interiors. Because of this, the separate effects of weight and interior size cannot be accurately determined by inference from observed choices in the real world, and policy analysis that depends on knowing the separate effects is thwarted.

To circumvent these problems, one can turn from the real world to the world of hypotheticals. That is, the researcher can present hypothetical choice situations to a sample of respondents and infer the value of factors entering the choice process from the respondents' stated choices in these hypothetical situations. For example, the researcher can describe several hypothetical autos to a consumer and ask the consumer which vehicle he would choose. Since the researcher makes up the autos that are described to the respondent, the researcher can (1) construct hypothetical vehicles that include characteristics that are not exhibited by currently available autos and (2) ensure that the set of hypothetical vehicles exhibits sufficient independent variation in each characteristic to allow the value of each to be estimated precisely.

The potential difficulty with this type of data is, of course, that respondents' choices in hypothetical situations will not necessarily be the same as if they were actually faced with the choice in the real world. Furthermore, the more dissimilar the hypothetical alternatives (e.g., hypothetical vehicles) are from real world alternatives, and hence the more useful the data could potentially be to the researcher, the less able the respondent will be to choose as he would if actually faced, somehow, with the choice in the real world.

Two studies have used the device of hypothetical choice situations for studying auto ownership decisions: one by Calfee (1980) and another by Charles River Associates (as reported by Beggs, Cardell, and Hausman, 1979, and Charles River Associates, 1980). In both of these studies, sets of hypothetical autos were presented to consumers and the consumers' preferences were elicited. Both studies included electric vehicles in the sets of hypothetical autos. Calfee presented several sets of autos to each consumer and asked which auto was preferred in each set; he used this information to estimate the "value" of each auto characteristic in the same way as the studies in section 7.2. Charles River Associates presented one set of hypothetical autos to each consumer and asked the consumer to rank order the autos by preference. The rankings were used to infer the "value" of each characteristic in a way that is similar to the studies of section 7.2, but incorporated the information concerning which auto was second most preferred, third most, and so on. (In real choice situations only the first choice is observed, not the second, third, and so on.)

The following auto characteristics were found to affect consumers' decisions in both of these studies: purchase price, operating cost, number of seats, top speed (or acceleration), and range. These results are quite consistent with those obtained by the studies of auto type choice in real situations, in which purchase price, operating cost, size (such as number of seats) entered. The fact that vehicle power (top speed, acceleration, or horsepower to weight ratio) entered the studies based on hypothetical choices but not those based on real choices could reflect either that (1) power is too highly correlated with other vehicle characteristics in the real world to allow its value to be estimated in studies with real choice data, or (2) relative power will affect consumers' choices between electric and gas vehicles (which have quite different power) but not their choices among gas vehicles.

7.4   Disaggregate, Noncompensatory Models Based on Both Real and Hypothetical Choice Situations

In all the studies discussed so far, it was assumed that the consumer trades off auto characteristics in the sense that a low value for one characteristic can be offset, in the consumer's evaluation, by a high value of another characteristic. For example, it is assumed that a consumer who wants a five-seat auto would choose a four-seat auto if the price were sufficiently low, or the gas mileage were sufficiently good, or there were some other characteristic that "compensated" for the small number of seats.

However, the consumer might actually make decisions in some noncompensatory manner. For example, if a household wants a five-seat auto, it might eliminate from consideration any auto that has fewer than five seats. That is, no matter how inexpensive or how good the gas mileage is, the household would never choose a four-seat auto; nothing could compensate for not having five seats.

In noncompensatory models, the consumer is assumed to have an importance ranking of characteristics of the alternatives, and, for each characteristic, have some minimum acceptable level, called a "threshold." It is easiest to think of the decision process as occurring in steps sequential over time (though this is not necessarily a part of the models). First, the consumer faces all the possible alternatives. He eliminates from consideration all the alternatives that do not meet the minimum acceptable standard (threshold) for the characteristic which he considers most important. Next, if more than one alternative remains after elimination in the first step, then the consumer looks at his second ranked characteristic and eliminates any alternatives that are not above the threshold for this characteristic. This process continues until only one alternative remains; that is the alternative which the consumer chooses.

To model this form of decisionmaking, two things must be learned by the researcher: the importance ranking of characteristics of the alternatives and the threshold for each characteristic. The importance ranking is essential since the process of successive elimination could result in different choices if applied in different orders. Similarly, the thresholds allow determination of which alternatives will be eliminated at each stage.[14]

Two studies of consumers' choices of which type of auto to own have been based on noncompensatory models of consumer behavior, namely, those by Recker and Golob (1978), and Murtaugh and Gladwin (1980). Recker and Golob presented consumers with a set of hypothetical, small, special purpose urban vehicles. The consumers were asked to tell the researcher how important they considered each characteristic of these autos; that is, in essence, consumers were asked to rank order the auto characteristics in terms of importance. This information was used, along with the researchers' observation of which auto the consumer said he preferred, to infer the threshold values for each characteristic.

The study by Murtaugh and Gladwin was somewhat different. Their approach was based on in-depth interviews with consumers who had recently purchased autos, eliciting the reasons for the consumer choosing the auto that he did. On the basis of the information obtained through numerous interviews, they constructed an algorithm that represented a noncompensatory decision process that they felt accurately reflected the decisions of most of the consumers they interviewed. The essential difference, therefore, between this study and that by Recker and Golob (aside from the fact that Recker and Golob used hypothetical choice situations and Murtaugh and Gladwin used real ones) is simply that Recker and Golob used statistical methods to determine the threshold values, whereas Murtaugh and Gladwin established threshold values on the basis of their extensive interviews without formal statistics.

Table 7.2 gives the order in which characteristics were considered by consumers in their noncompensatory choices. A couple of things are interesting. First, both studies found that vehicle size was the characteristic that households considered first. This is consistent with the studies discussed in sections 7.2 and 7.3. Note in the Recker and Golob study that size was a

Table 7.2
Noncompensatory models of auto type choice: order in which characteristics are considered

Recker and Golob	Murtaugh and Gladwin
Vehicle size	Vehicle size
Perceived safety	Vehicle purpose (for specific purposes or general use)
Flexibility of use	Price
Parking	Domestic or foreign
Number of passengers	
Fuel economy	
Ability to be seen	
Seating comfort	
Cargo space	

separate characteristic from the number of seats; therefore, vehicle size might denote weight in this study. Second, safety was found by Recker and Golob to be the second most important characteristic. Of the studies discussed so far only Winston and Mannering have found safety to be an important factor. This could easily be due to the fact that none of the other studies attempted to enter a variable for safety, which is notoriously difficult to measure in the real world. Recker and Golob used hypothetical choice situations and hence were able simply to specify the safety level of the vehicles they described.

Other explanations are also possible. Recker and Golob described small, special purpose vehicles; consumers might be more concerned with safety in these vehicles than in conventional autos. Also, the order in which characteristics are considered in the Recker and Golob model is based on the rank orderings that respondents state to the researcher. It is possible that respondents guess that safety is an important factor in their decisions (or feel that it "should" be) when indeed it is not. This possibility of respondents' not being able accurately to assess the relative importance of characteristics is one of the major drawbacks of this type of study. The difficulty becomes greater if the consumer does not actually choose on a noncompensatory basis, in which case the question of "which characteristic is most important" has no tangible meaning.

Neither of the studies based on noncompensatory models tested these models against compensatory models. Therefore, they do not provide evidence on how people make decisions concerning auto ownership. However, Gensch and Svestka (1978) examined consumers' choices of mode of travel (auto versus transit) with both noncompensatory and compensatory models. In particular, they compared the predictive ability of the two models and found that, for their sample, the noncompensatory model predicted mode choice better than the compensatory model. This provides indirect evidence in support of the noncompensatory model. This evidence should not be overemphasized, however. Aside from the fact that mode choice was examined instead of auto ownership, there are problems in the way that Gensch and Svestka made predictions with the compensatory model that impaired its performance: a person was predicted to take the mode for which there was the highest probability, rather than predicting aggregate mode shares by summing individual probabilities over people. However, the evidence provided by Gensch and Svestka is the only evidence available, and therefore is necessarily the best available.

7.5 Approximate Aggregate Demand Equations

Because of the difficulty and expense of collecting data on individual consumers, many studies have observed the total, or aggregate, demand for autos in an area (e.g., a state or the nation as a whole) and have related this aggregate demand to various explanatory variables, such as average auto prices in the area and average household income.

By definition, the true aggregate demand function for an area is the sum of the demand functions for all the individuals in the area. That is, if the demand function for person n is f_n, then the true aggregate demand function for an area is necessarily

$$F = \sum_{n \in S} f_n,$$

where S is the set of individuals in the area. The straightforward way to specify an aggregate demand function is, therefore, to specify demand functions at the individual level and sum them over individuals. Alternatively, one can specify an aggregate demand function and demonstrate that there exist individual demand functions that, when summed, equal the aggregate function. Aggregate demand functions obtained in either of these ways are called "consistent," since they are consistent with underlying demand at the individual level.

An aggregate demand equation that is consistent is not necessarily the true aggregate function. For example, it is possible for an aggregate demand function to be consistent, but only with individual demand functions that are unrealistically simplistic. By way of illustration, a linear aggregate demand function is consistent with linear individual demand functions; however, unless individual demand is truly linear (which is unlikely, particularly for auto choice), the linear aggregate demand function is, at best, an approximation to the true aggregate demand function.

Specifying and estimating demand equations that are consistent with realistic individual demand functions is difficult because of the complexity of such functions. Consequently it is customary to specify an aggregate demand function that is not necessarily consistent with realistic individual demand equations and consider it an approximation to the true aggregate demand function. In this section we discuss studies that have estimated approximate aggregate demand functions; in the next we examine two recent studies that estimated aggregate demand equations that are indeed consistent with a fairly realistic specification of individual demands.

Most studies that estimate approximate aggregate demand equations have examined only the total number of automobile purchases (or number of automobiles owned) and have ignored the consumers' choices of type of auto. These studies are the following: Wolff (1938), Roos and von Szelski (1939), Chow (1957, 1960), Nerlove (1957, 1958), Suits (1958, 1961), Kain and Beesley (1965), Dyckman (1966), Houthakker and Taylor (1966), Hamburger (1967), Evans (1969), Bos (1970), Hymans (1970a, 1970b), Wyckoff (1973), Juster and Wachtel (1974), Wildhorn et al. (1974), and Hess (1977).

Each of these models includes auto price and average income as explanatory variables. In addition, most of the models include some type of lagged dependent variable. Beyond this, however, the models differ as to which explanatory variables are included. Some variable, such as interest rates or money holdings, reflecting the ease of obtaining credit, is included in the models of Chow, Suits, Dyckman, Hamburger, Evans, and Juster and Wachtel. Wolff includes corporate profits as an explanatory variable. Suits includes a dummy variable for the years of World War II in order to reflect the disruption in buying patterns that occurred during those years. Kain and Beesley include population density as a proxy for the ease of reaching shopping and other destinations without an automobile. Hymans included an index of changes in stock prices as an indication of consumers' sentiments. Juster and Wachtel include an index of unemployment in their model. Finally, Wildhorn et al. included a dummy variable for years in which strikes of auto workers occurred. It is significant, however, that none of these models includes any auto characteristics other than price.

These studies examined the number of autos owned but not the type. Two studies have estimated approximate aggregate demand equations for the share of autos of each type that are owned (or purchased), namely, those by Chamberlain (1974) and Lave and Bradley (1980). Chamberlain's equations include the average price of autos and the price of fuel (which captures the difference in fuel economy, or operating cost, among types of autos). In addition, she included average income as an explanatory variable. Lave and Bradley entered no auto characteristics, but included several socioeconomic variables, such as average income, percent of people who are college educated, percent of population between the ages of 1 and 5, and so on. Neither of the studies examined auto characteristics other than price.

The more recent studies based on approximate aggregate demand equations have examined both the total number of autos and the share of autos of each type. These studies are Chase Econometrics Associates (1974), Energy and Environmental Analysis, Inc. (1975), Ayres et al. (1976), Difiglio and Kulash (1976), and Wharton Econometric Forecasting Associates, Inc. (1977).

The Chase model predicts the total number of new automobile sales and then divides total sales among classes on the basis of share equations. Five classes of automobiles were considered: subcompact, compact, intermediate, standard, and luxury. The predicted shares depend on the average price for automobiles of each class, the average fuel economy for automobiles of each class, the price of fuel, and the rate of unemployment, while predicted total sales depend on disposable income, automobile and fuel prices, credit conditions and previous purchases of autos.

The models of Energy and Environmental Analysis, Inc. (EEA), Difiglio and Kulash, and Ayres et al. are similar to the Chase model in that market shares by automobile class are determined as well as total new automobile purchases. The models of Difiglio and Kulash and Ayres et al. differ from that of Chase in that three auto classes are considered rather than five, and fewer explanatory variables appear. The EEA model, on the other and, includes all the explanatory variables that the Chase model includes, plus a variable reflecting the growth in vehicle miles traveled.

The last, and by far the most complete, aggregate econometric study is that by Wharton. This model is like the Chase model in that it has equations that determine the number of new automobiles purchased and the market share held by each automobile class. In addition, however, the model determines the number of used automobiles owned by automobile class. Consequently, the model can determine the effect of changes in new vehicle designs on consumers' choices of whether to own new or used automobiles.

The Wharton model includes a large array of independent variables. Among the socioeconomic variables that enter the model are the number of households, the number of licensed drivers, the number of persons driving to work, the number of persons between 20 and 29 years of age, the percent of the population living in urban areas, and average income. Rather than including variables for the average prices of automobiles in each class and the average fuel economy of automobiles in each class, the Wharton model includes only one variable, called the "cost per mile." From an intuitive point of view, this variable is the fixed cost of owning the automobile plus the yearly operating cost of a vehicle.

None of these models includes any noncost characteristics of autos, and as a consequence, consumers' responses to changes in seating capacity, luggage space, horsepower, etc., cannot be determined. This is a serious limitation, even if one is interested only in the effect of changes in cost. For example, increased fuel efficiency in a vehicle is generally achieved by changing noncost characteristics (e.g., size). Consequently, examining the effect of changes in operating cost without also considering the effect of concomitant changes in noncost characteristics can seriously bias the demand predictions.

7.6   Consistent Aggregate Demand Equations

Two studies have recently estimated aggregate demand equations with explicit account taken of the fact that aggregate demand is the sum of individual demands. Both of these studies were performed at Charles River Associates, one by Boyd and Mellman (1980) and the other by Cardell and Dunbar (1980), and both used the same model of aggregate demand. In particular, each study assumed that each consumer chooses the auto that maximizes his utility, with utility being a function of the characteristics of the auto and the tastes of the consumer. Under this assumption, different consumers choose different autos, even though all consumers face the same characteristics of the autos, because different consumers have different tastes and hence value the various auto characteristics differently. The distribution of tastes in the population was specified and aggregate demand equations were derived by aggregating individual demands in accordance with the distribution of tastes. Consequently, the estimated equations for aggregate demand in these studies are consistent with a realistic model of an individual consumer's behavior.[15]

Both of the studies that employed this approach were able to examine the effect of a variety of auto characteristics on consumers' choices of auto type. Cardell and Dunbar found six characteristics to be important factors in consumers' decisions: price, fuel economy, acceleration, frequency of repairs (as rated by *Consumer Reports*), luxury (as rated by *Consumer Reports*), and interior space. The Boyd and Mellman study found the first four of these to affect consumers' decisions, but entered styling and noise (as rated by *Consumer Reports*) in their model rather than luxury and interior space. In particular, Boyd and Mellman found that, when the styling variable was included, no measures of internal space, exterior size, or weight entered the model significantly.

These findings are somewhat consistent with the previously discussed demand analyses. Price and operating cost (i.e., fuel efficiency), are found to be important in both studies, while interior space entered one. Power (i.e., acceleration), which was found in the studies in section 7.2 and 7.4 not to be important but was relevant in the studies in section 7.3, entered strongly in both of these models. Apparently, the verdict on vehicle power is not yet in.

Neither of the models included any socioeconomic variables. This limits their usefulness in forecasting to periods during which socioeconomic variables (or, more precisely, the distribution of tastes in the population) do not change significantly. They could be used, for example, in performing "what if" analyses for the year in which they were estimated (e.g., what would demand for a particular vehicle have been if its fuel efficiency had been 10% better), but not for projecting demand over several years under various policy scenarios. There is no inherent limitation of the methodology that prevents socioeconomic variables from being included; this is an area in which further research promises to be quite fruitful.

8 Auto Ownership and Use: An Integrated System of Disaggregate Demand Models

8.1 Introduction

This chapter presents the new model of the demand for personal-use cars and light trucks. The model is similar to previous models based on "disaggregate," or household-level, analysis in that it

- is estimated on a sample of households so as to capture the behavioral factors conditioning households' choices;
- describes each household's choices as depending on the characteristics of each class and vintage of vehicle (such as its operating cost, purchase price, seating capacity, etc.) as well as the characteristics of the household (such as its income, size, number of workers, etc.); and
- can be used in a simulation framework to provide consistent forecasts of total vehicle demand and use within a region.

In addition, the model has several important characteristics and capabilities that previous models have not incorporated. In particular, the model

- can forecast the number of vehicles owned and the number of miles traveled annually, by class and vintage of vehicle;
- explicitly recognizes the interdependence, or "interrelatedness," of a household's choice of how many vehicles to own and its choice of which class and vintage of vehicles to own;
- recognizes that a household's choice of how many and what class/vintage of vehicle to own depends on how much the household drives, and vice versa; and
- reflects the fact that each household chooses a particular make and model from within its chosen class of vehicles, but does so without requiring a specification of the demand for each make and model.

The model consists of a system of submodels that separately describe the number of vehicles owned, the class and vintage of each vehicle, and the miles traveled in each vehicle. While different submodels are used to describe different choices by the household, the system of submodels constitutes an integrated whole in that (1) its overall structure is derived from economic theory in which the household chooses **jointly** the number of vehicles to own, the class/vintage of each vehicle, the make/model of each vehicle, and the amount to drive each vehicle, and (2) the parameters of each submodel are estimated using techniques that account for the inter-

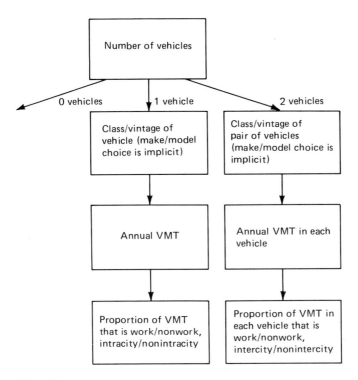

Figure 8.1
Household vehicle demand. Each box represents a separate submodel.

dependence among the households' choices. Consequently, the model em-
bodies two significant advantages: the specification of different submodels
for different choices facilitates understanding and use of the model; and
consistency in the structure and estimation of the submodels ensures that
the overall model accurately reflects the interdependent nature of a
household's choices.

The structure of the model is most readily explained in terms of prediction. The model consists of seven submodels, each of which predicts one of
the decisions represented in figure 8.1. First, the number of vehicles that the
household owns is predicted. If the household is predicted to own no
vehicles, then no further calculations are made. If the household is predicted
to own one vehicle, the class and vintage of its vehicle is then predicted,
followed by a prediction of annual VMT (vehicle miles traveled). Last, the
proportion of miles that the vehicle will be driven by the household in each

of four categories of travel is predicted. The four categories are short intracity work trips, other work trips, short intracity nonwork trips, and other nonwork trips.[1]

If a household is predicted to own two vehicles, then the model predicts the class and vintage of **each** of the vehicles. Next, the amount each vehicle is driven is predicted, followed by a prediction of the proportion of miles driven on each vehicle in each of the four categories of travel.

It is important to note that, while each household's decisions are predicted sequentially in the manner just described, the household is not assumed to **make** the decisions sequentially. Rather, the household simultaneously chooses the number of vehicles, class, and vintage of each vehicle and number of miles to drive, with each choice related to each other choice. The sequencing of the submodels is simply a convenience to the researcher and an aid to exposition, which is allowed by the particular form of the model (see the discussion on specification to follow and the general descriptions of GEV and continuous/discrete models in chapters 4 and 5).

While the model predicts choices of individual households, the ultimate purpose is to produce **aggregate** forecasts, such as the total number of vehicles by class and vintage in a region, state, or the nation as a whole. Aggregate forecasts for a particular geographic area are obtained by applying the model to each household in a sample of households from the area and aggregating the predictions for the sampled households. More specifically, for each household in a sample, the model is used to calculate the probability that the household will own a particular number of vehicles, each of a particular class and vintage, and the amount that the household will drive each of its vehicles. These calculations are performed for each sampled household separately, based upon the household's income, size, employment status, and location, as well as other factors, such as gas prices and fuel efficiency levels. Aggregate forecasts are obtained by taking a weighted sum of the predicted probabilities of each household in the sample, with the weights reflecting the sampling probability for the household. An illustration of this procedure is given in chapter 9, which presents forecasts for the state of California.

8.2   Model Specification

This section is relatively technical and need not be read for a general understanding of the model. General readers can skip to section 8.4, which describes the variables entering each submodel, the functional form relating the variables, and the estimated parameters of the functions.

The exact specification of the model, and its derivation from the economic theory of consumer behavior, is based on the recent work on GEV and discrete/continuous models discussed in chapters 4 and 5. The general form of the model is described first; the specific functions used in estimation are then presented as special cases and/or approximations of the general form.

We assume that each household chooses the number of vehicles to own, the class and vintage of each vehicle, the make and model of each vehicle, and the number of miles to travel in each vehicle so as to maximize its utility. The conditional indirect utility function of the household is denoted

$$V_{nc_n m_{c_n}} = f(Y, p_{nc_n m_{c_n}}, x_{nc_n m_{c_n}}), \qquad (8.1)$$

where

n is the number of vehicles ($n = 0, 1, 2, \ldots$);

c_n is the class/vintage combination of each of the n vehicles (i.e., c_n is a vector of length n whose elements denote the class/vintage combination of the vehicles);

m_{c_n} is the make/model of each of the n vehicles (i.e., m_{c_n} is a vector of length n whose elements denote the make/model of the vehicle(s), the make/model of each vehicle necessarily being within the class/vintage designated by c_n;

$V_{nc_n m_{c_n}}$ is the conditional indirect utility of the household, given that it owns n vehicles of class/vintage c_n and make/model m_{c_n}, expressed as a function of its income, the price of travel, and other explanatory variables;

Y is the income of the household;

$p_{nc_n m_{c_n}}$ is the cost per mile of traveling by vehicles of class/vintage c_n and make/model m_{c_n} (i.e., $p_{nc_n m_{c_n}}$ is a vector of length n whose elements are the cost per mile of traveling by vehicle(s) of class/vintage c_n and make/model m_{c_n}); and

$x_{nc_n m_{c_n}}$ is a vector of other explanatory variables, both observed and unobserved, that affect the utility that the household can obtain with n vehicles of class/vintage c_n and make/model m_{c_n}.

Given n, c_n, and m_{c_n}, the number of miles that the household will travel in the ith vehicle is, by Roy's identity, the (negative of the) derivative of the conditional indirect utility function with respect to the price per mile of traveling by the vehicle divided by the derivative with respect to income (see chapter 5 for a proof of this fact). This function can be denoted g_i:

$$VMT^i_{nc_n m_{c_n}} = -\frac{\partial V_{nc_n m_{c_n}}/\partial p^i_{nc_n m_{c_n}}}{\partial V_{nc_n m_{c_n}}/\partial Y}$$

$$= g^i(Y, p_{nc_n m_{c_n}}, x_{nc_n m_{c_n}}), \qquad i = 1, \ldots, n, \tag{8.2}$$

where

$VMT^i_{nc_n m_{c_n}}$ is the miles traveled by the ith vehicle, given that the household owns n vehicles of class/vintage c_n and make/model m_{c_n}; and $p^i_{nc_n m_{c_n}}$ is the cost per mile of traveling by the ith vehicle, given that the household owns n vehicles of class/vintage c_n and make/model m_{c_n}.

This equation represents the household's demand for travel in each vehicle, as a function of the cost of travel in all of its vehicles, the income of the household, and the other explanatory variables $x_{nc_n m_{c_n}}$.

The household chooses the number of vehicles to own, the class/vintage of each vehicle, and the make/model of each vehicle so that the conditional indirect utility function is maximized. That is, the household chooses n^* vehicles of class/vintage c_n^* and make/model $m_{c_n}^*$ if and only if

$$V_{n^* c_n^* m_{c_n}^*} > V_{nc_n m_{c_n}} \qquad \text{for all} \quad n, c_n, m_{c_n} \text{ other than } n^*, c_n^*, m_{c_n}^*.$$

Consequently, the probability that the household chooses n^*, c_n^*, and $m_{c_n}^*$ is simply

$$P_{n^* c_n^* m_{c_n}^*} = \text{Prob}(V_{n^* c_n^* m_{c_n}^*} > V_{nc_n m_{c_n}} \text{ for all } n, c_n, m_{c_n} \text{ other than } n^*, c_n^*, m_{c_n}^*).$$

To evaluate this probability, recall that $V_{nc_n m_{c_n}}$ is a function of $x_{nc_n m_{c_n}}$, which includes both observed and unobserved variables. Combining the effects of all unobserved variables into one composite unobserved variable, take the mean of $V_{nc_n m_{c_n}}$ over this unobserved variable and label this mean $\bar{V}_{nc_n m_{c_n}}$. Then, without loss of generality, $V_{nc_n m_{c_n}}$ can be decomposed into its mean and deviations from the mean:

$$V_{nc_n m_{c_n}} = \bar{V}_{nc_n m_{c_n}} + e_{nc_n m_{c_n}}.$$

Assume that $e_{nc_n m_{c_n}}$ for all n, c_n, and m_{c_n} are jointly distributed in accordance with a particular Generalized Extreme Value (GEV) function:

$$CDF(e_{nc_n m_{c_n}} \text{ for all } n, c_n, \text{ and } m_{c_n})$$

$$= \exp\left\{ -\sum_n \left[\sum_{c_n} \left[\sum_{m_{c_n}} [\exp(-e_{nc_n m_{c_n}})]^{1/(\theta)} \right]^{\theta/\lambda} \right]^\lambda \right\} \tag{8.3}$$

where θ and λ are parameters. Then, as discussed in chapter 4, the probability that a household will choose n^* vehicles of class vintage c_n^* and make/model $m_{c_n}^*$ can be expressed in the following manner.

Decompose the mean utility that the household obtains from n vehicles of class/cintage c_n and make/model m_{c_n} into three parts:

$$\bar{V}_{nc_n m_{c_n}} = \bar{V}_n + \lambda \bar{V}_{c_n|n} + \theta\lambda \bar{V}_{m_{c_n}|nc_n},$$

where

$\bar{V}_n$ is the mean of $\bar{V}_{nc_n m_{c_n}}$ over class/vintages and makes/models;
$\bar{V}_{c_n|n}$ is the mean of $\bar{V}_{nc_n m_{c_n}}$ over makes/models minus $\bar{V}_n$ divided by λ; and
$\bar{V}_{m_{c_n}|nc_n}$ is $\bar{V}_{nc_n m_{c_n}}$ minus the mean of $\bar{V}_{nc_n m_{c_n}}$ over makes/models divided by $\theta\lambda$.

Note that $\bar{V}_n$ depends only on factors that vary over n, $\bar{V}_{c_n|nc_n}$ depends on factors that vary over n and c_n but not over m_{c_n}, and $\bar{V}_{m_{c_n}|nc_n}$ depends on factors that vary over n, c_n, and m_{c_n}.

Similarly, let the joint probability of a household choosing n^* vehicles of class/vintage c_n^* and make/model $n_{c_n}^*$ be written as the product of marginal and conditional probabilities:

$$P_{n^* c_n^* m_{c_n}^*} = P_{n^*} \cdot P_{c_n^*|n^*} \cdot P_{m_{c_n}^*|n^* c_n^*},$$

where

P_{n^*} is the marginal probability of n^* vehicles (marginal over all class/vintages and make/models);
$P_{c_n^*|n^*}$ is the probability of class/vintage c_n^* (conditional on n^*, and marginal over all make/models); and
$P_{m_{c_n}^*|n^* c_n^*}$ is the conditional probability of make/model $m_{c_n}^*$ (conditional on n^* vehicles of class/vintage c_n^*).

Then, given the above distribution for $e_{nc_n m_{c_n}}$, these marginal and conditional probabilities can be written as

$$P_{n^*} = \frac{\exp(\bar{V}_{n^*} + \lambda I_{n^*})}{\sum_n \exp(\bar{V}_n + \lambda I_n)}; \tag{8.4}$$

$$P_{c_n^*|n^*} = \frac{\exp(\bar{V}_{c_n^*|n^*} + \theta J_{c_n^*})}{\sum_{c_n} \exp(\bar{V}_{c_n|n^*} + \theta J_{c_n})}; \tag{8.5}$$

$$P_{m_{c_n}^*|n^* c_n^*} = \frac{\exp(\bar{V}_{m_{c_n}^*|n^* c_n^*})}{\sum_{m_{c_n}} \exp(\bar{V}_{m_{c_n}|n^* c_n^*})}; \tag{8.6}$$

where

$$J_{c_n^*} = \ln \sum_{m_{c_n}} \exp(\bar{V}_{m_{c_n}|n^*c_n^*}), \tag{8.7}$$

$$I_{n^*} = \ln \sum_{c_n} \exp(\bar{V}_{c_n|n^*} + \theta J_{c_n}). \tag{8.8}$$

The submodels that constitute the vehicle choice model are represented by equations (8.4) and (8.5). The vehicle quantity submodel, which describes the number of vehicles the household chooses to own, is given by equation (8.4). In this equation, the probability of owning a certain number of vehicles depends on elements of $\bar{V}_n$. In addition, the utility that the household would obtain by its choice of class/vintages affects the household's probability of choosing a certain number of vehicles; this is represented by the term I_n.

Equation (8.5) represents the submodel that describes the household's choice of class and vintage of each vehicle, given the number of vehicles it chooses to own. The probability of choosing a particular class and vintage depends on elements of $\bar{V}_{c_n|n}$. In addition, the utility that the household would obtain by its choice of make/model within a class/vintage affects the household's probability of choosing a certain class and vintage; this is represented by the term J_{c_n}.

The submodel that describes the miles traveled in each vehicle is represented by equation (8.2). The number of miles traveled depends on the household's income (Y), the cost per mile of travel in vehicles ($p_{nc_n m_{c_n}}$), and the other explanatory variables $x_{nc_n m_{c_n}}$.

This discussion is based on a general indirect utility function, labeled f in equation (8.1), which gives rise to general travel demand functions, labeled g in equation (8.2), and choice models that, at least with respect to the arguments within the logit form, are fully general (equations (8.4), (8.5), and (8.6)). The task now is to choose a specific indirect utility function and from it derive the specific functions used for the VMT submodel and the specific arguments used in the vehicle quantity and vehicle class/vintage submodels.

The following conditional indirect utility function has convenient properties that will become evident. Therefore, assume that each household faces a conditional indirect utility function of the form

No vehicles:

$$V_{0c_0 m_{c_0}} = 0, \qquad \text{by normalization;}$$

One vehicle:

$$V_{1c_1m_{c_1}} = (1/(1 - \alpha_1))Y^{1-\alpha_1} + (1/\beta_1)\exp\{\delta_1 - \beta_1 p_{1c_1m_{c_1}}\}$$

$$+ \theta_{1c_1m_{c_1}}; \tag{8.9}$$

Two vehicles:

$$V_{2c_2m_{c_2}} = (1/(1 - \alpha_2))Y^{1-\alpha_2} + (1/\beta_2)\exp\{\delta_2 - \beta_2 p_{2c_2m_{c_2}}^1\}$$

$$- (1/\beta_2)\exp\{\delta_2 + \beta_2 p_{2c_2m_{c_2}}^2\}$$

$$+ \theta_{2c_2m_{c_2}};$$

and so on for $n = 3, 4, \ldots$, where

$\alpha_1, \alpha_2, \beta_1, \beta_2$ are parameters;
δ_1 is a weighted sum of both observed and unobserved characteristics of the household, with the weights being parameters;
δ_2 is another weighted sum (not necessarily the same as δ_1) of characteristics of the household, with the weights being parameters;
$\theta_{1c_1m_{c_1}}$ is a weighted sum of both observed and unobserved household characteristics and characteristics of a vehicle of class/vintage c_1 and make/model m_{c_1}; and
$\theta_{2c_2m_{c_2}}$ is a weighted sum of household characteristics and characteristics of the **pair** of vehicles of class/vintage c_2 and make/model m_{c_2} (recall that c_2 is a vector denoting the class/vintage of each of the two vehicles, and similarly for m_{c_2}).

Using Roy's identity, the miles traveled in each vehicle, given the number, class/vintage, and make/model of the vehicles is

One vehicle:

$$\ln \text{VMT} = \alpha_1 \ln Y - \beta_1 p_{1c_1m_{c_1}} + \delta_1; \tag{8.10}$$

Two autos:

$$\ln \text{VMT}^i = \alpha_2 \ln Y - \beta_2 p_{2c_2m_{c_2}}^i + \delta_2, \qquad \text{for} \quad i = 1, 2. \tag{8.11}$$

Equations (8.10) and (8.11) are the specific functions used in the sub-models describing vehicle miles traveled for one-vehicle and two-vehicle households. Note that because of the form of the two-vehicle indirect utility function, equation (8.11) represents the demand for travel in vehicle 1 or 2; that is, the forms of g^1 and g^2 in equation (8.2) are the same.

Since the conditional indirect utility function (8.9) is nonlinear in parameters of observed variables, a linear in parameters approximation to it in observed variables is used in estimation:

$$V_{0c_0m_{c_0}} = 0;$$

$$V_{1c_1m_{c_1}} = \psi_1 z_{1c_1m_{c_1}} + e'_{1c_1m_{c_1}}; \qquad (8.12)$$

$$V_{2c_2m_{c_2}} = \psi_2 z_{2c_2m_{c_2}} + e'_{2c_2m_{c_2}};$$

where

$z_{nc_nm_{c_n}}$ ($n = 1, 2$) are vector-valued functions of the observable characteristics of the household (i.e., Y and those entering δ_n and $\theta_{nc_nm_{c_n}}$) and observable characteristics of the class/vintage c_n and make/model m_{c_n} (i.e., $p_{nc_nm_{c_n}}$ and those entering $\theta_{nc_nm_{c_n}}$);
ψ_n ($n = 1, 2$) are vectors of parameters; and
$e'_{nc_nm_{c_n}}$ ($n = 1, 2$) are the errors in this approximation, which depend on both observed and unobserved variables.

Substituting the means of $\psi_1 z_{1c_1m_{c_1}}$ and $\psi_2 z_{2c_2m_{c_2}}$ over makes/models and vintages into equation (8.4) gives the specific functional form for the submodel that describes the number of vehicles the household will choose to own. This is the same as equation (8.4) with $\bar{V}_n$ replaced by a term that is linear in parameters.

Substituting the deviations of $\psi_1 z_{1c_1m_{c_1}}$ and $\psi_2 z_{2c_2m_{c_2}}$ from their means into equation (8.5) gives the specific functional form for the submodels that describe the class/vintages of the household's vehicles, given the number of vehicles the household will choose to own. This is the same as equation (8.5) with $V_{c_n|n}$ replaced by a term that is linear in parameters.

One final note is required to complete the discussion on model specification. There is no submodel in our estimated system that described the make/model of each of the household's vehicles; that is, equation (8.6) was not estimated. No such submodel was included for two reasons. First, forecasting vehicle demand with a model that includes a make/model component would necessitate developing forecasts of the characteristics of each future make and model of vehicle. This was considered to be infeasible, particularly for long run analysis. Second, the computations required to forecast with a make/model component are very burdensome because of the large number of makes and models available. As stated in section 7.2, previous applications of make/model models adopted several ad hoc forecasting procedures in order to keep these computations at a manageable level.

The household's choice of make and model of vehicle cannot be ignored, however, without biasing the results obtained in the class/vintage submodel. Recall that the class/vintage submodel (equation (8.5)) includes as an explanatory variable a term that reflects the utility that the household will obtain with its choice of make/model. This is the term J_{c_n} given by equation (8.7). If J_{c_n} is correlated with any other explanatory variable in the model, omitting it will bias estimates of the coefficients of the other variables; its inclusion prevents this bias.

Calculating J_{c_n} requires a make/model submodel (since, by equation (8.7), J_{c_n} is a function of the terms entering the choice probabilities for makes and models). McFadden (1978) has shown, however, that under fairly general assumptions J_{c_n} can be approximated by terms that are more directly observable. In particular, as the number of makes and models in a class/vintage grows large

$$J_{c_n} \to \ln(r_{c_n}) + \tfrac{1}{2} W_{c_n}^2, \tag{8.13}$$

where

r_{c_n} is the number of makes and models in class/vintage c_n, expressed as a proportion of the number of all makes and models; and
$W_{c_n}^2$ is the variance of $\bar{V}_{m_{c_n}|nc_n}$ around $\bar{V}_{c_n|n}$.

This approximation for J_{c_n} is adopted in the class/vintage submodel.

8.3   Data

The model was estimated on the sample of households that constitute the National Transportation Survey (NTS). This survey, administered by Cambridge Systematics, Inc., and Westat, Inc., and funded by the National Science Foundation, consists of 1,095 households contacted between mid-May and the end of June 1978. Households were sampled nationwide using a stratified random sampling procedure. The following information was obtained from each household:

• socioeconomic data, including household income and the age, sex, employment status, and education level of each household member;
• an inventory of the household's vehicles, specifying the make, model,

vintage, and date purchased of each vehicle currently owned;
• an estimate of the number of miles driven in each of the household's vehicles during the previous twelve months;
• information on whether the household had sold any vehicles during the previous twelve months, and, if so, the make, model, and vintage of each vehicle sold; and
• a one-day trip "diary" specifying the length, vehicle used, and purpose of each trip taken by a household member during the previous twenty-four hours.

Details of these data are described in Cambridge Systematics, Inc. (1980a).

The NTS household sample was augmented with data on the characteristics of more than 2,000 makes and models of 1967–1978 vintage vehicles. Data on front and rear shoulder room, luggage capacity, acceleration rate, braking distance, interior noise level, and repair record were obtained from *Consumer Reports*. Vehicle weight and turning radius were obtained from *Automotive News Almanac*. Prices for new vehicles were obtained from *Consumer Reports*, for used cars from the *Red Book*, and for used trucks from the *Used Truck Buyers Guide*. Gas mileage was obtained, when possible, from annual editions of *EPA Gas Mileage Guide for New Car Buyers*. Gas mileage of vehicles for which EPA figures were not available (particularly vintages prior to 1974, the year in which EPA began publishing such figures) were obtained from *Consumer Reports*; the *Consumer Reports* figures were converted to EPA-equivalent figures with an equation estimated on vehicles for which both EPA and *Consumer Reports* figures were available. Operating cost for each household was calculated using the gas price in the household's region (obtained from the *Oil and Gas Journal*) and the gas mileage, in miles per gallon, of the household's vehicle.

Complete details on the vehicle characteristics, particularly the way in which missing data were handled for each characteristic, are given in appendix A of Cambridge Systematics, Inc. (1980b).

Finally, for each NTS household, data were obtained on the number of public transit trips taken in the metropolitan area in which the household resides, and the population of the area. These data, collected from *National Urban Mass Transit Statistics*, were used to calculate the number of public transit trips taken per capita in the household's area of residence. This figure is used in the model as a measure of the quality of public transit service in the household's area of residence.

8.4   Estimation Results

As depicted in figure 8.1, seven submodels make up the complete model system. These submodels describe

- the number of vehicles each household chooses to own;
- the choice of class/vintage of vehicle for households choosing one vehicle;
- the choice of class/vintage of each vehicle for households choosing two vehicles;
- the number of miles traveled annually for households choosing one vehicle;
- the number of miles traveled annually by each vehicle for households choosing two vehicles;
- the proportion of miles traveled in each category of travel for households choosing one vehicle; and
- the proportion of miles traveled in each category of travel in each vehicle for households choosing two vehicles.

The estimation of each of these seven submodels is now described.

1   Vehicle Quantity Submodel

The vehicle quantity model calculates the probability that a household will choose to own a certain number of vehicles. This probability is given succinctly by equation (8.4). However, a more fully articulated description and interpretation is helpful.

A household is assumed to have a choice of owning zero, one, or two vehicles.[2] The probability of owning each number of vehicles depends on factors that reflect the household's need for vehicles and its willingness or ability to purchase vehicles. Let V_1 denote the weighted sum of factors that reflect a household's need or willingness to own one vehicle: $V_1 = \beta_1 z_1$, where z_1 is a vector of variables and β_1 is a vector of parameters to be estimated. Similarly, let V_2 denote the aggregate of factors that reflect a household's need or willingness to own two vehicles: $V_2 = \beta_2 z_2$, with analogous definitions. Given V_1 and V_2, the probability of owning one vehicle is specified as logit, namely[3]

$$P_1 = \frac{e^{V_1}}{e^{V_1} + e^{V_2} + 1}.$$

Note that as the need or willingness to purchase one vehicle, as captured in V_1, increases, the probability of owning one vehicle, P_1, also increases. The probability of owning two vehicles is

$$P_2 = \frac{e^{V_2}}{e^{V_1} + e^{V_2} + 1},$$

such that P_2 increases with V_2. The probability of owning no vehicles is simply 1.0 minus the probability of owning one or two vehicles:

$$P_0 = 1 - P_1 - P_2 = \frac{1}{e^{V_1} + e^{V_2} + 1},$$

such that when either V_1 or V_2 increases, P_0 decreases.

Among the variables entering V_1 and V_2 is one that represents the average utility that the household obtains in its choice of class and vintage of vehicle. (This is the term I_n in equation (8.4).) It is through this variable that interdependence of the vehicle quantity choice and the class/vintage choice is captured. Consequently, its inclusion is particularly important for the overall model specification.

Table 8.1 presents the variables entering the submodel and their estimated parameters, with the estimates obtained by the maximum likelihood method described in section 2.6.[4] Since factors that affect a household's need or willingness to own one vehicle also usually affect its need or willingness to own two vehicles, each explanatory variable enters both V_1 and V_2. Consequently, each variable is listed twice in the table, with a separate coefficient, or weight, estimated for owning one and two vehicles. With this information, the values of V_1 and V_2 that are implied by table 8.1 can be written explicitly as

$V_1 = 1.05$ (log of household income) $+ 1.08$ (number of workers)

$+ .181$ (number of members)

$- .0009$ (annual transit trips per capita in area)

$+ .635$ (average utility in class/vintage choice given one vehicle)

$- 1.79$

and

Table 8.1
Vehicle quantity submodel

Explanatory variable	Estimated coefficient	t-statistic
1 Log of household income, entering one-vehicle alternative	1.05	3.69
2 Log of household income, entering two-vehicle alternative	1.57	3.52
3 Number of workers in household, entering one-vehicle alternative	1.08	3.78
4 Number of workers in household, entering two-vehicle alternative	1.50	4.78
5 Log of number of members in household, entering one-vehicle alternative	.181	.43
6 Log of number of members in household, entering two-vehicle alternative	.197	.39
7 Annual number of transit trips per capita in household's area of residence, entering one-vehicle alternative	−.0009	1.82
8 Annual number of transit trips per capita in household's area of residence, entering two-vehicle alternative	−.0021	3.42
9 Average utility in class/vintage choice	.635	7.14
10 Alternative-specific constant for one-vehicle alternative	−1.79	2.97
11 Alternative-specific constant for two-vehicle alternative	−4.95	5.19

a. Model: multinomial logit, fitted by maximum likelihood method. Alternatives: (1) no vehicles, (2) one vehicle, (3) two vehicles. Number of observations: 634. Log likelihood at zero: −700.23. Log likelihood at covergence: −475.03.

$V_2 = 1.57$ (log of household income) $+ 1.50$ (number of workers)

$\quad + .197$ (number of members)

$\quad - .0021$ (annual transit trips per capita in area)

$\quad + .635$ (average utility in class/vintage choice given two vehicles)

$\quad - 4.95.$

Given the values of V_1 and V_2, the probability of owning zero, one, or two vehicles is calculated using these formulas.

The variables entering V_1 and V_2 and the estimated values of their coefficients are interpreted as follows. The first two variables arc thc log of the household's income, entering the alternatives of one and two vehicles separately. The estimated coefficients of these variables are positive, and the coefficient for the two-vehicle alternative is larger than that for the one-vehicle alternative. This indicates, as expected, that an increase in a household's income will increase its probability of choosing two vehicles over one and its probability of choosing one vehicle over none. Since it is the log of income that enters rather than income itself, increasing a household's income changes the relative probability of owning a particular number of vehicles less for higher income households than for lower income households.

The third through eighth variables in the model capture the effects on vehicle quantity demand of the number of workers in a household, household size, and the quality of transit in the household's area of residence. Instead of measuring directly the quality of transit for each household (which would be essentially impossible), a proxy variable is used. This variable is the number of transit trips taken per capita in the household's area of residence. Insofar as more people ride transit in areas where transit quality is good than in areas of relatively poor transit service, this proxy is a reasonable measure of transit quality.

The estimated coefficients of the third through eighth enter with the expected signs and relative magnitudes. The estimated parameters indicate that

• an increase in the number of workers in a household increases the probability of choosing two vehicles over one and the probability of choosing one vehicle over none;

• an increase in household size increases the probability of choosing two vehicles over one and of choosing one vehicle none; furthermore, the increase in these probabilities is less for larger households than smaller households; and

• an increase in the quality of transit in a household's area increases the probability of choosing one vehicle over two and the probability of choosing no vehicles over one.

The ninth explanatory variable is the term I_n discussed previously; it is a "feedback" variable from the class/vintage submodels and reflects the interdependence of the household's choice of how many vehicles to own with its choice of what class and vintage of vehicles to own. The variable enters with te anticipated sign and a large t-statistic, indicating its importance in explaining household's choices of how many vehicles to own.

The last two variables in the submodel are alternative-specific constants. The coefficients of these variables are chosen by the maximum likelihood method so that predicted shares of households in the three alternatives equal the actual shares in the estimation sample. Their signs and magnitudes have little interpretable content.

2   Class/Vintage Submodel for One-Vehicle Households

This submodel calculates, for each class and vintage of vehicles, the probability that a household that owns one vehicle will choose to own that class/vintage. The specification is given by equation (8.5) with $n^* = 1$, and is described more thoroughly in the following.

Denote V_i as a weighted sum of factors affecting the desirability to the household of owning a vehicle of class and vintage combination i (e.g., the desirability of a 1976 subcompact vehicle). This can be written as

$$V_i = \beta z_i,$$

where

z_i is a vector of characteristics of vehicles in class/vintage i and characteristics of the household; and
β is a vector of parameters to be estimated.

The probability that the household will choose to own a vehicle in class/vintage i is specified to be logit:

$$P_i = e^{V_i} / \sum_j e^{V_j},$$

where the summation in the denominator is over all possible classes and vintages of vehicles.

It is important to note that V_i includes variables that reflect the average utility that the household obtains in its choice of make and model of vehicle given that it chooses class/vintage i. (These are the variables $\ln(r_{c_n})$ and $(W_{c_n}^2)$ in equation (8.13), which are used to approximate J_{c_n} in equation (8.5).) These variables capture the interdependence of the class/vintage choice with the choice of a particular make and model of vehicle. Stated another way: Through these variables, the model incorporates the fact that a household chooses a make and model of vehicle within a class/vintage and chooses the class/vintage with knowledge of the makes and models within it.

As discussed in section 8.2, the exact function for the average utility associated with the make and model choice cannot be calculated without estimating a submodel of make/model choice. To avoid such estimation, the exact function is approximated by variables that McFadden (1978) has shown are arbitrarily close to the function when the number of makes and models of vehicles in each class/vintage is large. In particular, these variables are the number of makes and models within the class/vintage (expressed in logs) and the variance in the characteristics of makes and models around the average characteristics for the class/vintage (e.g., the variance of shoulder room around its average for makes and models within a given class/vintage).

For estimation, each household was assumed to have a choice among 12 classes of vehicles for each of 10 vintages, making a total of 120 alternatives from which to choose. The classes of vehicles are

1. subsubcompact domestic car (e.g., Chevette, Fiesta);
2. subcompact domestic car (e.g., Sunbird, Maverick);
3. compact domestic car (e.g., Firebird, Malibu);
4. midsize domestic car (e.g., Fairmont, Granada);
5. standard domestic car (e.g., Impala, Delta 88);
6. large domestic car (e.g., Olds 98, Lincoln);
7. small import car (e.g., Datsun 210, Toyota Corolla);
8. medium size import car (e.g., Datsun 510, Audi Fox);
9. luxury import car (e.g., all Mercedes, Datsun 810);
10. pickup trucks;
11. vans; and
12. utility vehicles (e.g., Jeep, Jimmy).

The 10 vintages are pre-1970, and the years 1970 through 1978.

For each class and vintage, the mean and variance of each vehicle characteristic were calculated over all makes and models in the class and vintage. In addition, the number of makes and models in each class/vintage was tabulated. These variables, along with socioeconomic characteristics of the household, entered the submodel.

Because of the large number of alternatives, estimation of this submodel on the full set of alternatives was considered infeasible. Consequently, a subset of the alternatives was employed for estimation. Fifteen alternatives were selected for each one-vehicle household. These alternatives included the household's chosen alternative (that is, the class/vintage that the household actually owned) and the alternative(s) that the household had chosen in the previous year (that is, the class/vintage(s) that the household owned in the previous year). If the household neither sold nor bought any vehicles during the year, then these two alternatives were the same, and that alternative was included only once. The remaining alternatives for each household were selected randomly.

This procedure of estimating on a subset of alternatives results, as described in section 2.6, in consistent estimates. Furthermore, tests indicate that, beyond a minimal number of alternatives, the estimated parameters are not sensitive to the number of alternatives included in estimation. A submodel with a given set of explanatory variables was estimated on fifteen alternatives and then separately on forty alternatives; essentially the same parameter estimates were obtained in both cases. (This result was also found by Cambridge Systematics, Inc., 1980b).

Table 8.2 presents the variables entering the submodel and their estimated parameters. For each class and vintage of vehicles, representative utility V_i can be written explicitly, using the information in table 8.2, as

$V_i = -.000380$ (average purchase price of $\times$ (dummy equaling one if
    vehicles in class/vintage)   household's income is below
                                                    \$12,000, and zero otherwise)

$-.00283$ (average purchase price $\times$ (dummy equaling one if
    of vehicles in class/   household's income is above
    vintage)   \$12,000, zero otherwise)

$-.3209$ (average operating cost $- 3.63$ (transaction cost
    of vehicles in class/   dummy for vehicles in
    vintage i)   class/vintage)

$+$ other variables listed in table 8.2.

Table 8.2
Class/vintage submodel for one-vehicle households[a]

Explanatory variable	Estimated coefficient	t-statistic
1 Purchase price in dollars, for households with incomes less than or equal to $12,000	−.000380	2.50
2 Purchase price in dollars, for households with incomes greater than $12,000	−.000283	2.06
3 Operating cost, in cents per mile	−.3209	1.55
4 Transaction cost dummy	−3.63	19.3
5 Front and rear shoulder room, in inches, for households with three or fewer members	.0228	.704
6 Front and rear shoulder room, in inches, for households with more than three members	.0359	1.05
7 Luggage space, in cubic feet, for households with three or fewer members	.0447	1.28
8 Luggage space, in cubic feet, for households with more than three members	.1033	1.93
9 Horsepower, for households with incomes greater than $25,000	.0149	1.78
10 Log of the number of makes and models in the class/vintage (expressed as a proportion of all makes and models)	.544	3.40
11 Variance of front and rear shoulder room around its mean for the class/vintage	.00186	1.95
12 Foreign car dummy	−.472	1.41
13 Vintage 1976–1978 dummy	1.24	2.12
14 Vintage 1972–1975 dummy	.60	2.09
15 Vintage 1976–1978 dummy for households with incomes greater than $12,000	.916	1.50
16 Pickup truck dummy	.639	3.95
17 Van dummy	.380	.234

a. Model: multinomial logit, fitted by maximum likelihood method. Alternatives: class/vintages. Number of observations: 274. Log likelihood at convergence: −371.67.

Given the value of V_i for each class/vintage, the probability that the household will own a vehicle of any particular class/vintage is calculated using the formula for P_i stated previously.

The variables entering V_i and the estimated values of their coefficients are interpreted as follows. The first two variables relate to the average purchase price of vehicles in the class/vintage. Two purchase-price variables are entered to allow for the possibility that lower income households are more affected by price than higher income households. The first price variable is the average price of vehicles in the class/vintage for households with incomes less than or equal to $12,000 per year in 1978 dollars (and zero for higher income households). The second variable is the average price of vehicles in the class/vintage for households with incomes greater than $12,000 (and zero for lower income households). Annual incomes of $12,000 was used to divide the households because that was the average income of one-vehicle households in the sample.

The estimated parameters for these two variables have the expected signs and relative magnitudes. The negative coefficients for these price variables indicate that an increase in the price of vehicles in a class/vintage decreases a household's probability of choosing that class/vintage (all other things held constant). The coefficient for the higher income households is lower than that of lower income households, indicating that an increase in the price of vehicles in a class/vintage decreases the probability of choosing the class/vintage more for lower income households than for higher income households.

The next variable in the submodel is the average operating cost of vehicles in the class/vintage. Its negative coefficient indicates that an increase in the operating cost of vehicles in a class/vintage decreases the probability that a household will choose that class/vintage (all other things held constant).

The ratio of the operating cost coefficient to the purchase price coefficient is a measure of the amount that a household would be willing to pay, in the form of a higher purchase price, in return for a one-cent per mile reduction in operating cost.[5] For lower income households, this is $844. That is, lower income households would be willing to pay up to $844 in extra purchase price for a one-cent per mile reduction in operating cost. For higher income households, the figure is $1,134.

To evaluate these figures, consider the following. If a household were rational (in the economist's sense of the word) and considered only its

Table 8.3
Number of miles traveled annually at which model's estimate of willingness to pay for reduced operating costs is consistent with "rational" behavior

Discount rate r	Real growth in gas prices g	Life of vehicle in years L	Implied miles traveled annually (M)	
			Lower income households	Higher income households
.03	.00	10	9,774	13,125
.03	.02	10	8,870	11,911
.03	.00	8	11,872	15,942
.03	.02	8	10,981	14,745
.05	.00	10	10,730	14,408
.05	.02	10	9,772	13,122
.05	.00	8	12,807	17,197
.05	.02	8	11,872	15,942

discount rate in real terms (labeled r), the real growth rate in gas prices (g), the life of the vehicle (L), and the miles traveled each year (M) in its calculation of life cycle costs, then it would evaluate the present value of the life cycle costs of a vehicle to be

$$P + \frac{1 - e^{(r-g)L}}{r - g} M \cdot C,$$

where P is the purchase price of the vehicle and C is its operating cost per mile (both in dollars). If $\beta_1 P + \beta_2 C$ is estimated, then, given the expression above for life cycle costs, the number of miles traveled annually must satisfy

$$M = (\beta_2/\beta_1)((r - g)/(1 - e^{-(r-g)L})).$$

For lower income households, the ratio of the estimated coefficients of the operating cost and purchase price terms in table 8.2 is $(-.3209 \times 100)/-.000380 = 84,447$, where multiplication by 100 reflects the fact that operating cost enters the submodel in cents per mile rather than dollars per mile. The analogous figure for higher income households is 113,392. For various values of r, g, and L, the number of miles that the household must travel per year in order for the above equation to be satisfied is given in table 8.3.

These figures are somewhat high, though not greatly so. This implies that households either (1) have lower discount rates and/or expect higher growth rates for gas prices than indicated in the chart, (2) are rational but calculate life cycle costs differently than was assumed (e.g., they might consider the resale value of the vehicle after a certain number of years rather than its useful life and think that resale value increases with fuel efficiency), or (3) are not rational in the economists's sense of the word or, equivalently, do not know how to make the necessary present value calculations (e.g., they might think that operating cost reductions translate into greater dollar savings than they actually do).

The fourth explanatory variable is a transaction cost dummy. This variable takes the value of one for vehicles in a class/vintage that the household did not own in the previous year and zero for a class/vintage of the vehicle that the household did own in the previous year. Assuming that no household sells a vehicle within a class/vintage and buys another one in the same class/vintage, this variable represents the psychic, search, and other transaction costs associated with buying a new vehicle. As its coefficient and t-statistic indicate, these factors are very important in a household's choices.[6]

The fifth and sixth variables relate to the average interior dimensions of the vehicles in each class/vintage. Interior dimension is measured as front and rear shoulder room (in inches). Two variables were entered to allow for the possibility that large households are more concerned with interior dimensions than smaller households. The fifth variable is equal to the average shoulder room of vehicles in the class/vintage for households with three or fewer members (and zero for larger households). The sixth variable is equal to the average shoulder room of vehicles in the class/vintage for households with more than three members (and zero for smaller households).

The estimated parameters for these two variables also have the expected signs and relative magnitudes. The positive coefficients indicate that an increase in the shoulder room of vehicles in a class/vintage will increase a household's probability of choosing the class/vintage (all other things held constant). The coefficient for the larger households is larger than that of smaller households, indicating that an increase in the shoulder room of vehicles in a class/vintage increases the probability of choosing the class/vintage more for large households than for smaller households.

The seventh and eighth variables capture the effect of luggage space. As with shoulder room, two variables are entered to allow for the possibility that larger households are more concerned about luggage space than are smaller households. The estimated coefficients of these variables are positive, indicating that an increase in the luggage capacity of vehicles in a class/vintage increases a household's probability of choosing the class/vintage. Again, households with more than three members have a larger coefficient than smaller households, and hence an increase in luggage space increases a larger household's probability of choosing the class/ vintage more than it does a smaller household's probability.

The ninth variable is the average horsepower of vehicles in each class/vintage for households with incomes over $25,000, and zero for households with lower incomes. This specification is based on the hypothesis that horsepower is a luxury for which high income households are willing to pay, but not low and middle income households. The positive coefficient of this variable indicates that an increase in the horsepower of vehicles in a class/vintage (with all other things held constant, including, significantly, the size of the vehicles as represented by shoulder room and luggage space) will increase the probability that high income households will choose the class/vintage. Furthermore, the ratio of the horsepower coefficient to the price coefficient indicates that high income households are willing to pay $53 for an extra unit of horsepower.

The tenth and eleventh variables capture the interdependence of a household's choice of class/vintage and its choice of make/model within the class/vintage. Recall that the specification of the class/vintage submodel (equation (8.5)) includes the term J_{c_n}, the utility that a household obtains in its choice of make/model, given its choice of class/vintage. However, since a submodel of make/model choice is not being estimated, this term is being approximated, as discussed previously (see equation (8.13)), by

1. the term $\ln(r_{c_n})$, where r is the number of makes and models in the class/vintage, expressed as a percentage of all makes and models (the tenth variable), and
2. variables that capture the variance of the utility of makes and models within a class/vintage around the mean utility for the class/vintage.

A number of variables were originally included in the approximation to the variance of the utility of makes and models. In particular, the variance of each vehicle characteristic was originally included in the submodel. However, the only variance found to have a significant positive coefficient[7,8] was that of shoulder room. This is the eleventh variable in the final submodel.

The importance of these last two variables is indicated by two things. First, the coefficient of $\ln(r_{c_n})$ is an estimate of θ, a parameter in the cumulative distribution function of the errors. To assure consistency with utility-maximization theory for all values of the explanatory variables, this term must be between zero and one (see McFadden, 1978). The estimated parameter is therefore within this consistent range. Second, the submodel was reestimated without the tenth and eleventh variables. The estimated coefficients of other variables changed considerably from those in table 8.2, indicating that ignoring the interdependence of the household's make/ model choice and its class/vintage choice may seriously bias estimation results.

The remaining six variables are dummies for particular classes and vintages. The foreign car dummy (which takes the value of one for any class/vintage consisting of foreign vehicles and zero otherwise) enters with a negative coefficient. This indicates that (all other things held constant) households would prefer domestic vehicles to foreign vehicles. This implies that the penetration of foreign vehicles in 1978 was due to their character- istics (e.g., operating cost and price) being considered superior to those of domestic vehicles, rather than a proforeign bias. Furthermore, the negative coefficient of the foreign vehicles dummy perhaps reflects the difficulty of repairing and servicing foreign vehicles, rather than any antiforeign bias per se.

Two vintage dummies (the thirteenth and fourteenth variables) were entered to allow for the possibility that households prefer newer vehicles to older ones. The coefficient for the 1976–1978 vintage dummy is greater than that for the 1972–1975 vintage dummy, indicating that this is so. Fur- thermore, both these vintage dummies are positive, indicating that vehicles built after 1971 are preferred to those built in or prior to 1971.

Another vintage dummy for 1976–1978 vehicles was entered for house- holds with incomes over $12,000. This specification reflects the hypothesis that a new vehicle is a luxury for which higher income households are more willing to pay than lower income households, and the positive estimated coefficient supports this.

The last two variables are dummies indicating that the class/vintage consists of pickup trucks and vans, respectively. The coefficients of these variables measure the difference in the utility that a household obtains from pickups and vans after all the other factors in the model have been ac- counted for. Since vehicle characteristics have different meanings for trucks and cars (e.g., shoulder room and luggage space), the positive coefficients of these dummy variables should not be interpreted as implying that pickup trucks and vans are preferred to cars. A direct comparison of utilities would be possible only if all characteristics (including luggage space) had the same meaning for cars and trucks, which they do not.

3 Class/Vintage Submodel for Two-Vehicle Households

A household that owns two vehicles has a choice of class and vintage for each of its two vehicles. Stated differently, a two-vehicle household has a choice of which **pair** of class/vintages to own. The third submodel calculates, for each pair of class/vintages, the probability that a household that owns two vehicles will choose to own that particular pair of class/vintages.

The submodel is specified similarly to that for class/vintage choice by one-vehicle households, except that now **pairs** of class/vintages are considered. In particular, the probability of owning pair i of class/vintages is specified to be logit:

$$P_i = \exp(V_i)/\sum_j \exp(V_j),$$

where $V_i = \beta z_i$ is a linear-in-parameters function of factors reflecting the desirability of class/vintage pair i, and the summation in the denominator is over all pairs of class/vintages.

Table 8.4 presents the list of variables reflecting the desirability of each class/vintage pair (i.e., elements of z_i) and the estimated coefficients of these variables (i.e., elements of β). As with the class/vintage submodel for one-vehicle households, estimation was performed on a subset of fifteen alternatives for each household. This subset included the class/vintage pair that the household owned in the current year and any class/vintage pair(s) that the household owned in the previous year (if different from the current class/vintage pair).

The explanatory variables of the model are similar to those of the one-vehicle submodel; however, the following differences should be noted:

1. Most explanatory variables (all except the ninth and thirteenth variables) are defined as the sum of the characteristics over both class/vintages in the pair. For example, the price variables are defined as sum of the average price of vehicles in one class/vintage in the pair **plus** the average price of vehicles in the other class/vintage. This specification implies that households are equally concerned with the characteristics of both of its

Table 8.4
Class/vintage submodel for two-vehicle households[a]

	Explanatory variable	Estimated coefficient	t-statistic
1	Purchase price of both vehicles, summed in dollars, for households with incomes less than or equal to $12,000	−.000531	2.09
2	Purchase price of both vehicles, summed in dollars, for household with incomes greater than $12,000 and less than or equal to $20,000	−.000383	2.28
3	Purchase price of both vehicles, summed in dollars, for households with incomes greater than $20,000	−.0001713	1.29
4	Operating cost of both vehicles, summed in cents per mile, for households with incomes less than or equal to $20,000	−.441	1.96
5	Operating cost of both vehicles, summed in cents per mile, for households with incomes greater than $20,000	−.330	1.35
6	Number of transactions required to obtain pair of vehicles	−4.48	13.5
7	Front and rear shoulder room of both vehicles, summed in inches, for households with three or fewer members	.0370	1.47
8	Front and rear shoulder room of both vehicles, summed in inches, for households with more than three members	.0533	2.09
9	Expected absolute difference in shoulder room of two vehicles, in inches	.0240	2.01
10	Horsepower for both vehicles, summed for household with incomes greater than $25,000	.00954	1.43
11	Log of the number of pairs of makes and models in the class/vintage pair (expressed as a proportion of all possible pairs of makes and models)	.307	1.70
12	Number of foreign cars in pair	−.662	1.64
13	Dummy indicating at least one class/vintage in the pair is "prestigious" (see text for classification of prestigious vehicles)	1.20	2.50
14	Number of vintage 1976–1978 vehicles in pair	.155	.167
15	Number if vintage 1972–1975 vehicles in pair	.931	2.84
16	Number of vintage 1976–1978 vehicles in pair, for households with incomes greater than $12,000	1.35	1.49
17	Number of pickup trucks in pair	2.05	1.70
18	Number of vans in pair	.679	.56
19	Number of utility vehicles in pair	−2.89	3.26

a. Number of observations: 241. Log likelihood at convergence: −130.55.

vehicles. For example, an extra dollar in price is considered just as onerous to the household whether it occurs in one vehicle or the other. For situations in which this does not seem reasonable other specifications are used.
2. The price of a class/vintage pair was entered separately for three income groups: households with incomes below $12,000, those with incomes between $12,000 ad $20,000, and those with incomes over $20,000. This grouping expands on that used in the one-vehicle submodel by differentiating households with incomes over $20,000 from those with incomes between $12,000 and $20,000. (Not enough one-vehicle households had incomes in excess of $20,000 to allow this differentiation in the one-vehicle submodel.) As expected, the price coefficients are successively smaller in magnitude for successively higher income groups.
3. Similar to differentiation in price response for households with incomes over $20,000, operating cost was entered separately for households with incomes over $20,000 and for households with incomes less than $20,000. As expected, the magnitude of the operating cost coefficient is smaller for high income households that for low income households.

The ratios of operating cost coefficients to price coefficients (recall that these are measures of the amount that a household would be willing to pay for a one-cent per mile reduction in operating cost) are similar to those obtained in the one-vehicle submodel. For two-vehicle households with incomes less than $12,000, the figure is $830; for one-vehicle households the figure was $844. Two-vehicle households with incomes between $12,000 and $20,000 are willing to pay an estimated $1,151; the comparable figure for one-vehicle households was $1,134. Two-vehicle households with incomes over $20,000 are estimated by the model to be willing to pay as much as $1,926 for a one-cent per mile reduction in operating cost. (There is no comparable figure for one-vehicle households since, as stated, few one-vehicle households had incomes in excess of $20,000.)
4. The specification of the shoulder room variables reflects the hypothesis that two-vehicle households would like to own vehicles of different sizes, for example, a large family car and smaller car for commuting. If this is the case, then the utility that a household obtains from two vehicles with shoulder room S_1 and S_2, respectively, is

$$V = \alpha(S_1 + S_2) + \beta|S_1 - S_2|, \quad \text{with} \quad \alpha > \beta.$$

The first term indicates that a household values extra shoulder room in either vehicle. The second term indicates that, for a given total amount of shoulder room, the household would prefer to have it distributed between the two vehicles in such a way that one vehicle has a lot while the other has comparatively little.

With this specification, a one inch increase in the shoulder room of the larger vehicle in a pair increases the utility that the household obtains from the pair by $\alpha + \beta$. A one inch increase in the shoulder room of the smaller vehicle increases the utility of the household by $\alpha - \beta$. The requirement that α exceed β ensures that an increase in the shoulder room of either vehicle will increase the household's utility.

While the household's utility depends on the shoulder room of the particular makes and models it chooses, variables entering the class/vintage submodel are averages over the makes and models within each class/vintage. For the first term in the preceding displayed equation, the average over pairs of makes and models within the two class/vintages is simply the sum of the average shoulder room for each class/vintage in the pair. However, for the second term, the average is **not** equal to the absolute value of the difference in the averages. That is,

$$E_{ij \in c^1 \times c^2}(S^i + S^j) = E_{i \in c^1}(S^i) + E_{j \in c^2}(S^j)$$

but

$$E_{ij \in c^1 \times c^2}|S^i - S^j| \neq |E_{i \in c^1}(S^i) - E_{j \in c^2}(S^j)|,$$

where

E is the expectation operator;
S^i is the shoulder room of make/model i; and
c^1, c^2 are the sets of makes and models in class/vintages 1 and 2, respectively.

However, under the assumption that shoulder room is normally distributed among makes and models within each class, it can be shown that[9]

$$E_{ij \in c^1 \times c^2}|S^i - S^j| = (S^i - S^j)\left(\Phi\left(\frac{S^i - S^j}{\sigma}\right) - \Phi\left(\frac{S^j - S^i}{\sigma}\right)\right)$$
$$+ 2\sigma \times \phi\left(\frac{S^i - S^j}{\sigma}\right),$$

(8.14)

where

Φ is the cumulative standard normal distribution;
ϕ is the probability density function for a standard normal deviate; and
σ is the variance of $(S^i - S^j)$.

The ninth variable in the submodel is this expression, with σ calculated under the assumption that the covariance of shoulder room in different class/vintages is zero.

The estimated coefficients of the shoulder room variables (the seventh through ninth variables) enter with the expected sign and with the appropriate relative magnitude. In particular, the coefficient for the sum of shoulder room for households with more than three members is larger than that for households with three or fewer members. Both of these coefficients are larger than the coefficient for the expected difference in shoulder room, which ensures that an increase in the shoulder room of either vehicle will increase the probability of a household choosing the class/vintage pair. The expected difference in shoulder room enters significantly, and omitting this variable substantially changes the estimated coefficients of other variables. We take this to indicate that the variable is important in explaining the choice of two-vehicle households.

5. Luggage space does not enter the submodel for two-vehicle households. In an initial specification, luggage space variables entered with negative coefficients and very small t-statistics. Since these households have two vehicles for carrying luggage, the result that they are not willing to pay for extra luggage space is perhaps not surprising.

6. The variance of shoulder room does not enter the submodel. In an initial specification, this variable entered with a negative sign and a very small t-statistic; as discussed previously, this variable must enter with a positive sign if it is to serve as an approximation to W^2 in equation (8.13). One reason for these results may be that the variance of shoulder room already enters the model indirectly through the expression for the expected difference in shoulder room (see equation (8.14)).

7. The model includes a dummy variable (the thirteenth variable) that indicates whether either of the class/vintages in the pair is a "prestigious" class/vintage. This variable was not originally included in the submodel; rather, it was suggested by the results of initial specifications. In particular, initial results indicated that households with two vehicles have a strong tendency to own at least one "prestigious" vehicle.

The determination of which class/vintages were considered prestigious was made on the basis of both a priori notions and trial-and-error experi-

Table 8.5
Vehicles designated as "prestigious" (denoted by ×)

		Vintage				
Class		New (1978)	1 year (1977)	2 years (1976)	3 years (1975)	4 years (1974)
1	Subsubcompact domestic car	×				
2	Subcompact domestic car	×				
3	Compact domestic car	×	×			
4	Midsize domestic car	×	×			
5	Standard domestic car	×	×	×		
6	Large domestic car	×	×	×	×	
7	Small import car	×				
8	Medium size import car	×	×	×		
9	Luxury import car	×	×	×	×	×
10	Pickup trucks	×	×			
11	Vans	×	×	×		
12	Utility vehicles	×	×	×	×	

mentation. The final result was that the class/vintages in table 8.5 were classified as prestigious. This classification follows a definite pattern: The prestige of a vehicle is related to both how new it is and how large it is. All new vehicles are prestigious, and larger vehicles (e.g., classes 6 and 9) retain their prestige longer than smaller vehicles. This dummy variable (the thirteenth variable) enters significantly with a large, positive coefficient. Furthermore, omitting the variable substantially changes the estimated coefficients of other variables, and hence we conclude that this variable is relevant in explaining the choices of two-vehicle households.[10]

4 Annual VMT Submodel for One-Vehicle Households

This submodel predicts the number of miles traveled annually by one-vehicle households. It is specified as a regression equation of the form

$$\log(\text{VMT}) = \beta z,$$

where VMT is vehicle miles traveled annually, z is a vector of explanatory variables, and β is a vector of parameters.

The parameters were estimated with an instrumental variables approach. This approach was required, rather than ordinary least squares, because the regression equation includes the operating cost of the household's vehicle as an explanatory variable, representing the cost of travel to the household. Since a household chooses which vehicle it owns, it effectively chooses the operating cost that it faces when driving, namely, the operating cost of its chosen vehicle. Therefore, the operating cost that a household faces is an endogenous variable, so that estimation with ordinary least squares is biased. To avoid this endogeneity bias, instrumental variables estimation was applied.[11] The exogenous variables used to predict operating cost are

gas price in area of residence;
household income;
household size;
type of housing unit;
population of household's area of residence;
number of transit trips in area of residence;
number of adults, adolescents;
number of workers;
age of household head;
education level of household head;
sex of household head; and
distance to work.[12]

Table 8.6 presents the estimated submodel of annual VMT for one-vehicle households. Increases in household income, household size, or the number of workers in the household increase the expected number of miles that a household drives annually. An increase in the operating cost of a household's vehicle or the quality of transit in the household's area (as measured by the number of transit trips per capita) decreases the amount that the household expects to drive. Households in large urban areas drive more, all other things held constant, than households in small urban areas, and those in small urban areas drive more than those in rural areas. The geographic dummies for the northeastern, midwestern, and southern United States indicate that households in the western United States (the omitted region) travel more than comparable households in other parts of the United States.

5   Annual VMT Submodel for Each Vehicle for Two-Vehicle Households

This submodel describes the number of miles traveled in each vehicle owned by a two-vehicle household. It is specified as a regression equation, with the dependent variable being the log of vehicle miles traveled in each vehicle.

Table 8.6
Submodel for annual vehicle miles traveled for one-vehicle households[a]

Explanatory variable	Estimated coefficient	t-statistic
1 Log of household income, in dollars	0.1406	1.49
2 Operating cost, in cents per mile	−0.2795	2.63
3 Log of household size	0.2131	1.71
4 Number of workers in household	0.17777	1.61
5 Number of transit trips per capita in household's area of residence	−0.000258	0.78
6 Dummy indicating that household lives in an urban area with more than one million population	0.1163	0.377
7 Dummy indicating that household lives in an urban area with less than one million population	0.0477	0.283
8 Dummy indicating household lives in north-eastern United States	−0.179	0.93
9 Dummy indicating household lives in midwestern United States	−0.074	0.40
10 Dummy indicating household lives in southern United States	−0.167	0.89
11 Intercept	8.709	15.4

a. Model: regression equation, fitted by ordinary least squares with instruments replacing operating cost. Dependent variable: log of annual VMT. Number of observations: 226. R-squared: .114.

Table 8.7 presents the estimated submodel. The variables and the interpretations of their coefficients are essentially the same as in the VMT submodel for one-vehicle households. However, the submodel for two-vehicle households contains one additional variable: a dummy indicating whether the vehicle for which VMT is being described is the newer of the two vehicles that a household owns. The positive coefficient for this variable indicates that two-vehicle households drive their newer vehicles more than their older ones.

6 Submodel for the Proportion of VMT in Each Category for One-Vehicle Households

For some forecasting purposes it is useful to have VMT by purpose, or category, of travel. The submodel presented here predicts the proportion of

Table 8.7
Submodel for annual miles traveled in each vehicle for two-vehicle households[a]

Explanatory variable	Estimated coefficient	t-statistic
1 Log of household income, in dollars	0.276	3.70
2 Operating cost, in cents per mile	−0.0351	0.472
3 Dummy indicating that vehicle is the newer of household's two vehicles	0.432	5.16
4 Log of household size	0.0833	0.721
5 Number of workers in household	0.0284	0.456
6 Number of transit trips per capita in household's area of residence	−0.000421	2.20
7 Dummy indicating that household lives in an urban area with more than one million population	0.200	1.06
8 Dummy indicating that household lives in an urban area with less than one million population	−0.0920	0.876
9 Dummy indicating household lives in north-eastern United States	−0.174	1.18
10 Dummy indicating household lives in midwestern United States	−0.107	0.930
11 Dummy indicating household lives in southern United States	−0.648	0.541
12 Intercept	6.27	15.8

a. Model: regression equation, fitted by ordinary least squares with instruments replacing operating cost. Dependent variable: log of annual VMT. Number of observations: 419. R-squared: .117.

a household's VMT in each of four categories of travel:

1. intracity work trips;
2. intracity nonwork trips;
3. non-intracity work trips; and
4. non-intracity nonwork trips.

The submodel is specified as a logit model with four alternatives representing the four categories of travel. Specifically, the proportion of VMT in category i is specified to be

$$P_i = \frac{e^{V_i}}{e^{V_1} + e^{V_2} + e^{V_3} + e^{V_4}},$$

where V_i is a weighted sum of explanatory variables relating to alternative i, with the weights being parameters.

Unlike the previous submodels, the specification of this submodel was not derived in section 8.2. Its specification is not behavioral in that it is not derived from a household's utility maximization. It is also not integrated with the other submodels in the system; that is, there is no representation of the interdependence of a household's choice of how much to drive in each category with its choice of how much to drive in total or its choices of how many and what class/vintage of vehicles to own. Consequently, this submodel should be viewed as an approximation to the "true" behavioral model, an approximation that, unlike the "true" behavioral model, can be of practical use in forecasting with readily available data.[13] However, forecasts derived using this submodel must be viewed with caution.

The parameters of the submodel were estimated on data obtained from the trip diary of each sampled household. As discussed in section 8.3, the trip diary contains information on the length of each trip taken by a household member during a twenty-four hour period. Each trip was classified as being in one of the four categories listed previously, and the VMT summed by category. The proportion of VMT in each category was simply these VMT figures by category divided by the total VMT for all trips in the diary.

The definition of work trip was straightforward: Any trip whose origin or destination was the place of work was considered a work trip. The definition of intracity trips was less clear-cut. Knowing only the origin and destination of a trip (such as home for the origin and a store for the destination) and its length, the question was, What trips could be considered "intracity"? Two criteria were used. First, since intracity trips are those within an urban area and not those from rural areas to urban areas, only households that live in SMSAs were classified as taking intracity trips. All trips by rural households were classified as nonintracity. Second, since intracity trips are not those from urban areas to rural areas or from one urban area to another, and since these trips are generally longer than those within an urban area, only trips of fifteen miles or less (one way) were classified as intracity trips. Any trips over fifteen miles in length were classified as nonintracity. In summary, trips taken by urban households of less than fifteen miles in length (one way) were classified as intracity, and all others classified as nonintracity.

Table 8.8 presents the estimated submodel. Urban households faced all

Table 8.8
Submodel for proportion of VMT in each category for one-vehicle households[a]

Explanatory variable	Estimated coefficient	t-statistic
1 Proportion of household members who work, entering alternative 1	2.26	1.81
2 Proportion of household members who work, entering alternative 3	2.28	4.13
3 Gas price in household's area of residence, in cents per gallon, entering alternative 1	.0120	1.222
4 Gas price in household's area of residence, in cents per gallon, entering alternative 2	.00942	3.634
5 Gas price in household's area of residence, in cents per gallon, entering alternative 3	−.00237	.388
6 Household size, entering alternative 1	.242	.759
7 Household size, entering alternative 2	.0892	.434
8 Household size, entering alternative 3	.242	1.92
9 Alternative-specific constant for alternative 1	−9.88	1.47
10 Alternative-specific constant for alternative 2	−5.46	3.07
11 Alternative-specific constant for urban households for alternative 3	−2.59	4.71
12 Alternative-specific constant for non-urban households for alternative 3	−.790	.195

a. Model: multinomial logit, fitted by maximum likelihood method. Alternatives: (1) intracity work; (2) intracity nonwork; (3) nonintracity work; (4) nonintracity nonwork. Log likelihood at zero: −26,620. Log likelihood at convergence: −16,150.

four alternatives; however, since rural households could not, by definition, take intracity trips, only the third and fourth alternatives were included in estimation for these households.

The variables in Table 8.8 and their estimated coefficients are readily interpretable. The proportion of household members who work enters the work trip alternatives (1 and 3) with positive coefficients, indicating that an increase in the number of workers in a household increases the proportion of the household's total VMT that is driven on work trips.

The price of gas in the household's region[14] enters the first and second alternatives with positive coefficients and enters the third alternative with a negative coefficient. (The coefficient for the fourth alternative is normalized

Table 8.9
Submodel for proportion of VMT in each category for two-vehicle households[a]

Explanatory variable	Estimated coefficient	t-statistic
1 Proportion of household members who work, entering alternative 1	2.40	2.16
2 Proportion of household members who work, entering alternative 3	1.87	3.67
3 Number of transit trips per capita in household's area of residence, entering alternative 1	−.0118	1.135
4 Number of transit trips per capita in household's area of residence, entering alternative 2	−.0127	1.545
5 Gas price in household's area of residence, in cents per gallon, entering alternative 1	.00954	3.46
6 Gas price in household's area of residence, in cents per gallon, entering alternative 2	.0124	2.96
7 Gas price in household's area of residence, in cents per gallon, entering alternative 3	.0023	1.31
8 Household size, entering alternative 1	.154	.583
9 Household size, entering alternative 2	−.294	1.46
10 Household size, entering alternative 3	.242	2.16
11 Alternative-specific constant for alternative 1	−6.40	2.45
12 Alternative-specific constant for alternative 2	−4.60	1.56
13 Alternative-specific constant for urban households for alternative 3	−2.55	4.32
14 Alternative-specific constant for urban households for alternative 3	−4.35	3.201

a. Model: multinomial logit, fitted by maximum likelihood method. Alternatives: (1) intracity work; (2) intracity nonwork; (3) nonintracity work; (4) nonintracity nonwork. Log likelihood at zero: −46,730. Log likelihood at convergence: −29,040.

to zero.) This indicates that an increase in gas price results in a household decreasing its nonintracity trips (alternatives 3 and 4) relative to intracity trips. Furthermore, the relative magnitudes of the gas price coefficients indicate that, as the gas price rises, the household reduces its nonwork trips more than its work trips.

Household size enters the first three alternatives with positive coefficients. (Again the coefficient for alternative 4 is normalized to zero.) The relative magnitudes of the coefficients indicate that, as household size increases **and** the proportion of workers stays constant, the household increases its number of work trips relative to nonwork trips, and increases its intracity nonwork trips relative to nonintracity nonwork trips. This is again a reasonable implication, since an increase in the number of workers in a household (required to keep the proportion of workers constant when household size increases) will generally increase the number of work trips in proportion to the increase in number of workers, but an increase in household size will generally increase the need for shopping trips less than proportionately.

7 Submodel for the Proportion of VMT in Each Category for Two-Vehicle Households

A submodel similar to that described previously was also estimated for households owning two vehicles. Table 8.9 presents the estimation results. The definition of alternatives, the estimation method, variables, and results are essentially the same as for one-vehicle households. The only significant difference is that the submodel includes one variable that was not found to be significant for one-vehicle households. This variable is the number of transit trips taken per capita in the household's area of residence, entering the intracity trip alternatives as a measure of the quality of transit for intracity travel. The estimated coefficient of this variable is negative in each of the intracity trips alternatives, indicating that, as expected, increases in the quality of transit in urban areas decreases the amount that households drive on intracity trips relative to nonintracity trips.

9 Demand Simulations for California

9.1 Introduction

The purpose of the model presented in chapter 8 is to address "what if" questions regarding the demand and use of vehicles. Such questions take the form "what would happen to vehicle demand and fuel consumption if...," with the remainder of the sentence describing some event or set of events. Particular "what if" questions arise when, for example,

• government officials need to decide how or whether to employ policy tools that are under their control in an effort to affect the demand for vehicles and fuel;
• auto manufacturers see that they can profit by anticipating the impact of possible changes in socioeconomic or other external factors;
• government agencies are responsible for anticipating and, to the extent possible, mitigating the ill effects that changes in external factors can have on the market for autos and fuel;
• a manufacturer wants to know whether the introduction of a new type of vehicle would be profitable;
• other manufacturers need to know how such an introduction would affect the demand for their existing vehicles.

An ideal setting in which to illustrate the use of the model in addressing such questions has been provided by the California Energy Commission. The Commission is mandated by the California legislature to examine factors that affect energy consumption within the state and to assess the impact of policies and programs that are directed toward reducing energy consumption. Gasoline consumption by personal use autos has been a special concern of the Commission, partially in response to the economic and political disruption of past gasoline shortages, but more generally in recognition of the magnitude of this component of energy consumption and the power of the state to affect it, relative to other components. The Commission has been particularly interested in the impact of programs that will facilitate introduction and widespread acceptance of nongasoline automobiles. Divisions within the Commission are examining methanol, liquid propane gas (LPG), diesel, and electricity as potentially important substitutes for gasoline in personal transportation.

To aid the Commission in its investigations, and to provide an example of how the model presented in chapter 8 can be used, the demand in California for various gasoline and nongasoline automobiles was simulated with the model under a set of conditions (i.e., inputs) specified by the Commission. In recognition of the fact that simulated demands from the model are entirely dependent on the specified inputs concerning fuel prices, vehicle technology, demographics, and so on, the Commission requested a series of simulations as follows. First, "base case" simulations were produced with all the inputs set at particular values that the Commission's staff decided were reasonable. Second, various "sensitivity" simulations were produced, each of which involved changing one of the inputs (e.g., the growth rate in income) and resimulating demand. By examining the base case simulations, it is possible to see what the entire set of assumed conditions, when considered simultaneously within the model, produce in terms of vehicle demand, use, and fuel consumption. Then by comparing the sensitivity results with the base case figures, the impacts of changes in input variables (some of which are under state control) are assessed.

In the following sections, the base case inputs are described, the simulated vehicle demands and fuel consumption that result from these inputs are discussed, and finally sensitivity analyses are presented. It is important to note that throughout these sections the term "simulations" is used rather than "forecasts," to emphasize the fact that outputs of the model are answers to "what if" questions, rather than forecasts per se. In the case of the base case simulations, the question is, "What would vehicle demand and fuel consumption be if all the conditions specified below were to occur?" Each of the sensitivity simulations asks the same question with one of the conditions changed. These questions are answered by the model without regard to the probability that the specified conditions will actually occur. Since, inevitably, the future will bring about conditions other than those specified, the output of the model cannot constitute predictions. The purpose and value of these simulations is to examine the implications of sets of inputs and to understand the relative impacts of various changes in conditions.

9.2   Base Case Inputs

To simulate vehicle demands with the model, three sets of inputs are required. First, the types, or classes, of vehicles that are available, and the characteristics of each of these classes, must be specified for each simulation year. That is, to simulate for the years 1980–2000, the purchase price, fuel efficiency, shoulder room, etc., of each class of vehicle that is assumed to be available must be specified for each of the twenty years. Second, simulation with the model requires a sample of households from the area for which the simulations are being produced, plus projections of socioeconomic variables. These projections include the number of households in the area, household income, and the number of members and workers in households. Third, projections of fuel prices are utilized.

Each of these three sets of inputs will be described for the base case simulations for the California Energy Commission. More details on the implementation of the model with these inputs are given in appendix A.

Vehicle Classes and Characteristics

Reflecting its interest in nongasoline powered vehicles, the Commission specified various classes of diesel, electric, methanol, and LPG vehicles in addition to gasoline cars and trucks. A total of twenty-five classes of vehicles were included in the simulations. Since many of these vehicles (e.g., methanol cars) are not currently available, the Commission specified the year that each vehicle would, for the purposes of simulation, be assumed to be available. For simulation years prior to this specified year, the simulations excluded the vehicle from the set of vehicles among which households chose.

The list of twenty-five classes and the years at which each was specified to be available are given in table 9.1. Since the Commission was interested in simulating demand for the period 1980–2000, it projected the characteristics of each of these twenty-five classes of vehicles for each of the twenty simulation years. That is, for each year from 1980–2000, the Commission projected the purchase price, fuel efficiency, shoulder room, luggage space, horsepower, and so on, for each class of vehicle.[1] These projections are given in appendix B.

Household Sample and Socioeconomic Projections

The model presented in chapter 8 operates at the level of individual households, while, for the purposes of the California Energy Commission, simulations of statewide demand are required. A sample enumeration approach, as described in section 6.1, was used to obtain aggregate demand figures. In particular, the model was run on each household within a sample drawn from California, and the demands of each household were simulated. Statewide demands were calculated by taking the weighted sum over

Table 9.1
Classes of vehicles assumed to be available in simulations for the California
Energy Commission

Class	First year available
1 Domestic and foreign gas mini car	1984
2 Domestic gas subcompact car	*
3 Domestic gas compact car	*
4 Domestic gas large car	*
5 Foreign regular gas car	*
6 Foreign luxury gas car	*
7 Domestic and foreign diesel mini car	1987
8 Domestic diesel subcompact car	1982
9 Domestic diesel compact car	1986
10 Domestic diesel large car	*
11 Foreign regular diesel car	*
12 Foreign luxury diesel car	*
13 Domestic and foreign electric car	1987
14 Domestic and foreign methanol compact car	1986
15 Domestic and foreign methanol large car	1986
16 Domestic and foreign LPG compact car	1984
17 Domestic and foreign LPG large car	1984
18 Small gas pickups and utility vehicles	*
19 Large gas pickups and utility vehicles	*
20 Small diesel pickups and utility vehicles	*
21 Large diesel pickups and utility vehicles	*
22 Small gas vans and other vehicles	1985
23 Large gas vans and other vehicles	1985
24 Small diesel vans and other vehicles	1985
25 Large diesel vans and other vehicles	1982

* Available from first simulation year.

households of these individual demands, with the weights representing the sampling probability of each household.

The sample consisted of 105 households drawn at random from a state-wide household survey collected by the California Department of Trans-portation (Caltrans). The survey is described in detail in a report by Caltrans (1981). For each household, the following information was uti-lized: income, number of persons in household, number of workers, num-ber of vehicles owned at time of survey, class and vintage of each vehicle, and a weight assigned to the household by Caltrans that reflects the sampling procedure that Caltrans used.

Since the model calculates statewide demands on the basis of a sample of household, simulations of statewide totals for future years require updat-ing the sample for projected changes in demographic characteristics. In particular, the sample is adjusted for each simulation year so that it will "look like" a sample that would be drawn in that year. This updating is accomplished by (1) adjusting the characteristics of the households in the sample (e.g., changing their income to represent projected growth in in-come) and/or (2) adjusting the weight attached to each sampled household to reflect projected changes in the number of households of each type.

Both of these updating methods were used in simulations for the Com-mission. The income of each household was adjusted in each simulation year on the basis of a specified growth rate. For the base case, this rate was set by the Commission at 0.81% annually. That is, the income of each household was increased in each consecutive simulation year by 0.81% in real terms.[2]

The weight of each household was adjusted on the basis of projected changes in the number of households with each number of members and workers. Categorizing on the basis of the number of members and number of workers in a household, the Commission determined, using census data, that in 1980 the number of households in California in each category was as given in table 9.2. The Commission projected that by 2000 the number of households in each category would be as given in table 9.3. The Com-mission also specified that, for each simulation year between 1980 and 2000, the number of households in each category was to be calculated by linear interpolation between the numbers for that category in 1980 and 2000. Note that these projections represent a 1.7% average annual growth rate in the total number of households in California.

The weight assigned to each household was adjusted from one simula-

Table 9.2[a]
Number of households by category in California in 1980

Number of members	Number of workers		
	0	1	2+
1	1,140,946	1,146,135	—
2	708,862	966,483	988,154
3	196,324	534,548	749,057
4+	908,480[b]		1,291,209

a. Based on census data for 1980. Total number of households: 8,630,198.
b. There were 908,480 households with 4+ members and 0 or 1 worker. That is, there is only one cell including both 0 and 1 worker households with 4+ members.

Table 9.3[a]
Projected number of households by category in California in 2000

Number of members	Number of workers		
	0	1	2+
1	11,584,004	1,810,486	—
2	1,164,891	1,249,829	1,799,251
3	248,130	643,141	904,839
4+	1,251,696[b]		1,508,914

a. Based on projected census data for 2000. Total number of households: 12,165,181.
b. There were 1,251,696 households with 4+ members and 0 or 1 worker. That is, there is only one cell including both 0 and 1 worker households with 4+ members.

tion year to the next to reflect the projected changes in the total number of households in each category, where a category represents a particular number of members and workers. Denote the weight assigned by Caltrans to household n as c_n. The weighted number of sampled households in category k, labeled S_K, is the summation of c_n over all households in category k. Denote as N_K^t the number of households in the state that the Commission projects will be in category k in simulation year t. The weight attached to each household in category k in simulation year t is then $(N_K^t/S_K) \cdot c_n$. Thus, for each simulation year, the weighted number of households in each category in the sample will necessarily equal the projected number in the state. Stated intuitively, the weighted sample in each simulation year will "look like" a random sample of households taken that year.

Fuel Price Projections

Projections of fuel prices, inclusive of taxes, were specified by the Commission. Prices for 1980, 1981, and 1982 are from historical data. For years starting with 1983, the Commission calculated prices based on annual growth rates covering different periods of the simulation. The four liquid fuels, gasoline, diesel, methanol, and LPG, had the following annualized real price growth rates (exclusive of taxes):

1983–1987: 1%;
1988–1994: 3%;
1995–2000: 4.5%.

Electricity prices were projected throughout the period to increase at an average annual rate of 1.8% in real terms.

9.3   Base Case Simulations

Using the inputs specified by the California Energy Commission, personal use vehicle holdings, vehicle miles traveled (VMT), and fuel consumption were simulated with the model for California and the years 1980–2000. The salient results are presented and discussed in the following, with detailed outputs given in appendix C.

Total Vehicle Holdings and VMT

The total number of personal use vehicles and VMT on these vehicles are simulated to be as given in table 9.4. Vehicle holdings are simulated to

Table 9.4
Simulated number of vehicles and miles traveled

	1980	1990	2000
Number of vehicles (millions)	13.76	18.39	21.67
VMT (billions)	141.1	222.5	263.0

increase over the twenty year period at an average rate of 2.3% annually. Much of this growth can be attributed to the increased numbers of households projected for California. For the purpose of these base case simulations, the total number of households in California was projected by the Commission to grow at an average rate of 1.7% annually. Consequently, the growth in vehicle holdings is only slightly greater than the growth in the number of households. In fact, the average number of vehicles per household is simulated to increase only 12% over the twenty year period, from 1.59 in 1980 to 1.78 in 2000. This increase is due primarily to the projected increase in real incomes.

VMT is simulated to increase somewhat more rapidly than vehicle holdings. In particular, VMT is simulated to increase at an average rate of 3.2% annually, with annual VMT per vehicle increasing from 10,254 in 1980 to 12,136 in 2000. This increased vehicle use is a reasonable consequence of the vehicle technology inputs. As is evident from the data in appendix B, fuel efficiency for each class of vehicles is projected to improve substantially over time. Furthermore, new, more fuel efficient classes of vehicles (such as minis and methanol vehicles) are projected to be available in the future. These improvements in fuel efficiency translate into decreased operating costs. Since operating cost (which is in cents per mile) is the price attached to travel, decreases in operating cost will necessarily increase the amount that people drive their vehicles.

Both vehicle holdings and VMT are simulated to increase over time at decreasing rates. That is, the percentage increase in holdings and VMT from 1980 to 1990 is greater than that from 1990 to 2000. This growth pattern is attributable to the fact that improvements in fuel efficiency have a larger impact on the operating cost of vehicles with relatively poor fuel efficiency, so that as fuel efficiency for a class of vehicles steadily improves over time, the effect on operating cost becomes less and less. For example, assuming for convenience a fuel price of $1 per gallon, an increase in fuel efficiency from fifteen miles per gallon to twenty miles per gallon decreases

Table 9.5
Simulated vehicle holdings by fuel type

	1980	1990	2000
Gas	13,656,327	17,199,989	19,920,293
Diesel	100,346	1,068,320	1,463,319
Electric	—	8,503	66,581
Methanol	—	47,450	114,471
LPG	—	68,461	105,326

operating cost by 25% (from 6.7 cents per mile to 5 cents per mile), while an increase in fuel efficiency from twenty miles per gallon to twenty-five miles per gallon decreases operating cost by only 20% (from 5 cents per mile to 4 cents per mile). Since the impact of fuel efficiency improvements is greater during the earlier periods, the growth in vehicle ownership and VMT is also greater.

Vehicle Holdings by Fuel Type

The California Energy Commission was particularly interested in determining the potential demand for nongasoline powered vehicles and the extent to which the introduction of these vehicles would reduce gas consumption in the state. To examine this issue, various classes of diesel, electric, methanol, and LPG vehicles were included in the base case set of vehicle classes. Simulations of vehicle holdings by fuel type are shown in table 9.5.

The general conclusion to be drawn from the simulation results is that, given the projected characteristics of the vehicle and the projected fuel prices, gas vehicles would continue to dominate the market, even in the face of the introduction of alternative fueled vehicles. The only nongasoline vehicles to capture a nonnegligible portion of the market are diesels, which are simulated to comprise 6.7% of all vehicles owned in 2000. The demand for electric, methanol, and LPG vehicles is simulated to be very low: 0.3% for electric vehicles, 0.5% for methanol cars, and 0.5% for LPG cars by the year 2000.

The reason for the low demand for the alternative fueled vehicles can be seen by examining the vehicle technology data in appendix B. The prices of the electric, methanol, and LPG vehicles are considerably higher than those for comparable gas vehicles, while operating costs are only slightly lower (if

Table 9.6
Comparison of price and operating costs in 2000 for alternative fueled vehicles

Class	Price (in 1978 dollars)	Operating cost (cents per mile in 1978 dollars)
3 Compact gas cars	5,182	3.41
4 Large gas cars	7,618	3.72
13 Electric cars	9,606	1.29
14 Compact methanol cars	6,008	3.49
15 Large methanol cars	8,528	3.97
16 Compact LPG cars	6,344	3.04
17 Large LPG cars	8,938	3.20

at all). For purposes of comparison, relevant figures are given in table 9.6 for the year 2000. LPG vehicles cost over $1,000 more than comparable gas cars and have operating costs that are lower by only about half a cent per mile. Electric vehicles cost $4,428 more than compact gas cars, but are only about two cents per mile cheaper to run. Methanol cars both cost more and are more expensive to operate than comparably sized gas cars.

It is important to note that these results do not imply that alternative fueled vehicles will not be able to complete effectively with gasoline vehicles in the future. (Again, the results are simulations, not predictions.) What the results do imply is that vehicle characteristics and/or fuel prices must be **substantially** different from those projected by the Commission for alternative fueled vehicles to succeed in the marketplace. These vehicles can constitute an important portion of the market if (1) technology improvements allow these vehicles to be built much more cheaply than the Commission projects, (2) gasoline vehicles do not improve in fuel efficiency anywhere near as much as the Commission projects, or (3) gasoline prices increase much more than the Commission projected while other fuels' prices do not rise as quickly. In addition, the normal market mechanism can be affected by government intervention in various ways to increase demand for nongas vehicles; however, these interventions would need to be severe in order to have much impact. (Some of these issues are examined in section 9.4.)

A word of caution is in order regarding the use of the model to simulate demand for nongasoline vehicles. The simulations of vehicle ownership are based on the model described in chapter 8 in which consumers evaluate vehicles on the basis of their operating cost, price, seating capacity, horsepower, and other characteristics. Since the model was estimated on data from a period in which nongasoline vehicles were not generally available, characteristics that nongasoline vehicles possess, but gasoline vehicles do not, are not included in the model. Consequently, factors that could affect consumers' evaluation of nongasoline vehicles, such as uncertainty about the performance of the vehicles, are not incorporated into the results. Furthermore, the simulations are for demand only, and do not reflect any supply side constraints (such as limited production capacity for new vehicles or limited fuel availability for alternative fuels). These factors will cause the true demand for alternative fueled vehicles to be less than that simulated by the model. However, since the model already simulates very low demand for nongasoline vehicles, any biases caused by these factors will not affect the general conclusions drawn from the base case results.

Vehicle Holdings by Size and Class

Table 9.7 presents simulated vehicle holdings by size and class. The most interesting aspect of these data is that the share held by each class does not change much over time. For example, compact cars are simulated to comprise 12.7% of the vehicle stock in 1980 and 12.6% in 2000; large cars would comprise 35.5% in 1980 and 34.6% in 2000; and so on.

The only deviations from this pattern are the minis and foreign regular vehicles. Minis, which were not available in 1980, are simulated to capture a sizable 8% of the market by 2000, while foreign regular vehicles are simulated to fall from 22.3% of total holdings in 1980 to 15.4% in 2000. These results imply that the demand for minis will be drawn primarily from foreign regular vehicles, an implication that seems quite reasonable given that currently the most popular small vehicles are foreign.

Fuel Consumption by Personal Vehicles

The simulation results for fuel consumption are presented for each fuel type in table 9.8. The most notable result is that gas consumption is simulated to drop substantially, by 22% over the twenty year period. As discussed above, VMT per vehicle increases over the twenty year period and any shifts to nongasoline vehicles or smaller classes of gas vehicles is minimal. Consequently, the reduction in gas consumption can only result from increased fuel efficiency of gas vehicles. Examining the projections of vehicle char-

Table 9.7
Simulated vehicle holdings by size class

Size class		1980		1990		2000	
		Number	% of total	Number	% of total	Number	% of total
1, 7, 13	Mini	0	0	1,060,023	5.8	1,733,375	8.0
2, 8	Subcompact	1,200,234	8.7	1,525,333	8.3	1,801,959	8.3
3, 9, 14, 16	Compact	1,751,689	12.7	2,327,387	12.7	2,738,856	12.6
4, 10, 15, 17	Large	4,878,170	35.5	6,513,994	35.4	7,496,352	34.6
5, 11	Foreign regular	3,079,415	22.4	3,071,908	16.7	3,339,510	15.4
6, 12	Foreign luxury	482,297	3.5	659,163	3.6	854,060	3.9
18, 20	Small pickups and utility vehicles	706,531	5.1	809,076	4.4	871,235	4.0
19, 21	Large pickups and utility vehicles	1,106,302	8.0	1,587,104	8.6	1,824,846	8.4
22, 24	Small vans and other	0	0	19,397	0.1	32,763	0.2
23, 25	Large vans and other	557,036	4.0	819,339	4.5	977,033	4.5
Sum		13,756,673	100.0	18,392,723	100.0	21,669,990	100.0

Table 9.8
Simulated fuel consumption by personal use vehicles

	1980	1990	2000
Gasoline (billions of gallons)	8.75	7.76	6.80
Diesel (billions of gallons)	0.056	0.425	0.437
Electricity (billions of kilowatt-hours)	0	0.028	0.174
Methanol (billions of gallons)	0	0.037	0.064
LPG (billions of gallons)	0	0.036	0.041

acteristics in appendix B makes it clear that this is indeed the case. Fuel efficiency of gas vehicles is projected to double over the twenty year period; subcompacts are projected to improve from 21.02 miles per gallon in 1980 to 46.95 miles per gallon in 2000, compacts from 19.13 miles per gallon to 39.08 miles per gallon, and large domestic vehicles from 17.12 miles per gallon to 35.83 miles per gallon. It is important to note, of course, that gas consumption will not fall as dramatically, and could easily increase, if these projected improvements in fuel efficiency are not actually achieved.

Diesel consumption is simulated to increase sevenfold over the twenty year period. This result reflects the increased holdings of diesel vehicles. Similarly, consumption of methanol, LPG, and electricity is simulated to be small, reflecting the small demand for vehicles powered by these fuels.

9.4 Sensitivity Analyses

Perhaps the most valuable way to use a simulation model is to run it numerous times with changes in inputs. Comparing the results of these simulations provides information about the impact of each input in isolation from other factors. This information is an aid to government agencies and vehicle manufacturers in deciding whether a particular type of intervention is warranted (e.g., increasing gasoline prices through higher taxes, while all other factors remain the same; introducing a new vehicle in the market) and in anticipating the effects of demographic changes (e.g., larger than expected rises in income; lower employment than expected).

Recognizing the value of multiple simulations, the California Energy Commission requested that the model be rerun with various changes in the base case inputs. Specifically, six scenarios were simulated, each of which

Table 9.9
Simulated effects of greater income growth

Year 2000	VMT (billions)	Number of vehicles (millions)	Gas consumption (billions of gallons)
Base case	262.99	21.67	6.804
Scenario 1	299.05	22.70	7.845
Percent change	13.7	4.75	12.1
Implied income elasticity	0.29	0.10	0.31

provides information about the impact of an input variable in which the Commission was particularly interested. These scenarios, and their simulation results, are presented in the following.

Scenario 1: Greater Income Growth

Given the prominence of income in the economic decisions of households, an important question to address is, To what extent do vehicle holdings, vehicle miles traveled (VMT), and fuel consumption change in response to changes in income? To answer this question, the model was run with income projected to grow at an annual rate that is 2% higher than was used in the base case: 2.81% rather than 0.81%. The income of each household in 1980 is the same under the scenario and the base case but in each subsequent year is higher in the scenario. By the year 2000, each household's income under the scenario is 48% higher than under the base case.

Highlights of the simulation results for this scenario are given for the year 2000 in table 9.9, along with comparable base case figures. The detailed results are given in appendix D.1. The simulated responses are in the right direction and have plausible magnitudes. The elasticity[3] of VMT with respect to income is larger than the elasticity of the number of vehicles with respect to income, implying that households will adjust the amount that they drive on each vehicle for changes in income as well as adjusting the number of vehicles they own. Gas consumption is more sensitive to income than VMT. This result is due to the fact that, as incomes increase, households switch to larger, more expensive, and less fuel efficient vehicles, thus increasing their fuel consumption per mile. These shifts are evident in the detailed outputs in appendix D.1.

Table 9.10
Simulated effects of moderately higher gas price increases

Year 2000	VMT (billions)	Number of vehicles (millions)	Gas consumption (billions of gallons)
Base case	262.99	21.67	6.804
Scenario 2	243.22	21.03	5.903
Percent change	−7.5	−2.95	−13.24
Implied price elasticity	−0.27	−0.11	−0.47

Scenario 2: Moderate Gas Price Increases

In the base case, gas prices, in real terms, were assumed to rise at 1% each year from 1983 to 1987, 3% yearly from 1988 to 1994, and 4.5% yearly from 1995 to 2000. To assess the impact of moderately higher gas prices, the model was run with gas prices that rise 2% from 1983 to 1987, 4% for 1988–1994, and 5.5% for 1995–2000. With these higher growth rates, the price of gas in 2000 is 27.7% higher under the scenario than in the base case.

The highlights of the simulation results are shown in table 9.10, with details given in appendix D.2. The estimated responses are in the expected direction and have plausible magnitudes. The VMT elasticity is greater (in magnitude) than the vehicle holdings elasticity, implying that households adjust the amount they drive each vehicle, in addition to adjusting the number of vehicles they own, in response to gas price increases. The elasticity of gas consumption with respect to gas price is larger than the VMT elasticity. This reflects the fact that, when gas prices rise, households switch to nongas vehicles (such as diesel) and to smaller, more fuel efficient gas vehicles, thus reducing gas consumption more than VMT. The detailed results in appendix D.2 evidence these shifts explicitly.

Scenario 3: High Gas and Diesel Prices, with No Electric, Methanol, and LPG Vehicles

This scenario is intended to examine the response of households to fairly large, steady increases in fuel prices (both gas and diesel) when there is no possibility of switching to alternative fueled vehicles. In particular, gas and diesel prices are projected to rise at 7% per year, in real terms, starting in 1983, and electric, methanol, and LPG vehicles are removed from the set of

Table 9.11
Simulated effects of higher fuel price increases with no alternative fueled vehicles

Year 2000	VMT (billions)	Number of vehicles (millions)	Gas consumption (billions of gallons)
Base case	262.99	21.67	6.804
Scenario 3	179.56	18.71	4.232
Percent change	−31.7	−13.7	−37.8
Implied price elasticity	−0.27	−0.12	−0.32

vehicle classes available to the households. By the year 2000, gas prices under the scenario are 115% higher than in the base case, and diesel prices are 117% higher.

A summary of the simulation results is given in table 9.11, with details in appendix D.3. VMT and vehicle holdings drop considerably more, in absolute terms, than in scenario 2, in which gas and diesel prices rise less and the possibility of switching to alternative fueled vehicles is available. It is interesting to note, however, that the estimated elasticities of VMT and vehicle holdings are essentially the same as in scenario 2.

Gas consumption drops more in this scenario than in scenario 2, as would be expected with the higher gas price. However, the **elasticity** of gas consumption to price is lower (in magnitude) in this scenario than in scenario 2. This result reflects the fact that in scenario 2 households can reduce their gas consumption by switching to nongas vehicles. This option is not feasible in the current scenario since diesel prices are rising as fast as gas prices, making it not advantageous to switch to diesel vehicles, and alternative fueled vehicles are not available. Consequently, the normalized response (i.e., elasticity) is smaller in this scenario than in scenario 2.

Scenario 4: Reduced Employment

In this scenario the number of workers per household was reduced by reducing the number of households in categories with one or more workers and increasing the number of households with no workers. The number of households in each size/workers category for the year 2000 was changed from that given in table 9.3 to that in table 9.12. The total number of households is unchanged; households were simply shifted to categories for fewer workers. Also, as in the base case, the number of households in each

Table 9.12[a]
Alternative projection of number of households by category, representing
reduced employment

Number of members	Number of workers		
	0	1	2+
1	2,010,577	1,383,913	—
2	1,455,383	1,386,692	1,371,896
3	396,766	703,690	695,654
4+	1,599,577[b]		1,161,033

a. Based on projections for the year 2000.
b. There were 1,599,577 households with 4+ members and 0 or 1 worker. That
is, there is only one cell including both 0 and 1 worker households with 4+
members.

Table 9.13
Simulated effects of reduced employment

Year 2000	VMT (billions)	Number of vehicles (millions)	Gas consumption (billions of gallons)
Base case	262.99	21.67	6.804
Scenario 4	256.22	21.24	6.619
Percent change	−2.57	−1.98	−2.72
Implied employment elasticity	0.17	0.13	0.18

category for simulation years between 1980 and 2000 was calculated by
linear interpolation between the numbers in the category in 1980 and 2000.

With the scenario defined in this way, the average number of workers per
household in 2000 is 14.8% lower in this scenario than in the base case. Note
that, while employment was reduced, income stayed constant. Thus, implicitly, earnings per worker increases in this scenario. The estimated effects
of the scenario reflect both the reduced employment and increased earnings
per worker. The results are summarized in table 9.13. The simulated responses are in the expected direction with plausible relative magnitudes.
The VMT elasticity is greater than the vehicle holdings elasticity, implying
that the households drive each vehicle less as their employment levels drop.
Furthermore, gas consumption drops more than VMT, in percentage

Table 9.14
Simulated effects of eliminating alternative fueled vehicles

Year 2000	VMT (billions)	Number of vehicles (millions)	Fuel consumption (billions of gallons)	
			Gas	Diesel
Base case	262.99	21.67	6.804	0.436
Scenario 5	262.87	21.64	6.888	0.442
Percent change	−0.05	−0.14	1.24	1.25

terms, reflecting the fact that households switch to smaller, more fuel efficient vehicles as their employment levels reduce. This effect is small, however, as indicated by the fact that the reduction in gas consumption is only slightly greater than in VMT.

Scenario 5: No Alternative Fueled Vehicles

Under the base case, electric, methanol, and LPG vehicles were simulated to comprise, in combination, no more than 1.3% of vehicle holdings by the year 2000. The purpose of the current scenario is to determine what would happen in the market if these vehicles were eliminated. For example, would households that would choose these vehicles (if available) simply not own any vehicles, or would they switch to gas and diesel vehicles? If they switch, would they switch to diesel vehicles more than gas vehicles?

The model was run with electric, methanol, and LPG vehicles removed from the set of vehicle classes among which households choose. The results are shown in table 9.14. All of the simulated changes are small (as expected, given the small share held by alternative fueled vehicles in the base case) and in the correct directions. The magnitude of the changes indicates that nearly all the households that were simulated to choose alternative fueled vehicles in the base case were also simulated to switch to gas and diesel vehicles when the alternative fueled vehicles were not available. This implication is evident by the fact that 1.3% of the vehicles in the base case were alternative fueled, and yet the number of vehicles owned dropped by only 0.14%. Furthermore, since fuel consumption for gas and fuel consumption for diesel increase by nearly the same percentage, the simulations indicate that households that switched from alternative fueled vehicles switch to gas and diesel vehicles fairly proportionately.

Table 9.15
Simulated effects of reduced prices for electric vehicles

Year 2000	Number of EVs	VMT on EVs (millions)	Electricity consumption (millions of kilowatt-hours KWH)
Base case	66,581	813	173.6
Scenario 6	126,834	1,559	331.6
Percent change	90.5	91.8	91.0

Scenario 6: Reduced Prices for Electric Vehicles

In the base case, demand for electric vehicles (EVs) was simulated to be very small, with less than 67,000 EVs being held in 2000. Since the prices of EVs are very high, the Commission was interested in determining the impact on EV demand of reducing the purchase price of EVs by $4,000 (in 1978 dollars). This reduction could be accomplished through improvements in production processes, or, more directly, by rebates given by the government to households that purchase EVs.

The highlights of the simulation results of this scenario are given in table 9.15, with details given in appendix D.6. The $4,000 price reduction (which represents about 40% of the price of an EV) is simulated nearly to double the number of EVs owned, total VMT on EVs, and electricity consumption. While this is a large increase, the number of EVs as a proportion of all vehicle holdings is still simulated to be small (0.6%). The reason EVs are simulated not to be popular even with the price reduction is that (1) their price, with the $4,000 reduction, is still higher than most gas vehicles, and (2) their size is very small, while size, according to the estimates presented in chapter 8, is a very important factor in affecting households' choices of vehicles.

9.5   Conclusions

What can the California Energy Commission learn from the base case and scenario simulations? The most striking conclusion concerns the alternative fueled vehicles that the Commission is studying. If the Commission feels that the projections of fuel prices and vehicle technology that they specified for the simulations are reasonable, then it seems that an emphasis on alternative fueled vehicles would be misplaced and that programs directed toward improving the fuel efficiency of gasoline vehicles would probably be more effective in reducing gasoline consumption. Several aspects of the simulation results indicate this conclusion. First, given the projected characteristics of methanol, LPG, and electric vehicles, these vehicles are simulated to capture only a negligible portion of the market. The difference in gasoline consumption whether or not alternative fueled vehicles are available in the market is simulated to be very small, on the order of 1%. And offering rebates on the purchase of these vehicles does not, according to the simulations, improve the situation much (at least for electric cars). The basic problem is that, given the Commission's projections of fuel prices and vehicle characteristics, the alternative vehicles are too expensive to purchase for the small savings in operating cost that they offer the consumer.

Despite the limited impact of alternative fueled vehicles, gasoline consumption is nevertheless simulated to decrease substantially over time. This result is **not** due to changes in household behavior; vehicle holdings and miles traveled increase, and the distribution of vehicles by class stays approximately the same. Rather, the reduction in gasoline consumption is nearly entirely due to the increased fuel efficiency that the Commission projects for gasoline vehicles. This indicates (again, if the Commission believes its projections are reasonable) that programs directed toward assuring that the projected fuel efficiency improvements are actually attained would be quite effective in reducing gas consumption. The Corporate Average Fuel Efficiency standards, by which auto manufacturers are required to meet certain levels of average fuel efficiency for the fleet of vehicles that they sell, is an example at the federal level of such a program. The state government is less able than Congress to regulate manufacturers. However, incentives and funds for research and development in areas of gasoline vehicle technology would probably be more effective at reducing gasoline consumption than similar R&D in alternative fuels.

Related to these conclusions is the fact that, under the Commission's projected inputs, mini gasoline cars would be able to capture a sizable (though not large) part of the market if they were introduced on a widespread basis. These small, two-seater cars are new and relatively untested in the market; however, the technology clearly exists to produce them. Programs directed toward demonstrating and marketing these minis could be expected by the Commission to be more effective at reducing gasoline consumption than similar programs for electric or other alternative vehicles.

It is important to note that none of these conclusions is stated as a general, or absolute, fact. Rather, the conclusions are all of the form, "If the Commission feels that its projections of vehicle characteristics, demographics, and fuel prices are reasonable, then the model indicates that it should also think that ...." As stated at the beginning of this chapter, simulation models are not predictors of the future; they are means for addressing "what if" questions. Used in this way, they can be very effective as an aid to thinking and decisionmaking.

Appendix A   Implementation of Model for Simulations

A.1   Calculation of Aggregate Totals

The model presented in chapter 8 operates at the level of individual house-holds. For the California Energy Commission, demand simulations were required for the state as a whole rather than for individual households. The method for obtaining aggregate, statewide simulations from the household level model is described in this section.

Estimates of statewide totals are obtained by (1) simulating the demands of each household within a sample from the state, and (2) taking the weighted sum of the simulated household demands over all sampled house-holds, with the weights reflecting the sampling proportion of each house-hold. The details of this procedure are the following. Consider a sample of N households, with each household labeled $n = 1, \ldots, N$. Each sampled household has some weight associated with it, representing the number of households similar to it in the population. (This weight, for samples based on exogenous factors, is the inverse of the probability that the household was chosen for the sample.) Label the weight for household n as w_n. Note that if the sample is purely random, then w_n is the same for all n; if the sample is stratified random, then w_n is the same for all n within a stratum.

For each sampled household, the following probabilities are calculated with the model.

Vehicle Quantity Submodel:

P_0^n = probability that household n chooses to own no vehicles;

P_1^n = probability that household n chooses to own one vehicle;

P_2^n = probability that household n chooses to own one or two vehicles.

Class/Vintage Submodel for One Vehicle:

$P_{i|1}^n$ = probability that household n chooses to own a vehicle in class/vintage i, given that it chooses to own one vehicle (for each class/vintage).

Class/Vintage Submodel for Two Vehicles:

$P_{ij|2}^n$ = probability that household n chooses to own a vehicle in class/vintage i and a vehicle in class/vintage j, given that it chooses to own two vehicles (for each pair of class/vintages).

The VMT submodels calculate the vehicle miles traveled for each class and vintage of vehicle:

VMT_{i1}^n = vehicle miles traveled by household n, given that it chooses to own one vehicle of class/vintage i;

VMT_{ij2}^n = vehicle miles traveled by household n in a vehicle of class/vintage i, given that the household chooses to own two vehicles, with one being a vehicle in class/vintage j in addition to the vehicle in class/vintage i.

With these calculated numbers, the **expected** number of vehicles that household n will own of class/vintage i can be determined as follows:

N_i^n = expected number of vehicles that household n will own of class/vintage i

= (probability of owning one vehicle) × (probability of choosing class/vintage i, given one vehicle)

+ (probability of owning two vehicles) × (probability of choosing a pair of vehicles that includes one in class/vintage i)

$$= [P_1^n \times P_{i|1}^n] + \left[P_2^n \times \sum_j P_{ij|2}^n \right] + [P_2^n \times P_{ii|2}^n],$$

where the last term allows for the possibility that the household can own two vehicles of the same class/vintage. Similarly, the expected VMT that household n will drive on vehicles of class/vintage i is

$$VMT_i^n = [P_1^n \times P_{i|1}^n \times VMT_{i1}^n]$$

$$+ \left[P_2^n \times \sum_j P_{ij|2}^n \times VMT_{ij2}^n \right]$$

$$+ P_2^n \times P_{ii|2}^n \times VMT_{ii2}^n.$$

Estimates of statewide totals are calculated once the expected number of vehicles and VMT in each class/vintage have been calculated for each sampled household. The total number of vehicles of class/vintage i in the state is calculated as the weighted sum of the expected number for each sampled household:

$$\bar{N}_i = \sum_n w_n N_i^n.$$

Similarly, the total statewide VMT on vehicles in class/vintage i is

$$\overline{\text{VMT}}_i = \sum_n w_n \text{VMT}_i^n.$$

Fuel consumption is calculated as the last step. The amount of fuel consumed by vehicles in class/vintage i is estimated as the number of miles traveled divided by average fuel efficiency (miles per gallon) for vehicles in that class/vintage:

F_i = statewide fuel consumption by personal use vehicles in class/vintage i

$\quad = \overline{\text{VMT}}_i/e_i,$

where e_i is the fuel efficiency of vehicles in class/vintage i.

A.2   Inputs

Vehicles

The California Energy Commission, with assistance from Energy and Environmental Analysis, Inc., calculated the average characteristics of each class of vehicle built from 1971 to 1980 and projected the characteristics of vehicles that would be built in the simulation years 1980–2000. These data are given in appendix B. For the 1971–1980 vehicles, the price given in appendix B is the cost of buying that vehicle in the first simulation year, 1980 (e.g., the cost of buying a 1975 compact in 1980, given that it is five years old). For vehicles projected to be built after 1980, the price represents the cost of buying that vehicle new when it is produced (e.g., the cost of buying a 1990 compact in 1990). To represent the fact that vehicles decrease in price as they become older, depreciation rates were applied to the price of each vehicle in moving from one simulation year to another.

The depreciation rates are given in table A.1. While the same depreciation rates were applied in all years to all classes of vehicles, the model is capable of handling different rates in different years and for different classes.

Socioeconomic Variables

The sample of households and projections of socioeconomic variables is described in section 9.2.

Fuel Prices

The projections of fuel price that the Commission specified are shown in table A.2. All prices are listed in 1978 cents/gallon except electricity, which is in 1978 cents/kilowatt-hours.

Table A.1
Depreciation rates used in simulations

Age of vehicle (years)	Price as proportion of price when new (both prices in 1978 dollars)
1	0.82
2	0.67
3	0.54
4	0.43
5	0.35
6	0.28
7	0.23
8	0.19
9+	0.12

Transit Trips per Capita

For each household, the model takes as input the number of transit trips per capita that are taken in the household's metropolitan area. As discussed in chapter 8, this variable is used as a proxy for the quality of transit in the household's area, which affects the household's ownership and usage of autos.

The Commission's projections were obtained from System Design Concepts, Inc. For each of the seven metropolitan areas with transit service the actual number in 1980 and the projected number for 2004 are given in table A.3; the figures for years 1981–2000 were calculated by linear interpolation. For households living in other areas of California, the number of transit trips per capita in the area was projected to be zero throughout the simulation period.

A.3 Sampling of Class/Vintage Pairs for Two-Vehicle Households

The class/vintage submodel for two-vehicle households calculates, for each household, the probability that the household will choose each pair of class/vintages. For a reasonable number of classes and vintages of vehicles, the number of pairs of class/vintages is very large. For example, with 25 classes of vehicles and 10 vintages (for a total of 250 class/vintages), there are over 30,000 pairs of class/vintages.

Table A.2
Projected fuel prices, as specified by the California Energy Commission (in 1978
cents per gallon or per KWH)

Year	Gas	Diesel	Electric	Methanol	LPG
1980	97.50	89.70	4.312		
1981	97.50	88.92	4.231		
1982	85.02	82.68	4.764	54.60	65.52
1983	89.70	87.36	4.816	57.72	68.64
1984	89.70	86.58	4.809	56.94	67.86
1985	89.70	87.36	4.985	57.72	67.86
1986	89.70	87.36	5.096	56.94	68.64
1987	89.70	87.36	5.174	57.72	68.64
1988	92.04	89.70	5.275	58.50	69.42
1989	93.60	91.26	5.378	60.06	71.76
1990	98.94	93.60	5.385	61.62	73.32
1991	97.50	95.16	5.478	62.40	74.10
1992	100.62	97.50	5.504	63.96	76.44
1993	102.96	99.84	5.541	65.52	78.00
1994	106.08	101.40	5.469	67.08	80.34
1995	109.20	105.30	5.698	70.20	82.68
1996	113.88	109.98	5.900	71.76	85.80
1997	118.56	113.88	6.006	74.88	89.70
1998	123.24	118.56	6.117	78.00	93.60
1999	128.70	124.02	6.201	81.12	96.72
2000	133.38	128.70	6.141	84.24	101.40
2001	140.40	134.16	6.234	87.36	105.30
2002	145.86	139.62	6.327	92.04	109.20
2003	152.10	145.08	6.423	95.94	114.66
2004	158.34	152.10	6.518	99.84	119.34

Table A.3
Number of transit trips per capita used in simulations

Metropolitan area	Actual for 1980	Projected by Commission for 2004
Anaheim/Santa Ana/Garden Grove	15.20	9.86
Fresno	16.49	14.50
Los Angeles/Long Beach	57.24	58.99
Sacramento	19.33	20.33
San Diego	20.96	18.76
San Francisco/Oakland	98.73	85.43
San Jose	19.96	19.41

While a large number of pairs of class/vintages poses no theoretical problem, it entails a practical problem due to the high cost of calculating probabilities for each pair of class/vintages. Early runs of the model, in which the probability of each class/vintage pair was calculated, cost much more money that was considered feasible to spend on a per run basis. Consequently, the code was rewritten to sample, for each household, every ninth class/vintage pair and calculate the probability of only the sampled pairs. This reduced the cost of running the entire model by a factor of nearly nine (since nearly all the costs were incurred in the class/vintage submodel for two-vehicle households).

To assure that all class/vintage pairs were represented, the sampling of pairs was cycled across households. That is, the first household was programmed to sample the first, tenth, nineteenth, and so on, class/vintage pairs. The second household sampled the second, eleventh, twentieth, and so on, class/vintage pairs. And so on, to the ninth household, with sampled the ninth, eighteenth, twenty-seventh, and so on pairs. The ninth household completed a cycle with each class/vintage pair selected once by one of the first nine households. The cycle was then repeated with the tenth household choosing the first, tenth, nineteenth, and so on class/vintage pairs.

A.4   Recalibration of Alternative-Specific Constants

Each of the submodels that are logit (i.e., all except the VMT submodels) take the form

$$P_i = \frac{e^{bz_i + a_i}}{\sum_j e^{bz_j + a_j}},$$

where z_i is a vector of variables relating to alternative i, b is a vector of parameters, and a_i is a constant term. The constant a_i represents the average impact of all variables that are not included in the model.

In estimation, the value of each a_i is determined along with the other model parameters, b. The estimated value of a_i is the average in the estimation sample of the unincluded terms. It is chosen by the estimation routine so that the number of households in the sample predicted to choose each alternative is exactly equal to the number in the sample that actually chose it.

In simulating demands for the California Energy Commission, a sample is used that is different from the estimation sample. (The simulation sample is from California, while the estimation sample is nationwide.) Since the average of unincluded variables is necessarily different for the simulation sample, new values of a_i needed to be calculated, in the manner described in section 6.3. For each submodel, new values of a_i were chosen so that the simulated number of households choosing alternative i in the first year of simulation, 1980, exactly equaled the number of households that actually chose that alternative in 1980. The procedure for calibrating each a_i is described in the following for each submodel.

Vehicle Quantity Submodel

Two alternative specific constants were estimated in the vehicle quantity submodel: a_1 for the alternative of owning one vehicle and a_2 for the alternative of owning two vehicles. As shown in table 8.1, the estimated values of a_1 and a_2 are -1.79 and -4.95, respectively.

Let A_1 denote the proportion of households in the simulation sample that chose to own one vehicle, and A_2 denote the proportion that chose two vehicles. The model was run with the original values of a_1 and a_2, labeled a_1^0 and a_2^0, and the number of households that would choose to own one and two vehicles was simulated. Let the simulated proportion of households choosing one and two vehicles be denoted S_1^0 and S_2^0, respectively, where the superscripts refer to the fact that the simulation is based on a_1^0 and a_2^0.

The model with its original values of a_1 and a_2 underpredicts the share of households choosing to own one vehicle if A_1 is greater than S_1^0 and overpredicts if S_1^0 is greater than A_1 (similarly for the share choosing two vehicles). To correct the misprediction (or, more precisely, to adjust the constants so that they represent the average of unincluded variables in the simulation sample), a_1 and a_2 are adjusted to new values using the formula

$$a_i^1 = a_i^0 + \ln(A_i/S_i^0), \qquad i = 1, 2.$$

Note that if A_i is greater than S_i^0 so that the model is underpredicting the share of households choosing i vehicles, then the adjustment increases a_i. Conversely, if S_i^0 is greater than A_i and the model is overpredicting, a_i is adjusted downward.

The adjustment just described completes the first iteration of the recalibration procedure. For the second iteration, the model is run with the new values of a_i (that is, with a_1^1 and a_2^1) and new simulation shares are obtained, labeled S_1^1 and S_2^1. If S_1^1 and S_2^1 are not equal to A_1 and A_2, respectively, then the constants are adjusted again, using the formula

$$a_i^2 = a_i^1 + \ln(A_i/S_i^1), \qquad i = 1, 2,$$

where a_i^2 is the twice-adjusted value of a_i. This process is continued, obtaining new values of a_1 and a_2 with each iteration, until the simulated proportion of households choosing each number of vehicles equals (or is very close to) the actual proportion in the sample.

In the sample of households used for the base case simulations, 34.3% owned one vehicle and 55.2% owned two vehicles. Using the procedure described, the constants were recalibrated to values of -9.795 for the alternative of owning one vehicle and -13.087 for the alternative of owning two vehicles. These values replace, in the simulation code, the values of table 8.1.

Class/Vintage Submodels

A separate constant for each class and vintage of vehicle was not calibrated, due to the unwieldy number of class/vintages that were considered available for the simulations. Rather, one constant was estimated for each class of vehicles and applied to all vintages within that class. The procedure for estimating these constants is the following. First, the model was run to simulate the number of vehicles in each class/vintage. Second, the simulated number of vehicles in each class was calculated by summing over vintages the number simulated in each class/vintage. Third, the class specific constants in the model were adjusted using the formula last displayed for the vehicle quantity submodel.

Table A.4
Class distribution of vehicles owned in California in 1980

Class	Percent
2 Domestic gas subcompact car	8.7
3 Domestic gas compact car	12.7
4 Domestic gas large car	35.2
5 Foreign regular gas car	22.3
6 Foreign luxury gas car	3.2
10 Domestic diesel compact car	0.3
11 Foreign regular diesel car	0.1
12 Foreign luxury diesel car	0.3
18 Small gas pickups and utility vehicles	5.1
19 Large gas pickups and utility vehicles	8.0
21 Large diesel pickups and utility vehicles	0.05
23 Large gas vans and other vehicles	4.0

Rather than using, as the basis for recalibration, the share of vehicles in each class in the sample, the Commission provided information on the share of personal use vehicles in each class in California. By using the true statewide proportions for 1980 rather than the sample proportions, the effect of sampling errors are mitigated.

The proportion of personal use vehicles owned in each class that was available in 1980 is given in table A.4. The values of the constants that were obtained for each class of vehicle available in 1980 are given in table A.5. For classes of vehicles that were not available in 1980 (such as methanol vehicles), the procedure described previously cannot be used to obtain constants. Rather, constants for these vehicles must be assigned on the basis of reasonable notions concerning the similarity of different classes of vehicles.

Recall that the constant for each class of vehicles captures the average effect of all variables that are not not included in the model. The task, therefore, is to determine which class of vehicles available in 1980 most closely corresponds, with respect to factors not included in the model, to each new class of vehicle. The constant for the corresponding class of existing vehicles is assigned to the new class of vehicles.

For example, mini gas cars were not available in 1980, and so a constant for that class could not be estimated. It seems reasonable, however, to

Table A.5
Constants calibrated for each vehicle class

Classes of vehicles available in 1980	Constant
2 Domestic gas subcompact car	1.378
3 Domestic gas compact car	1.749
4 Domestic gas large car	2.298
5 Foreign regular gas car	2.276
6 Foreign luxury gas car	1.798
10 Domestic diesel compact car	−1.244
11 Foreign regular diesel car	−1.468
12 Foreign luxury diesel car	−0.169
18 Small gas pickups and utility vehicles	−0.038
19 Large gas pickups and utility vehicles	0.997
21 Large diesel pickups and utility vehicles	−2.347
23 Large gas vans and other vehicles	−4.955

assume that the unincluded factors affecting the desirability of subcompact gas cars, which were available in 1980 and for which a constant was calibrated, are similar to those of mini gas cars (or at least more similar than any other class of vehicle available in 1980). Consequently, mini gas cars were assigned a constant equal to the value calibrated for subcompact gas cars.

The assignment of constants for each new class of vehicle that was used in producing the base case simulations is given in table A.6. Note that each new, non-gas-powered vehicle is assigned the constant for an existing diesel class. This assignment reflects the fact that the unobserved factors that will probably be most important in determining the demand for these new vehicles—namely, uncertainty by the public about new types of vehicles, questions regarding the difficulty of customers' obtaining the alternative fuels, and so on—are currently being experienced for diesel vehicles.

Submodels for Proportion of VMT in Each Category

The Commission provided the following estimates of the proportion of VMT in each category:

1. short intracity work trips, 0.20;
2. short intracity nonwork trips, 0.54;

Table A.6
Constants assigned to vehicle classes not available in 1980

New class	Class available in 1980 that was judged most similar in unincluded factors	Value of constant
1 Gas mini cars	2 Gas subcompact cars	1.378
7 Diesel mini cars	11 Foreign regular diesel cars	−1.468
8 Domestic diesel sub-compact cars	11 Foreign regular diesel cars	−1.468
9 Domestic diesel compact cars	11 Foreign regular diesel cars	−1.468
13 Electric cars	11 Foreign regular diesel cars	−1.468
14 Methanol compact cars	11 Foreign regular diesel cars	−1.468
15 Methanol large cars	10 Large diesel cars	−1.244
16 LPG compact cars	11 Foreign regular diesel cars	−1.468
17 LPG large cars	10 Large diesel cars	−1.244
20 Small diesel pickups and utility vehicles	21 Large diesel pickups and utility vehicles	−2.347
22 Small gas vans	23 Large gas vans and other vehicles	−4.955
24 Small diesel vans	23 Large gas vans and other vehicles	−4.955
25 Large diesel vans	23 Large gas vans and other vehicles	−4.955

3. other work trips, 0.20;
4. other nonwork trips, 0.06.

These proportions were taken as the actual proportions of VMT in each category, and the procedure described previously for the vehicle quantity submodel was used to calibrate an alternative-specific constant for each of these categories. The resulting constants are

1. short intracity work trips, 5.414;
2. short intracity nonwork trips, 6.806;
3. other work trips, 2.024;
4. other nonwork trips, 0.0.

Appendix B   Projected Auto Characteristics[1]

Key to tables (see table B.1):

Column		Description
a	Vintage	Year in which the vehicle was manufactured.
b	Number of models	The number of makes and models of this class manufactured in the year designated in column a.
c	Price	The average price, in 1978 dollars, over all makes and models in the class. For vintages 1976–1979, the price is as seen in 1980 (e.g., the price given for a 1976 vehicles is the cost of buying a 1976 vehicle of this class in 1980). For vintages 1980–2000, prices are for new cars in the year manufactured (e.g., the price given for a 1990 vehicle is the cost of buying a 1990 vehicle of this class in 1990).
d	Shoulder room	Front and rear shoulder room in inches, averaged over all makes and models in the class.
e	Variance of d	Variance of shoulder room across all makes and models in the class, in inches squared.
f	Luggage space	Average luggage space in cubic feet for makes and models in the class, for classes of autos; zero for truck classes.
g	MPG	Miles per gallon, averaged over makes and models in the class.
h	HP	Horsepower, averaged over makes and models in the class.

Table B.1
Projected auto characteristics

a Vintage	b Number of models	c Price (1978$)	d Shoulder room	e Variance of d	f Luggage space	g MPG	h HP
Class 1:	**domestic gas mini car (two-seater)**						
1976							
1977							
1978							
1979							
1980							
1981							
1982							
1983							
1984							
1985	2	3200	92	10	7	44	60
1986	2	3200	92	10	7	44	60
1987	3	3200	92	10	7	44	60
1988	4	3200	92	10	7	44	60
1989	4	3265	92	10	7	46.6	58
1990	4	3305	92	10	7	48	57
1991	4	3345	92	10	7	49.5	55
1992	4	3414	92	10	7	51.2	54
1993	4	3458	92	10	7	52.7	54
1994	4	3502	92	10	7	54.2	54
1995	4	3547	92	10	7	55.0	54
1996	4	3592	92	10	7	55.8	54
1997	4	3592	92	10	7	55.8	54
1998	4	3610	92	10	7	55.8	54
1999	4	3625	92	10	7	55.8	54
2000	4	3640	92	10	7	55.8	54
Class 2:	**domestic gas subcompact car**						
1976	13	3920	97	11	9	18.90	87
1977	13	3920	97	11	9	18.90	87
1978	15	3961	98	15	9	19.64	86
1979	15	3961	99	15	9	19.64	86
1980	15	4020	99	15	9	21.06	86
1981	14	4102	100	15	9	23.58	84
1982	14	4167	99	80	9	25.65	81
1983	14	4223	99	80	9	26.48	82
1984	14	4260	98	180	9	28.11	82
1985	14	4273	98	180	9	29.20	82
1986	14	4371	98	180	9	32.47	78
1987	14	4371	98	180	9	33.07	78
1988	14	4416	98	180	9	34.40	77
1989	14	4452	98	180	9	35.42	77
1990	14	4494	98	180	9	34.95	76
1991	14	4512	98	180	9	36.60	75

Table B.1 (continued)

a Vintage	b Number of models	c Price (1978$)	d Shoulder room	e Variance of d	f Luggage space	g MPG	h HP
1992	14	4512	98	180	9	37.10	75
1993	14	4572	98	180	9	38.65	73
1994	14	4631	98	180	9	40.23	70
1995	14	4690	98	180	9	41.88	68
1996	14	4702	98	180	9	41.88	68
1997	14	4714	98	180	9	42.13	67
1998	14	4726	98	180	9	42.38	66
1999	14	4726	98	180	9	42.64	65
2000	14	4726	98	180	9	42.64	65
Class 3:	**domestic gas compact car**						
1976	14	4125	110	14	13	14.67	106
1977	14	4125	110	14	13	14.67	106
1978	14	4179	110	14	13	15.50	103
1979	14	4200	110	14	13	15.81	103
1980	14	4370	110	14	13	19.30	96
1981	14	4444	110	14	13	20.88	93
1982	14	4484	110	14	13	22.12	90
1983	14	4484	110	14	13	22.12	90
1984	14	4583	110	14	13	25.12	87
1985	14	4646	109	15	13	26.77	84
1986	14	4676	109	15	13	27.57	83
1987	14	4690	109	15	13	27.99	83
1988	14	4740	109	15	13	29.40	82
1989	14	4790	109	15	13	30.80	81
1990	14	4845	109	15	13	32.40	80
1991	14	4890	109	15	13	32.40	80
1992	14	4935	109	15	13	33.41	78
1993	14	4983	109	15	13	34.44	76
1994	14	5033	109	15	13	35.52	74
1995	14	5033	109	15	13	36.61	72
1996	14	5048	109	15	13	37.01	72
1997	14	5063	109	15	13	37.42	72
1998	14	5078	109	15	13	37.83	72
1999	14	5078	109	15	13	37.83	72
2000	14	5078	109	15	13	37.83	72
Class 4:	**domestic gas large car**						
1976	33	6626	118	74	18	12.95	150
1977	34	6637	117	75	18	13.62	142
1978	35	6680	116	75	18	14.74	134
1979	35	6730	116	75	18	15.37	128
1980	35	6801	116	75	18	17.02	125
1981	34	6875	116	75	18	18.55	123
1982	34	6963	116	75	18	20.38	119

Table B.1 (continued)

a Vintage	b Number of models	c Price (1978$)	d Shoulder room	e Variance of d	f Luggage space	g MPG	h HP
1983	34	7015	115	75	18	21.23	116
1984	34	7072	115	75	18	22.41	113
1985	34	7153	114	75	18	24.10	110
1986	34	7257	114	75	18	27.08	105
1987	34	7257	114	75	18	27.08	105
1988	34	7285	114	75	18	27.89	103
1989	34	7315	114	75	18	28.73	101
1990	34	7345	114	75	18	29.59	99
1991	34	7375	114	75	18	30.48	97
1992	34	7375	114	75	18	30.48	97
1993	34	7429	114	75	18	31.42	96
1994	34	7473	114	75	18	32.40	95
1995	34	7518	114	75	18	33.40	94
1996	34	7563	114	75	18	34.44	93
1997	34	7563	114	75	18	34.44	93
1998	34	7573	114	75	18	34.82	93
1999	34	7584	114	75	18	35.20	93
2000	34	7595	114	75	18	35.60	93
Class 5:	**foreign gas mini car**						
1976							
1977							
1978							
1979							
1980							
1981							
1982							
1983							
1984	3	3200	92	10	7	46	55
1985	5	3200	92	10	7	46	55
1986	7	3200	92	10	7	46	55
1987	8	3200	92	10	7	46	55
1988	8	3254	92	10	7	47.84	54
1989	8	3308	92	10	7	49.75	53
1990	8	3362	92	10	7	52.00	52
1991	8	3414	92	10	7	54.07	51
1992	8	3454	92	10	7	54.07	51
1993	8	3500	92	10	7	55.69	51
1994	8	3540	92	10	7	57.36	50
1995	8	3595	92	10	7	59.66	50
1996	8	3640	92	10	7	62.04	50
1997	8	3640	92	10	7	62.04	50
1998	8	3640	92	10	7	62.04	50
1999	8	3640	92	10	7	62.04	50
2000	8	3640	92	10	7	62.04	50

Table B.1 (continued)

a Vintage	b Number of models	c Price (1978$)	d Shoulder room	e Variance of d	f Luggage space	g MPG	h HP
Class 6:	**foreign gas regular car**						
1976	42	4303	95	185	9	24.18	77
1977	43	4311	95	185	9	24.42	77
1978	44	4319	95	185	9	24.64	76
1979	44	4335	95	185	9	25.63	75
1980	41	4352	96	190	9	26.82	74
1981	38	4390	97	190	9	28.14	73
1982	38	4422	98	200	9	29.18	72
1983	38	4474	98	200	9	30.60	71
1984	38	4511	99	200	9	31.88	70
1985	38	4548	99	200	9	33.22	70
1986	38	4580	99	200	9	34.55	70
1987	38	4628	99	200	9	35.93	69
1988	38	4648	99	200	9	36.72	69
1989	38	4670	99	200	9	37.62	68
1990	38	4697	99	200	9	38.65	68
1991	38	4723	99	200	9	39.62	67
1992	38	4767	99	200	9	39.62	67
1993	38	4811	99	200	9	40.84	67
1994	38	4856	99	200	9	42.11	67
1995	38	4891	99	200	9	43.42	67
1996	38	4891	99	200	9	44.77	67
1997	38	4903	99	200	9	44.77	67
1998	38	4915	99	200	9	45.26	67
1999	38	4927	99	200	9	45.75	67
2000	38	4927	99	200	9	46.26	67
Class 7:	**foreign gas luxury car**						
1976	23	11,093	82	702	9	14.14	131
1977	23	11,104	82	702	9	14.35	128
1978	25	11,115	82	702	9	14.71	125
1979	26	11,150	82	702	9	15.40	125
1980	28	11,233	82	702	9	17.26	123
1981	29	11,288	82	702	9	17.94	121
1982	29	11,343	82	702	9	18.65	120
1983	30	11,405	82	702	9	19.59	118
1984	30	11,465	82	702	9	20.41	116
1985	30	11,525	82	702	9	21.43	115
1986	30	11,580	82	702	9	22.50	114
1987	30	11,630	82	702	9	23.62	113
1988	30	11,680	82	702	9	24.69	112
1989	30	11,731	82	702	9	25.92	111
1990	30	11,786	82	702	9	27.22	110
1991	30	11,846	82	702	9	28.03	108
1992	30	11,908	82	702	9	28.88	106

Table B.1 (continued)

a Vintage	b Number of models	c Price (1978$)	d Shoulder room	e Variance of d	f Luggage space	g MPG	h HP
1993	30	11,978	82	702	9	29.89	104
1994	30	12,040	82	702	9	30.93	102
1995	30	12,100	82	702	9	32.02	100
1996	30	12,127	82	702	9	32.43	99
1997	30	12,154	82	702	9	32.85	98
1998	30	12,181	82	702	9	33.28	97
1999	30	12,208	82	702	9	33.71	96
2000	30	12,236	82	702	9	34.12	95

Class 8: domestic diesel mini car (two-seater)

a Vintage	b	c	d	e	f	g	h
1976							
1977							
1978							
1979							
1980							
1981							
1982							
1983							
1984							
1985							
1986							
1987							
1988	2	3500	92	10	7	58.00	40
1989	3	3554	92	10	7	60.32	39
1990	4	3608	92	10	7	62.73	38
1991	4	3664	92	10	7	65.57	37
1992	4	3718	92	10	7	68.20	36
1993	4	3718	92	10	7	68.20	36
1994	4	3740	92	10	7	69.56	36
1995	4	3763	92	10	7	70.95	36
1996	4	3786	92	10	7	72.37	36
1997	4	3786	92	10	7	72.37	36
1998	4	3786	92	10	7	72.37	36
1999	4	3786	92	10	7	72.37	36
2000	4	3786	92	10	7	72.37	36

Class 9: domestic diesel subcompact car

a Vintage	b	c	d	e	f	g	h
1976							
1977							
1978							
1979							
1980							
1981							
1982	1	4567	102	15	7	39.00	51
1983	1	4567	102	15	7	39.00	51

Table B.1 (continued)

a Vintage	b Number of models	c Price (1978$)	d Shoulder room	e Variance of d	f Luggage space	g MPG	h HP
1984	3	4642	102	15	7	43.15	50
1985	5	4700	102	15	7	46.37	49
1986	8	4775	102	15	7	51.30	48
1987	8	4775	102	15	7	51.30	48
1988	8	4809	102	15	7	52.90	48
1989	8	4833	102	15	7	54.69	48
1990	8	4877	102	15	7	56.46	48
1991	8	4901	102	15	7	58.30	48
1992	8	4901	102	15	7	58.30	48
1993	8	4918	102	15	7	59.23	48
1994	8	4935	102	15	7	60.18	48
1995	8	4952	102	15	7	61.14	48
1996	8	4970	102	15	7	62.12	48
1997	8	4970	102	15	7	62.12	48
1998	8	4970	102	15	7	62.12	48
1999	8	4970	102	15	7	62.12	48
2000	8	4970	102	15	7	62.12	48

Class 10:   domestic diesel compact car

a Vintage	b Number of models	c Price (1978$)	d Shoulder room	e Variance of d	f Luggage space	g MPG	h HP
1976							
1977							
1978							
1979							
1980							
1981							
1982							
1983							
1984							
1985							
1986	2	5100	109	10	13	37.0	62
1987	6	5100	109	15	13	37.0	62
1988	8	5154	109	15	13	38.66	61
1989	8	5208	109	15	13	40.40	60
1990	8	5262	109	15	13	42.22	59
1991	8	5316	109	15	13	44.16	58
1992	8	5316	109	15	13	44.16	58
1993	8	5384	109	15	13	45.97	58
1994	8	5452	109	15	13	47.86	58
1995	8	5520	109	15	13	49.82	58
1996	8	5588	109	15	13	51.86	58
1997	8	5588	109	15	13	51.86	58
1998	8	5603	109	15	13	52.43	58
1999	8	5618	109	15	13	53.00	58
2000	8	5633	109	15	13	53.60	58

Table B.1 (continued)

a Vintage	b Number of models	c Price (1978$)	d Shoulder room	e Variance of d	f Luggage space	g MPG	h HP
Class 11:	**domestic diesel large car**						
1976							
1977							
1978	2	7433	120	0	20	22.1	120
1979	6	7455	118	15	18	22.9	110
1980	15	7490	116	15	18	23.8	100
1981	15	7562	116	15	18	24.9	98
1982	19	7640	116	20	18	27.1	96
1983	19	7676	115	20	18	27.96	94
1984	24	7768	115	20	18	29.56	92
1985	28	7840	114	20	18	31.63	90
1986	28	7940	114	20	18	35.14	89
1987	28	7977	114	20	18	35.97	89
1988	28	8044	114	20	18	37.98	88
1989	28	8074	114	20	18	39.12	87
1990	28	8104	114	20	18	40.29	86
1991	28	8134	114	20	18	42.30	85
1992	28	8158	114	20	18	43.14	85
1993	28	8215	114	20	18	44.69	85
1994	28	8272	114	20	18	46.30	85
1995	28	8329	114	20	18	47.97	85
1996	28	8386	114	20	18	49.69	85
1997	28	8386	114	20	18	49.69	85
1998	28	8401	114	20	18	50.24	85
1999	28	8416	114	20	18	50.79	85
2000	28	8431	114	20	18	51.35	85
Class 12:	**foreign diesel mini car**						
1976							
1977							
1978							
1979							
1980							
1981							
1982							
1983							
1984							
1985							
1986							
1987	2	3500	92	5	7	62.00	40
1988	4	3554	92	10	7	64.48	39
1989	5	3608	92	10	7	67.05	38
1990	5	3664	92	10	7	70.00	37
1991	5	3718	92	10	7	72.88	36

Table B.1 (continued)

a Vintage	b Number of models	c Price (1978$)	d Shoulder room	e Variance of d	f Luggage space	g MPG	h HP
1992	5	3718	92	10	7	72.88	36
1993	5	3740	92	10	7	74.33	36
1994	5	3763	92	10	7	75.82	36
1995	5	3786	92	10	7	77.34	36
1996	5	3786	92	10	7	77.34	36
1997	5	3786	92	10	7	77.34	36
1998	5	3786	92	10	7	77.34	36
1999	5	3786	92	10	7	77.34	36
2000	5	3786	92	10	7	77.34	36
Class 13:	**foreign diesel regular car**						
1976							
1977							
1978	2	4800	103	10	15	41.90	50
1979	2	4800	103	10	15	41.90	50
1980	2	4810	103	10	15	42.73	50
1981	4	4825	103	10	15	43.90	50
1982	4	4830	102	10	13	44.21	49
1983	6	4858	102	10	13	45.62	49
1984	8	4887	101	10	12	47.08	48
1985	10	4915	101	10	12	48.58	48
1986	10	4944	100	10	12	50.14	47
1987	10	4944	100	10	12	50.14	47
1988	10	5000	100	10	12	51.89	46
1989	10	5056	100	10	12	53.71	45
1990	10	5112	100	10	12	55.59	45
1991	10	5168	100	10	12	57.54	45
1992	10	5168	100	10	12	57.54	45
1993	10	5206	100	10	12	59.34	45
1994	10	5244	100	10	12	61.24	45
1995	10	5282	100	10	12	63.19	45
1996	10	5320	100	10	12	65.22	45
1997	10	5320	100	10	12	65.22	45
1998	10	5332	100	10	12	65.93	45
1999	10	5349	100	10	12	66.66	45
2000	10	5356	100	10	12	67.40	45
Class 14:	**foreign diesel luxury car**						
1976	3	13,175	110	12	12	24.0	71
1977	3	13,175	110	12	12	24.0	71
1978	4	13,235	110	12	12	24.5	75
1979	6	13,335	110	12	12	25.72	75
1980	8	13,395	110	12	12	27.00	75
1981	10	13,455	110	12	12	28.36	75
1982	10	13,670	110	12	12	30.77	80

Table B.1 (continued)

a Vintage	b Number of models	c Price (1978$)	d Shoulder room	e Variance of d	f Luggage space	g MPG	h HP
1983	10	13,700	110	12	12	31.08	84
1984	12	13,730	110	12	12	32.33	84
1985	12	13,760	110	12	12	32.68	84
1986	12	13,790	110	12	12	33.04	84
1987	12	13,870	110	12	12	34.36	83
1988	12	13,980	110	12	12	36.08	82
1989	12	14,090	110	12	12	37.88	81
1990	12	14,200	110	12	12	39.78	80
1991	12	14,310	110	12	12	41.76	79
1992	12	14,310	110	12	12	41.76	79
1993	12	14,327	110	12	12	42.42	79
1994	12	14,334	110	12	12	43.10	79
1995	12	14,361	110	12	12	43.79	79
1996	12	14,378	110	12	12	44.50	79
1997	12	14,378	110	12	12	44.50	79
1998	12	14,378	110	12	12	44.50	79
1999	12	14,378	110	12	12	44.50	79
2000	12	14,378	110	12	12	44.50	79
Class 15:	**domestic electric car**						
1976							
1977							
1978							
1979							
1980							
1981							
1982							
1983							
1984							
1985							
1986							
1987							
1988	1	4800	102	0	6	4.35	30
1989	3	4800	102	5	6	4.35	30
1990	3	4800	102	5	6	4.35	30
1991	3	4800	102	5	6	4.35	30
1992	3	4800	102	5	6	4.35	30
1993	3	4800	102	5	6	4.35	30
1994	3	5000	102	5	6	4.6	35
1995	3	5000	102	5	6	4.6	35
1996	3	5000	102	5	6	4.6	35
1997	3	5000	102	5	6	4.6	35
1998	3	5000	102	5	6	4.6	35
1999	3	5000	102	5	6	4.6	35
2000	3	5000	102	5	6	4.6	35

Table B.1 (continued)

a Vintage	b Number of models	c Price (1978$)	d Shoulder room	e Variance of d	f Luggage space	g MPG	h HP
Class 16:	**foreign electric car**						
1976							
1977							
1978							
1979							
1980							
1981							
1982							
1983							
1984							
1985							
1986							
1987	1	4800	97	0	6	4.50	28
1988	3	4800	97	5	6	4.50	28
1989	3	4800	97	5	6	4.50	28
1990	3	4800	97	5	6	4.50	28
1991	3	4800	97	5	6	4.50	28
1992	3	4800	97	5	6	4.50	28
1993	3	4800	97	5	6	4.50	28
1994	3	5000	97	5	6	4.75	33
1995	3	5000	97	5	6	4.75	33
1996	3	5000	97	5	6	4.75	33
1997	3	5000	97	5	6	4.75	33
1998	3	5000	97	5	6	4.75	33
1999	3	5000	97	5	6	4.75	33
2000	3	5000	97	5	6	4.75	33
Class 17:	**methanol compact car**						
1976							
1977							
1978							
1979							
1980							
1981							
1982							
1983							
1984							
1985							
1986	2	4976	109	8	13	16.50	83
1987	4	4990	109	12	13	16.80	82
1988	6	5040	109	15	13	17.64	82
1989	6	5090	109	15	13	18.51	81
1990	6	5145	109	15	13	19.44	80
1991	6	5145	109	15	13	19.44	80

Table B.1 (continued)

a Vintage	b Number of models	c Price (1978$)	d Shoulder room	e Variance of d	f Luggage space	g MPG	h HP
1992	6	5190	109	15	13	20.04	78
1993	6	5235	109	15	13	20.66	76
1994	6	5283	109	15	13	21.31	74
1995	6	5333	109	15	13	21.96	72
1996	6	5333	109	15	13	21.96	72
1997	6	5348	109	15	13	22.20	72
1998	6	5363	109	15	13	22.45	72
1999	6	5378	109	15	13	22.70	72
2000	6	5378	109	15	13	22.70	72

Class 18: methanol large car

a Vintage	b Number of models	c Price (1978$)	d Shoulder room	e Variance of d	f Luggage space	g MPG	h HP
1976							
1977							
1978							
1979							
1980							
1981							
1982							
1983							
1984							
1985							
1986	2	7557	114	8	18	14.50	105
1987	6	7557	114	12	18	14.50	105
1988	10	7585	114	16	18	14.92	103
1989	10	7615	114	16	18	15.37	101
1990	10	7645	114	16	18	15.83	99
1991	10	7675	114	16	18	16.30	97
1992	10	7675	114	16	18	16.30	97
1993	10	7729	114	16	18	16.80	96
1994	10	7773	114	16	18	17.33	95
1995	10	7818	114	16	18	17.86	94
1996	10	7863	114	16	18	18.42	93
1997	10	7863	114	16	18	18.42	93
1998	10	7873	114	16	18	18.62	93
1999	10	7884	114	16	18	18.83	93
2000	10	7895	114	16	18	19.04	93

Class 19: LPG/LNG compact car

a Vintage
1976
1977
1978
1979
1980
1981
1982

Table B.1 (continued)

a Vintage	b Number of models	c Price (1978$)	d Shoulder room	e Variance of d	f Luggage space	g MPG	h HP
1983							
1984	1	5183	109	0	13	23.26	76
1985	3	5246	109	10	13	24.79	76
1986	6	5276	109	15	13	25.53	75
1987	6	5290	109	15	13	25.91	75
1988	6	5340	109	15	13	27.22	73
1989	6	5390	109	15	13	28.57	72
1990	6	5445	109	15	13	30.00	70
1991	6	5445	109	15	13	30.00	70
1992	6	5490	109	15	13	30.93	69
1993	6	5535	109	15	13	31.89	68
1994	6	5583	109	15	13	32.89	67
1995	6	5633	109	15	13	33.90	66
1996	6	5633	109	15	13	33.90	66
1997	6	5648	109	15	13	34.27	66
1998	6	5663	109	15	13	34.65	66
1999	6	5678	109	15	13	35.00	66
2000	6	5678	109	15	13	35.00	66
Class 20:	**LPG/LNG large car**						
1976							
1977							
1978							
1979							
1980							
1981							
1982							
1983							
1984	2	7672	114	0	18	20.75	102
1985	6	7753	114	10	18	22.31	100
1986	10	7857	114	16	18	25.07	96
1987	10	7857	114	16	18	25.07	96
1988	10	7885	114	16	18	25.82	94
1989	10	7915	114	16	18	26.60	92
1990	19	7945	114	16	18	27.40	90
1991	10	7975	114	16	18	28.22	88
1992	10	7975	114	16	18	28.22	88
1993	10	8029	114	16	18	29.09	86
1994	10	8073	114	16	18	30.03	85
1995	10	8118	114	16	18	30.93	84
1996	10	8163	114	16	18	31.89	83
1997	10	8163	114	16	18	31.89	83
1998	10	8273	114	16	18	32.24	83
1999	10	8384	114	16	18	32.59	83
2000	10	8395	114	16	18	32.96	83

Table B.1 (continued)

a Vintage	b Number of models	c Price (1978$)	d Shoulder room	e Variance of d	f Luggage space	g MPG	h HP
Class 21:	**pickups**						
1976	11	3718	25	0	0	14.30	116
1977	9	4328	25	0	0	14.30	123
1978	9	5547	25	0	0	14.50	121
1979	9	4364	25	0	0	15.39	121
1980	9	4384	25	0	0	15.15	121
1981	9	4367	25	0	0	17.54	121
1982	9	4419	25	0	0	18.87	121
1983	9	4437	25	0	0	19.61	121
1984	9	4452	25	0	0	20.83	121
1985	9	4464	25	0	0	21.28	121
1986	9	4504	25	0	0	22.22	121
1987	9	4544	25	0	0	23.26	121
1988	9	4584	25	0	0	23.81	121
1989	9	4624	25	0	0	25.00	121
1990	9	4665	25	0	0	25.64	121
1991	9	4710	25	0	0	21.74	121
1992	9	4755	25	0	0	27.03	121
1993	9	4800	25	0	0	27.78	121
1994	9	4845	25	0	0	28.57	121
1995	9	4889	25	0	0	30.30	121
1996	9	4893	25	0	0	30.30	121
1997	9	4897	25	0	0	31.25	121
1998	9	4901	25	0	0	31.25	121
1999	9	4906	25	0	0	31.25	121
2000	9	4910	25	0	0	31.25	121
Class 22:	**vans**						
1976	5	3910	25	0	0	15.60	115
1977	5	4655	25	0	0	15.00	117
1978	5	5863	25	0	0	14.90	117
1979	5	4981	25	0	0	12.20	117
1980	5	5016	25	0	0	11.91	117
1981	5	5051	25	0	0	12.50	117
1982	5	5142	25	0	0	13.89	117
1983	5	5191	25	0	0	15.15	117
1984	5	5240	25	0	0	16.13	117
1985	5	5289	25	0	0	16.95	117
1986	5	4504	25	0	0	18.18	117
1987	5	5402	25	0	0	18.52	117
1988	5	5458	25	0	0	19.23	117
1989	5	5516	25	0	0	20.00	117
1990	5	5573	25	0	0	20.83	117
1991	5	5627	25	0	0	20.83	117

Table B.1 (continued)

a Vintage	b Number of models	c Price (1978$)	d Shoulder room	e Variance of d	f Luggage space	g MPG	h HP
1992	5	5681	25	0	0	21.74	117
1993	5	5735	25	0	0	22.22	117
1994	5	5788	25	0	0	22.73	117
1995	5	5841	25	0	0	23.26	117
1996	5	5861	25	0	0	23.26	117
1997	5	5882	25	0	0	23.81	117
1998	5	5903	25	0	0	24.39	117
1999	5	5923	25	0	0	23.81	117
2000	5	5944	25	0	0	24.39	117
Class 23:	**utility vehicles**						
1976	4	4531	46	0	0	14.10	97
1977	4	4881	46	0	0	14.10	97
1978	4	6138	46	0	0	14.10	100
1979	4	6496	46	0	0	12.05	100
1980	4	6547	46	0	0	12.35	100
1981	4	6805	46	0	0	15.63	100
1982	4	6687	46	0	0	14.49	100
1983	4	6726	46	0	0	15.87	100
1984	4	6765	46	0	0	17.24	100
1985	4	6804	46	0	0	18.18	100
1986	4	6860	46	0	0	19.23	100
1987	4	6917	46	0	0	19.61	100
1988	4	6973	46	0	0	20.41	100
1989	4	7031	46	0	0	20.83	100
1990	4	7088	46	0	0	21.74	100
1991	4	7142	46	0	0	22.22	100
1992	4	7196	46	0	0	23.26	100
1993	4	7250	46	0	0	23.26	100
1994	4	7303	46	0	0	24.39	100
1995	4	7356	46	0	0	25.00	100
1996	4	7377	46	0	0	25.00	100
1997	4	7397	46	0	0	25.00	100
1998	4	7418	46	0	0	25.64	100
1999	4	7438	46	0	0	25.64	100
2000	4	7459	46	0	0	26.32	100

Appendix C   Base Case Simulations

Key to vehicle classes:

1   Domestic and foreign gas mini car
2   Domestic gas subcompact car
3   Domestic gas compact car
4   Domestic gas large car
5   Foreign regular gas car
6   Foreign luxury gas car
7   Domestic and foreign diesel mini car
8   Domestic diesel subcompact car
9   Domestic diesel compact car
10   Domestic diesel large car
11   Foreign regular diesel car
12   Foreign luxury diesel car
13   Domestic and foreign electric car
14   Domestic and foreign methanol compact car
15   Domestic and foreign methanol large car
16   Domestic and foreign LPG compact car
17   Domestic and foreign LPG large car
18   Small gas pickups and utility vehicles
19   Large gas pickups and utility vehicles
20   Small diesel pickups and utility vehicles
21   Large diesel pickups and utility vehicles
22   Small gas vans and other vehicles
23   Large gas vans and other vehicles
24   Small diesel vans and other vehicles
25   Large diesel vans and other vehicles

Table C.1
Base case simulations

```
PERSONAL VEHICLE DATA FOR 1980
                  NO.                              FUEL USE
CLASS           VEHICLES          VMT          GALLONS OR KWH
  1                 0.              0.               0.
  2           1200234.    11987366138.        637321029.
  3           1751689.    16912420828.       1139495292.
  4           4841224.    45774033488.       3510605096.
  5           3060928.    35454261152.       1441566918.
  6            439457.     4489275747.        277274992.
  7                 0.              0.               0.
  8                 0.              0.               0.
  9                 0.              0.               0.
 10             36946.      506580053.         21761131.
 11             13487.      192686157.          4579377.
 12             42840.      567051088.         23166773.
 13                 0.              0.               0.
 14                 0.              0.               0.
 15                 0.              0.               0.
 16                 0.              0.               0.
 17                 0.              0.               0.
 18            706531.     7783091586.        410279148.
 19           1099229.    11124244583.        912085738.
 20                 0.              0.               0.
 21              7073.       93515959.          6089797.
 22                 0.              0.               0.
 23            557036.     6237578164.        425972433.
 24                 0.              0.               0.
 25                 0.              0.               0.


PERSONAL VEHICLES OWNED THIS YEAR
CARS:         11386804.
TRUCKS:        2369869.
TOTAL:        13756673.

CAR VMT BY USE CATEGORIES
  1:SHORT-URBAN-WORK TRIP MILES:        23039483362.
  2:SHORT-URBAN-NONWORK TRIP MILES:     62313548123.
  3:OTHER WORK TRIP MILES:              23543678325.
  4:OTHER NONWORK TRIP MILES:            6986964839.

TRUCK VMT BY USE CATEGORIES
  1:SHORT-URBAN-WORK TRIP MILES:         5993191731.
  2:SHORT-URBAN-NONWORK TRIP MILES:     12801371921.
  3:OTHER WORK TRIP MILES:               4952055707.
  4:OTHER NONWORK TRIP MILES:            1491810933.

TOTAL VMT BY USE CATEGORIES
  1:SHORT-URBAN-WORK TRIP MILES:        29032675093.
  2:SHORT-URBAN-NONWORK TRIP MILES:     75114920044.
  3:OTHER WORK TRIP MILES:              28495734033.
  4:OTHER NONWORK TRIP MILES:            8478775772.

PERSONAL VMT
CAR VMT:         115883674650.
TRUCK VMT:        25238430292.
TOTAL VMT:       141122104942.

FUEL USE BY PERSONAL VEHICLES:   CARS          TRUCKS          TOTAL
  GASOLINE (GALS):          7006263328.    1748337319.    8754600647.
  DIESEL (GALS):              49507281.       6089797.      55597078.
  ELECTRICITY (KWH):                 0.             0.             0.
  METHANOL (GALS):                   0.             0.             0.
  LPG (GALS):                        0.             0.             0.
```

Table C.1 (continued)

```
PERSONAL VEHICLE DATA FOR 1990
                 NO.                              FUEL USE
CLASS        VEHICLES           VMT           GALLONS OR KWH
  1          1029941.       13132988744.         284190163.
  2          1460523.       17253443128.         559109925.
  3          2243711.       26155309272.         969136814.
  4          6237942.       75340089946.        2915716651.
  5          3020936.       38156445249.        1071821786.
  6           553330.        6596447769.         295708660.
  7            21579.         303879670.           4761618.
  8            64810.         795457121.          15613307.
  9            36983.         496026222.          12674261.
 10           206834.        2522422122.          72922270.
 11            50972.         620091336.          13019241.
 12           105833.        1281868290.          40595763.
 13             8503.         124574703.          27683267.
 14            18881.         239908167.          13455166.
 15            28569.         379320140.          23650021.
 16            27812.         332132207.          13407471.
 17            40649.         513933014.          22432775.
 18           720080.        8355117723.         360333184.
 19          1521167.       17562808006.         992829497.
 20            88996.         995621104.          24967240.
 21            65937.         764813196.          31366623.
 22             8112.         107717550.           4664271.
 23           404248.        5170130852.         307257047.
 24            11285.         146042283.           3706878.
 25           415091.        5108341964.         205321971.

PERSONAL VEHICLES OWNED THIS YEAR
CARS:          15157806.
TRUCKS:         3234917.
TOTAL:         18392723.

CAR VMT BY USE CATEGORIES
   1:SHORT-URBAN-WORK TRIP MILES:            35559500128.
   2:SHORT-URBAN-NONWORK TRIP MILES:        103188445500.
   3:OTHER WORK TRIP MILES:                  34624559930.
   4:OTHER NONWORK TRIP MILES:               10871831544.

TRUCK VMT BY USE CATEGORIES
   1:SHORT-URBAN-WORK TRIP MILES:             8917054278.
   2:SHORT-URBAN-NONWORK TRIP MILES:         19973250228.
   3:OTHER WORK TRIP MILES:                   7095128083.
   4:OTHER NONWORK TRIP MILES:                2225160089.

TOTAL VMT BY USE CATEGORIES
   1:SHORT-URBAN-WORK TRIP MILES:            44476554405.
   2:SHORT-URBAN-NONWORK TRIP MILES:        123161695728.
   3:OTHER WORK TRIP MILES:                  41719688014.
   4:OTHER NONWORK TRIP MILES:               13096991633.

PERSONAL VMT
CAR VMT:         184244337102.
TRUCK VMT:        38210592678.
TOTAL VMT:       222454929780.

FUEL USE BY PERSONAL VEHICLES:   CARS           TRUCKS            TOTAL
   GASOLINE (GALS):          6095683999.     1665083999.      7760767998.
   DIESEL (GALS):             159586459.      265362711.       424949170.
   ELECTRICITY (KWH):          27683267.              0.        27683267.
   METHANOL (GALS):            37105187.              0.        37105187.
   LPG (GALS):                 35840246.              0.        35840246.
```

Table C.1 (continued)

```
PERSONAL VEHICLE DATA FOR 2000
                 NO.                          FUEL USE
CLASS         VEHICLES        VMT         GALLONS OR KWH
   1          1575712.    19310742519.      333254112.
   2          1706210.    20311180566.      488489126.
   3          2537452.    29949484330.      826850701.
   4          7099563.    86704561906.     2508807827.
   5          3280048.    41453842821.      899899839.
   6           724638.     8810965937.      273917043.
   7            91082.     1103742758.       14875781.
   8            95749.     1140377941.       17957314.
   9           110954.     1318596513.       26145284.
  10           267406.     3355219145.       69351915.
  11            59462.      731986548.       11972117.
  12           129422.     1591465026.       37347832.
  13            66581.      813041489.      173637536.
  14            48166.      550105123.       24694141.
  15            66305.      777893202.       39231019.
  16            42284.      489165191.       15361984.
  17            63078.      768689617.       25286355.
  18           772997.     9042392368.      310712020.
  19          1743173.    20149615852.      882657349.
  20            98238.     1115756965.       22981138.
  21            81673.      945756818.       30885317.
  22            12632.      156378810.        5572647.
  23           467831.     5958271511.      273913280.
  24            20131.      242634067.        5196099.
  25           509202.     6199340590.      200129311.

PERSONAL VEHICLES OWNED THIS YEAR
CARS:        17964113.
TRUCKS:       3705877.
TOTAL:       21669990.

CAR VMT BY USE CATEGORIES
   1:SHORT-URBAN-WORK TRIP MILES:        43365049618.
   2:SHORT-URBAN-NONWORK TRIP MILES:    134405927606.
   3:OTHER WORK TRIP MILES:              32266852566.
   4:OTHER NONWORK TRIP MILES:           9143230843.

TRUCK VMT BY USE CATEGORIES
   1:SHORT-URBAN-WORK TRIP MILES:        10501711832.
   2:SHORT-URBAN-NONWORK TRIP MILES:     25169986768.
   3:OTHER WORK TRIP MILES:               6361121227.
   4:OTHER NONWORK TRIP MILES:            1777327154.

TOTAL VMT BY USE CATEGORIES
   1:SHORT-URBAN-WORK TRIP MILES:        53866761450.
   2:SHORT-URBAN-NONWORK TRIP MILES:    159575914374.
   3:OTHER WORK TRIP MILES:              38627973793.
   4:OTHER NONWORK TRIP MILES:           10920557996.

PERSONAL VMT
CAR VMT:        219181060632.
TRUCK VMT:       43810146982.
TOTAL VMT:      262991207614.

FUEL USE BY PERSONAL VEHICLES:   CARS          TRUCKS          TOTAL
GASOLINE (GALS):            5331218647.    1472855295.    6804073942.
DIESEL (GALS):              177650243.     259191865.     436842108.
ELECTRICITY (KWH):          173637536.            0.      173637536.
METHANOL (GALS):            63925161.             0.       63925161.
LPG (GALS):                 40648340.             0.       40648340.
```

Appendix D   Scenarios

D.1   Scenario 1: Income Growth

```
PERSONAL VEHICLE DATA FOR 1990
             NO.                              FUEL USE
CLASS      VEHICLES           VMT          GALLONS OR KWH
  1         966375.      12747429725.        275864795.
  2        1445173.      17736910247.        573279900.
  3        2238221.      27200373928.       1006023517.
  4        6544108.      82346906747.       3181016799.
  5        2909875.      37950781841.       1063605269.
  6         597134.       7452164328.        332812331.
  7          19947.        290622348.          4557589.
  8          62392.        793572052.         15528567.
  9          36688.        510554185.         13035600.
 10         212872.       2698267484.         77768126.
 11          48473.        609929430.         12779335.
 12         111707.       1405764109.         44454149.
 13           8029.        122249728.         27166606.
 14          19741.        261494351.         14639479.
 15          31075.        428469067.         26697699.
 16          27862.        347382369.         13992307.
 17          43696.        574204894.         25010729.
 18         739485.       8987858900.        387210538.
 19        1696816.      20490450443.       1156178778.
 20          88304.       1034295022.         25880597.
 21          74926.        906641519.         37094460.
 22           8501.        118126866.          5111273.
 23         451933.       6007326502.        356254034.
 24          11361.        154029850.          3904139.
 25         438161.       5651233414.        226748239.
```

```
PERSONAL VEHICLES OWNED THIS YEAR
CARS:        15323369.
TRUCKS:       3509486.
TOTAL:       18832856.
```

```
CAR VMT BY USE CATEGORIES
  1:SHORT-URBAN-WORK TRIP MILES:        37897255232.
  2:SHORT-URBAN-NONWORK TRIP MILES:    108262532899.
  3:OTHER WORK TRIP MILES:              35903085074.
  4:OTHER NONWORK TRIP MILES:           11414203628.
```

```
TRUCK VMT BY USE CATEGORIES
  1:SHORT-URBAN-WORK TRIP MILES:        10142676611.
  2:SHORT-URBAN-NONWORK TRIP MILES:     22844569226.
  3:OTHER WORK TRIP MILES:               7856000816.
  4:OTHER NONWORK TRIP MILES:            2506715865.
```

```
TOTAL VMT BY USE CATEGORIES
  1:SHORT-URBAN-WORK TRIP MILES:        48039931842.
  2:SHORT-URBAN-NONWORK TRIP MILES:    131107102125.
  3:OTHER WORK TRIP MILES:              43759085890.
  4:OTHER NONWORK TRIP MILES:           13920919492.
```

```
PERSONAL VMT
CAR VMT:       193477076833.
TRUCK VMT:      43349962517.
TOTAL VMT:     236827039350.
```

```
FUEL USE BY PERSONAL VEHICLES:   CARS          TRUCKS          TOTAL
  GASOLINE (GALS):          6432602611.     1904754623.    8337357234.
  DIESEL (GALS):             168123367.      293627435.     461750802.
  ELECTRICITY (KWH):          27166606.              0.      27166606.
  METHANOL (GALS):            41337178.              0.      41337178.
  LPG (GALS):                 39003036.              0.      39003036.
```

```
PERSONAL VEHICLE DATA FOR 2000
                NO.                              FUEL USE
CLASS         VEHICLES          VMT           GALLONS OR KWH
  1          1461080.      19220381288.          331294224.
  2          1702521.      21938497976.          526256622.
  3          2582920.      33297855178.          917750297.
  4          7674834.     102260151404.         2953039439.
  5          3146662.      42753199885.          925371734.
  6           792815.      10470364835.          324603811.
  7            82596.       1067931500.           14382239.
  8            91823.       1177726943.           18488561.
  9           110154.       1416100961.           28023613.
 10           292110.       3957094550.           81551055.
 11            57246.        756858934.           12345191.
 12           145351.       1923711811.           45030144.
 13            64491.        841700589.          179609619.
 14            51644.        644330550.           28844707.
 15            73755.        943321364.           47486396.
 16            44373.        560265073.           17560433.
 17            70498.        931252374.           30571855.
 18           841659.      10772323594.          369798529.
 19          2072131.      26118968121.         1143086779.
 20           101700.       1263103262.           25989206.
 21            96853.       1213485647.           39596438.
 22            13885.        188584281.            6713933.
 23           546234.       7546735610.          346760120.
 24            20963.        277591322.            5940127.
 25           562991.       7508104726.          242185927.
```

```
PERSONAL VEHICLES OWNED THIS YEAR
CARS:          18444873.
TRUCKS:         4256417.
TOTAL:         22701290.
```

```
CAR VMT BY USE CATEGORIES
  1:SHORT-URBAN-WORK TRIP MILES:        50287116833.
  2:SHORT-URBAN-NONWORK TRIP MILES:    148976175732.
  3:OTHER WORK TRIP MILES:              34791498741.
  4:OTHER NONWORK TRIP MILES:          10105953907.
```

```
TRUCK VMT BY USE CATEGORIES
  1:SHORT-URBAN-WORK TRIP MILES:        13071598582.
  2:SHORT-URBAN-NONWORK TRIP MILES:     31853041713.
  3:OTHER WORK TRIP MILES:               7773247842.
  4:OTHER NONWORK TRIP MILES:            2191008425.
```

```
TOTAL VMT BY USE CATEGORIES
  1:SHORT-URBAN-WORK TRIP MILES:        63358715415.
  2:SHORT-URBAN-NONWORK TRIP MILES:    180829217446.
  3:OTHER WORK TRIP MILES:              42564746583.
  4:OTHER NONWORK TRIP MILES:          12296962332.
```

```
PERSONAL VMT
CAR VMT:       244160745214.
TRUCK VMT:      54888896562.
TOTAL VMT:     299049641776.
```

```
FUEL USE BY PERSONAL VEHICLES:   CARS          TRUCKS          TOTAL
  GASOLINE (GALS):          5978316127.    1866359361.    7844675488.
  DIESEL (GALS):             199820802.     313711698.     513532501.
  ELECTRICITY (KWH):         179609619.             0.     179609619.
  METHANOL (GALS):            76331104.             0.      76331104.
  LPG (GALS):                 48132288.             0.      48132288.
```

D.2   Scenario 2: Moderate Gas Price Increases

```
PERSONAL VEHICLE DATA FOR 1990
                NO.                               FUEL USE
CLASS         VEHICLES          VMT            GALLONS OR KWH
  1           1062837.      13408776637.          290089887.
  2           1451636.      16844205249.          544439831.
  3           2192114.      25100824445.          927138720.
  4           6087157.      72005321994.         2777978178.
  5           3066063.      37958219317.         1064901776.
  6            538446.       6177258665.          276245716.
  7             24151.        341889838.            5357389.
  8             72258.        890669248.           17476505.
  9             41293.        555269955.           14188536.
 10            231374.       2827633046.           81761667.
 11             56862.        695291197.           14597924.
 12            118151.       1432214048.           45361565.
 13              9520.        139936729.           31097051.
 14             21080.        267964689.           15029142.
 15             31813.        422348588.           26332001.
 16             31039.        371092107.           14979879.
 17             45237.        572248702.           24978573.
 18            684874.       7860813208.          338651771.
 19           1390345.      15815596071.          891979879.
 20             99042.       1109464478.           27819478.
 21             73741.        855301393.           35075864.
 22              7713.        101195225.            4379574.
 23            365308.       4609782731.          273132419.
 24             12526.        162133489.            4115384.
 25            462053.       5680810905.          228343282.


PERSONAL VEHICLES OWNED THIS YEAR
CARS:           15081033.
TRUCKS:          3095603.
TOTAL:          18176636.


CAR VMT BY USE CATEGORIES
   1:SHORT-URBAN-WORK TRIP MILES:          35090035568.
   2:SHORT-URBAN-NONWORK TRIP MILES:      103304255325.
   3:OTHER WORK TRIP MILES:                32127607041.
   4:OTHER NONWORK TRIP MILES:              9759266518.

TRUCK VMT BY USE CATEGORIES
   1:SHORT-URBAN-WORK TRIP MILES:           8547999647.
   2:SHORT-URBAN-NONWORK TRIP MILES:       19322291576.
   3:OTHER WORK TRIP MILES:                 6390103986.
   4:OTHER NONWORK TRIP MILES:             1934702291.

TOTAL VMT BY USE CATEGORIES
   1:SHORT-URBAN-WORK TRIP MILES:          43638035215.
   2:SHORT-URBAN-NONWORK TRIP MILES:      122356546901.
   3:OTHER WORK TRIP MILES:                38517711028.
   4:OTHER NONWORK TRIP MILES:            11693968809.

PERSONAL VMT
CAR VMT:        180011164453.
TRUCK VMT:       36195097500.
TOTAL VMT:      216206261953.


FUEL USE BY PERSONAL VEHICLES:   CARS          TRUCKS            TOTAL
  GASOLINE (GALS):          5880794107.    1508143643.      7388937749.
  DIESEL (GALS):             178743588.     295354008.       474097596.
  ELECTRICITY (KWH):          31097051.             0.        31097051.
  METHANOL (GALS):            41361144.             0.        41361144.
  LPG (GALS):                 39958452.             0.        39958452.
```

```
PERSONAL VEHICLE DATA FOR 2000
                NO.                        FUEL USE
CLASS        VEHICLES        VMT        GALLONS OR KWH
  1         1670530.    19863666584.      342426697.
  2         1664840.    18812404628.      451211917.
  3         2364078.    26437806584.      728834393.
  4         6599272.    75688019038.     2187648507.
  5         3352551.    39890801630.      864181585.
  6          685117.     7533986806.      233821535.
  7          122315.     1508222453.       20323599.
  8          127634.     1543263283.       24298512.
  9          148915.     1790748864.       35500938.
 10          362135.     4583802185.       94761978.
 11           79718.      997204410.       16307679.
 12          174493.     2157126669.       50631452.
 13           89243.     1107535177.      236508419.
 14           64430.      740193259.       33218505.
 15           89179.     1049373865.       52921249.
 16           56701.      660738197.       20748504.
 17           84170.     1031753330.       33938368.
 18          653118.     7392552389.      253791425.
 19         1335507.    14717131973.      643878079.
 20          131366.     1504525171.       30984035.
 21          111215.     1293046733.       42222348.
 22           10415.      124432169.        4430259.
 23          345272.     4192377061.      192515129.
 24           26580.      322068523.        6896828.
 25          678535.     8276248223.      267167416.

PERSONAL VEHICLES OWNED THIS YEAR
CARS:           17735321.
TRUCKS:          3292007.
TOTAL:          21027328.

CAR VMT BY USE CATEGORIES
   1:SHORT-URBAN-WORK TRIP MILES:         41034506288.
   2:SHORT-URBAN-NONWORK TRIP MILES:     134512120301.
   3:OTHER WORK TRIP MILES:               23807022659.
   4:OTHER NONWORK TRIP MILES:            6042997713.

TRUCK VMT BY USE CATEGORIES
   1:SHORT-URBAN-WORK TRIP MILES:          9145818834.
   2:SHORT-URBAN-NONWORK TRIP MILES:      23251826859.
   3:OTHER WORK TRIP MILES:                4346453671.
   4:OTHER NONWORK TRIP MILES:            1078282878.

TOTAL VMT BY USE CATEGORIES
   1:SHORT-URBAN-WORK TRIP MILES:         50180325122.
   2:SHORT-URBAN-NONWORK TRIP MILES:     157763947160.
   3:OTHER WORK TRIP MILES:               28153476330.
   4:OTHER NONWORK TRIP MILES:            7121280591.

PERSONAL VMT
CAR VMT:          205396646961.
TRUCK VMT:         37822382243.
TOTAL VMT:        243219029203.

FUEL USE BY PERSONAL VEHICLES:   CARS          TRUCKS          TOTAL
   GASOLINE (GALS):          4808124635.    1094614892.    5902739526.
   DIESEL (GALS):             241824159.     347270627.     589094786.
   ELECTRICITY (KWH):         236508419.             0.     236508419.
   METHANOL (GALS):            86139753.             0.      86139753.
   LPG (GALS):                 54686872.             0.      54686872.
```

D.3   Scenario 3: High Gas and Diesel Prices with No Electric, Methanol, and LPG Vehicles

```
PERSONAL VEHICLE DATA FOR 1990
                NO.                            FUEL USE
CLASS         VEHICLES          VMT         GALLONS OR KWH
  1           1220218.      14685452045.       317394684.
  2           1452319.      15560153407.       497715542.
  3           2057591.      21808187735.       795317029.
  4           5720550.      61904095189.      2358866618.
  5           3332865.      37706095453.      1052463410.
  6            493598.       4842575908.       214299010.
  7             29163.        398464319.         6238877.
  8             79746.        948735814.        18475535.
  9             42541.        536537107.        13680629.
 10            226771.       2586188038.        73784730.
 11             61768.        718785526.        15053959.
 12            111287.       1258796577.        39745755.
 13                 0.                0.                0.
 14                 0.                0.                0.
 15                 0.                0.                0.
 16                 0.                0.                0.
 17                 0.                0.                0.
 18            562018.       6185525916.       265249226.
 19            976349.      10452341746.       584008469.
 20             95623.       1044285835.        26108248.
 21             57634.        637741454.        25925634.
 22              6548.         81986519.         3540667.
 23            258347.       3087297194.       180832684.
 24             12664.        159183205.         4029451.
 25            378476.       4444277681.       177239091.

PERSONAL VEHICLES OWNED THIS YEAR
CARS:           14828416.
TRUCKS:          2347659.
TOTAL:          17176075.

CAR VMT BY USE CATEGORIES
   1:SHORT-URBAN-WORK TRIP MILES:          32811034093.
   2:SHORT-URBAN-NONWORK TRIP MILES:      101019321119.
   3:OTHER WORK TRIP MILES:                22997379366.
   4:OTHER NONWORK TRIP MILES:              6126332539.

TRUCK VMT BY USE CATEGORIES
   1:SHORT-URBAN-WORK TRIP MILES:           6374421543.
   2:SHORT-URBAN-NONWORK TRIP MILES:       15136875476.
   3:OTHER WORK TRIP MILES:                 3625971307.
   4:OTHER NONWORK TRIP MILES:              955371224.

TOTAL VMT BY USE CATEGORIES
   1:SHORT-URBAN-WORK TRIP MILES:          39185455636.
   2:SHORT-URBAN-NONWORK TRIP MILES:      116156196595.
   3:OTHER WORK TRIP MILES:                26623350673.
   4:OTHER NONWORK TRIP MILES:              7081703762.

PERSONAL_VMT
CAR VMT:        162954067117.
TRUCK VMT:       26092639550.
TOTAL VMT:      189046706667.

FUEL USE BY PERSONAL VEHICLES:    CARS          TRUCKS          TOTAL
GASOLINE (GALS):            5236056294.      1033631045.    6269687339.
DIESEL (GALS):              166979485.        233302424.     400281909.
ELECTRICITY (KWH):                  0.                0.             0.
METHANOL (GALS):                    0.                0.             0.
LPG (GALS):                         0.                0.             0.
```

```
PERSONAL VEHICLE DATA FOR 2000
                NO.                          FUEL USE
CLASS       VEHICLES          VMT          GALLONS OR KWH
  1        2057423.       21695616240.        372712897.
  2        1664475.       15564354914.        370120847.
  3        2078081.       19317006835.        530155546.
  4        5804533.       53944244000.       1554070068.
  5        3807307.       36432613149.        784121363.
  6         607503.        4896557285.        151196735.
  7         144692.        1601919524.         21545144.
  8         134596.        1451173653.         22742812.
  9         134562.        1381291048.         27237186.
 10         337661.        3584680063.         73651496.
 11          84210.         914469789.         14872723.
 12         140169.        1482147928.         34569622.
 13              0.                 0.                 0.
 14              0.                 0.                 0.
 15              0.                 0.                 0.
 16              0.                 0.                 0.
 17              0.                 0.                 0.
 18         402858.        4086299953.        139920663.
 19         612522.        5744826374.        250463258.
 20         100068.        1067576615.         21947860.
 21          53793.         542311994.         17651719.
 22           6559.          69910257.          2482439.
 23         162040.        1681748003.         76988810.
 24          21918.         246659883.          5275411.
 25         359993.        3852275720.        124051895.

PERSONAL VEHICLES OWNED THIS YEAR
CARS:         16995212.
TRUCKS:        1719752.
TOTAL:        18714964.

CAR VMT BY USE CATEGORIES
   1:SHORT-URBAN-WORK TRIP MILES:        31078631752.
   2:SHORT-URBAN-NONWORK TRIP MILES:    122068143704.
   3:OTHER WORK TRIP MILES:               7667292738.
   4:OTHER NONWORK TRIP MILES:            1452006234.

TRUCK VMT BY USE CATEGORIES
   1:SHORT-URBAN-WORK TRIP MILES:         3902307362.
   2:SHORT-URBAN-NONWORK TRIP MILES:     12431720804.
   3:OTHER WORK TRIP MILES:                813933005.
   4:OTHER NONWORK TRIP MILES:            143647630.

TOTAL VMT BY USE CATEGORIES
   1:SHORT-URBAN-WORK TRIP MILES:        34980939114.
   2:SHORT-URBAN-NONWORK TRIP MILES:    134499864507.
   3:OTHER WORK TRIP MILES:               8481225743.
   4:OTHER NONWORK TRIP MILES:            1595653864.

PERSONAL VMT
CAR VMT:       162266074428.
TRUCK VMT:      17291608800.
TOTAL VMT:     179557683228.

FUEL USE BY PERSONAL VEHICLES:   CARS          TRUCKS          TOTAL
   GASOLINE (GALS):         3762377457.      469855170.    4232232627.
   DIESEL (GALS):            194618982.      168926885.     363545868.
   ELECTRICITY (KWH):                0.              0.              0.
   METHANOL (GALS):                  0.              0.              0.
   LPG (GALS):                       0.              0.              0.
```

D.4   Scenario 4: Reduced Employment

PERSONAL VEHICLE DATA FOR 1990

CLASS	NO. VEHICLES	VMT	FUEL USE GALLONS OR KWH
1	1022666.	13004730200.	281447825.
2	1444605.	16976054844.	550618307.
3	2217440.	25757307387.	954477414.
4	6162595.	74133018217.	2870454904.
5	3011223.	37870422600.	1064402483.
6	546234.	6460611797.	289675706.
7	21297.	299244328.	4689482.
8	63916.	782438556.	15366818.
9	36240.	485632846.	12409041.
10	203497.	2476846082.	71649440.
11	50441.	612329069.	12862168.
12	103152.	1248579801.	39544994.
13	8194.	120372929.	26749540.
14	18458.	233242837.	13085490.
15	28002.	372600982.	23237982.
16	27328.	326071506.	13165327.
17	39694.	500022184.	21847433.
18	699510.	8086839592.	348811925.
19	1490112.	17194012847.	971930627.
20	87274.	972339342.	24393897.
21	63836.	739215848.	30315818.
22	7962.	105656786.	4575952.
23	397769.	5078354278.	302161829.
24	11028.	142525353.	3617468.
25	407769.	5020449699.	201782639.

PERSONAL VEHICLES OWNED THIS YEAR
```
CARS:       15004981.
TRUCKS:      3165261.
TOTAL:      18170242.
```

CAR VMT BY USE CATEGORIES
```
  1:SHORT-URBAN-WORK TRIP MILES:        32713153122.
  2:SHORT-URBAN-NONWORK TRIP MILES:    105227255521.
  3:OTHER WORK TRIP MILES:              32636450811.
  4:OTHER NONWORK TRIP MILES:           11082666711.
```

TRUCK VMT BY USE CATEGORIES
```
  1:SHORT-URBAN-WORK TRIP MILES:         8202499926.
  2:SHORT-URBAN-NONWORK TRIP MILES:     20142290279.
  3:OTHER WORK TRIP MILES:               6744488524.
  4:OTHER NONWORK TRIP MILES:            2250115015.
```

TOTAL VMT BY USE CATEGORIES
```
  1:SHORT-URBAN-WORK TRIP MILES:        40915653048.
  2:SHORT-URBAN-NONWORK TRIP MILES:    125369545801.
  3:OTHER WORK TRIP MILES:              39380939336.
  4:OTHER NONWORK TRIP MILES:           13332781726.
```

PERSONAL VMT
```
CAR VMT:     181659526165.
TRUCK VMT:    37339393745.
TOTAL VMT:   218998919910.
```

FUEL USE BY PERSONAL VEHICLES:	CARS	TRUCKS	TOTAL
GASOLINE (GALS):	6011076639.	1627480333.	7638556972.
DIESEL (GALS):	156521944.	260109821.	416631765.
ELECTRICITY (KWH):	26749540.	0.	26749540.
METHANOL (GALS):	36323472.	0.	36323472.
LPG (GALS):	35012760.	0.	35012760.

```
PERSONAL VEHICLE DATA FOR 2000
              NO.                        FUEL USE
CLASS       VEHICLES        VMT        GALLONS OR KWH
  1         1568807.     19107421515.    329824068.
  2         1679123.     19793901407.    476524892.
  3         2490243.     29198781346.    806093114.
  4         6953248.     84337647237.   2441025029.
  5         3271700.     40998927331.    890866448.
  6          706256.      8483215837.    263810779.
  7           90635.      1092913028.     14732254.
  8           94398.      1117952627.     17619431.
  9          108613.      1285023920.     25483351.
 10          260261.      3256101658.     67336040.
 11           58784.       720330021.     11788036.
 12          124133.      1524212049.     35775341.
 13           65380.       797010626.    170240244.
 14           46900.       531072860.     23864470.
 15           63926.       750009236.     37822783.
 16           41317.       476637983.     14969243.
 17           60811.       736065204.     24235591.
 18          736384.      8558877458.    294114649.
 19         1673210.     19335521865.    846939129.
 20           95388.      1075499200.     22157509.
 21           76604.       884758566.     28893611.
 22           12245.       151210359.      5388982.
 23          452092.      5753929831.    264674700.
 24           19441.       233441901.      4999265.
 25          494611.      6021227133.    194411639.

PERSONAL VEHICLES OWNED THIS YEAR
CARS:         17684534.
TRUCKS:        3559974.
TOTAL:        21244509.

CAR VMT BY USE CATEGORIES
  1:SHORT-URBAN-WORK TRIP MILES:         37478150337.
  2:SHORT-URBAN-NONWORK TRIP MILES:     138275235477.
  3:OTHER WORK TRIP MILES:               29041551960.
  4:OTHER NONWORK TRIP MILES:             9412286112.

TRUCK VMT BY USE CATEGORIES
  1:SHORT-URBAN-WORK TRIP MILES:          9051104316.
  2:SHORT-URBAN-NONWORK TRIP MILES:      25353653534.
  3:OTHER WORK TRIP MILES:                5809253012.
  4:OTHER NONWORK TRIP MILES:             1800455450.

TOTAL VMT BY USE CATEGORIES
  1:SHORT-URBAN-WORK TRIP MILES:         46529254653.
  2:SHORT-URBAN-NONWORK TRIP MILES:     163628889011.
  3:OTHER WORK TRIP MILES:               34850804972.
  4:OTHER NONWORK TRIP MILES:            11212741563.

PERSONAL VMT
CAR VMT:        214207223886.
TRUCK VMT:       42014466313.
TOTAL VMT:      256221690199.

FUEL USE BY PERSONAL VEHICLES:   CARS           TRUCKS          TOTAL
  GASOLINE (GALS):            5208144329.    1411117461.    6619261789.
  DIESEL (GALS):              172734453.      250462025.     423196477.
  ELECTRICITY (KWH):          170240244.              0.     170240244.
  METHANOL (GALS):             61687253.              0.      61687253.
  LPG (GALS):                  39204834.              0.      39204834.
```

D.5 Scenario 5: No Alternative Fueled Vehicles

```
PERSONAL VEHICLE DATA FOR 1990
               NO.                          FUEL USE
CLASS       VEHICLES         VMT         GALLONS OR KWH
  1         1034642.     13204791949.       285744700.
  2         1469184.     17372068628.       562918097.
  3         2258761.     26355057599.       976443622.
  4         6283334.     75952164401.      2939177754.
  5         3038120.     38412632133.      1078965788.
  6          556858.      6646689866.       297932193.
  7           21680.       305556921.         4787911.
  8           65180.       800954404.        15720104.
  9           37261.       500241182.        12781525.
 10          208350.      2543282365.        73518905.
 11           51278.       624475742.        13110793.
 12          106663.      1293433813.        40959674.
 13               0.               0.               0.
 14               0.               0.               0.
 15               0.               0.               0.
 16               0.               0.               0.
 17               0.               0.               0.
 18          722966.      8397165850.       362120270.
 19         1526960.     17644131129.       997380814.
 20           89292.       999965694.        25075339.
 21           66235.       769082635.        31538368.
 22            8171.       108578590.         4701532.
 23          407203.      5212270951.       309741200.
 24           11368.       147229088.         3736837.
 25          417996.      5148401005.       206921536.

PERSONAL VEHICLES OWNED THIS YEAR
CARS:          15131310.
TRUCKS:         3250192.
TOTAL:         18381501.

CAR VMT BY USE CATEGORIES
   1:SHORT-URBAN-WORK TRIP MILES:          35486169485.
   2:SHORT-URBAN-NONWORK TRIP MILES:      103073684489.
   3:OTHER WORK TRIP MILES:                34593600467.
   4:OTHER NONWORK TRIP MILES:            10857894560.

TRUCK VMT BY USE CATEGORIES
   1:SHORT-URBAN-WORK TRIP MILES:           8970646970.
   2:SHORT-URBAN-NONWORK TRIP MILES:       20079609920.
   3:OTHER WORK TRIP MILES:                 7138818483.
   4:OTHER NONWORK TRIP MILES:             2237749569.

TOTAL VMT BY USE CATEGORIES
   1:SHORT-URBAN-WORK TRIP MILES:          44456816455.
   2:SHORT-URBAN-NONWORK TRIP MILES:      123153294410.
   3:OTHER WORK TRIP MILES:                41732418950.
   4:OTHER NONWORK TRIP MILES:            13095644129.

PERSONAL VMT
CAR VMT:         184011349002.
TRUCK VMT:        38426824942.
TOTAL VMT:       222438173944.

FUEL USE BY PERSONAL VEHICLES:   CARS          TRUCKS           TOTAL
   GASOLINE (GALS):          6141182154.    1673943816.     7815125970.
   DIESEL (GALS):             160878913.     267272081.      428150993.
   ELECTRICITY (KWH):                 0.             0.              0.
   METHANOL (GALS):                   0.             0.              0.
   LPG (GALS):                        0.             0.              0.
```

```
PERSONAL VEHICLE DATA FOR 2000
                 NO.                          FUEL USE
        VEHICLES          VMT         GALLONS OR KWH
CLASS
   1    1591231.    19511829864.          336725102.
   2    1726586.    20566630587.          494617013.
   3    2571461.    30368743395.          838412471.
   4    7197038.    87927498744.         2544207153.
   5    3317967.    41969281417.          911094711.
   6     733081.     8920719083.          277326206.
   7      91963.     1115623189.           15035896.
   8      96879.     1155054424.           18187855.
   9     112397.     1337024376.           26509953.
  10     271014.     3402866219.           70335754.
  11      60179.      741553258.           12128342.
  12     131256.     1615406586.           37908723.
  13          0.             0.                   0.
  14          0.             0.                   0.
  15          0.             0.                   0.
  16          0.             0.                   0.
  17          0.             0.                   0.
  18     779399.     9120656427.          313396423.
  19    1757208.    20312537140.          889782099.
  20      98952.     1124288092.           23156734.
  21      82428.      954819175.           31180420.
  22      12794.      158423141.            5645441.
  23     474031.     6038135475.          277584584.
  24      20390.      245857573.            5265095.
  25     515726.     6279435192.          202713803.

PERSONAL VEHICLES OWNED THIS YEAR
CARS:       17901053.
TRUCKS:      3740928.
TOTAL:      21641982.

CAR VMT BY USE CATEGORIES
  1:SHORT-URBAN-WORK TRIP MILES:         43202583143.
  2:SHORT-URBAN-NONWORK TRIP MILES:     134094558724.
  3:OTHER WORK TRIP MILES:               32213355448.
  4:OTHER NONWORK TRIP MILES:             9121733828.

TRUCK VMT BY USE CATEGORIES
  1:SHORT-URBAN-WORK TRIP MILES:         10608630262.
  2:SHORT-URBAN-NONWORK TRIP MILES:      25403270344.
  3:OTHER WORK TRIP MILES:                6427507630.
  4:OTHER NONWORK TRIP MILES:             1794743978.

TOTAL VMT BY USE CATEGORIES
  1:SHORT-URBAN-WORK TRIP MILES:         53811213406.
  2:SHORT-URBAN-NONWORK TRIP MILES:     159497829067.
  3:OTHER WORK TRIP MILES:               38640863078.
  4:OTHER NONWORK TRIP MILES:            10916477807.

PERSONAL VMT
CAR VMT:       218632231143.
TRUCK VMT:      44234152214.
TOTAL VMT:     262866383357.

FUEL USE BY PERSONAL VEHICLES:   CARS          TRUCKS           TOTAL
  GASOLINE (GALS):          5402382655.    1486408548.     6888791203.
  DIESEL (GALS):            180106523.      262316052.      442422575.
  ELECTRICITY (KWH):                0.              0.              0.
  METHANOL (GALS):                  0.              0.              0.
  LPG (GALS):                       0.              0.              0.
```

D.6   Scenario 6: Reduced Price for Electric Vehicles

PERSONAL VEHICLE DATA FOR 1990

CLASS	NO. VEHICLES	VMT	FUEL USE GALLONS OR KWH
1	1028802.	13116347221.	283833415.
2	1459303.	17237480128.	558590377.
3	2241940.	26133210323.	968314328.
4	6231753.	75259072001.	2912608177.
5	3018233.	38117183862.	1070721452.
6	552900.	6591248644.	295473672.
7	21547.	303392981.	4754044.
8	64752.	794631098.	15597160.
9	36960.	495659745.	12664838.
10	206639.	2519693218.	72844268.
11	50924.	619425456.	13005277.
12	105761.	1280907335.	40565222.
13	26703.	378742507.	84165002.
14	18862.	239659404.	13440994.
15	28556.	379120687.	2363578.
16	27785.	331779766.	13393231.
17	40622.	513565027.	22416931.
18	719715.	8350072619.	360111063.
19	1520097.	17548863013.	992043924.
20	88937.	994801636.	24946753.
21	65905.	764389193.	31348839.
22	8108.	107641694.	4661027.
23	404067.	5167420214.	307097795.
24	11278.	145928115.	3703907.
25	414866.	5105048026.	205189738.

PERSONAL VEHICLES OWNED THIS YEAR
CARS: 15162043.
TRUCKS: 3232972.
TOTAL: 18395015.

CAR VMT BY USE CATEGORIES
    1:SHORT-URBAN-WORK TRIP MILES: 35572363405.
    2:SHORT-URBAN-NONWORK TRIP MILES: 103228087961.
    3:OTHER WORK TRIP MILES: 34634910642.
    4:OTHER NONWORK TRIP MILES: 10875757395.

TRUCK VMT BY USE CATEGORIES
    1:SHORT-URBAN-WORK TRIP MILES: 8910847547.
    2:SHORT-URBAN-NONWORK TRIP MILES: 19959105549.
    3:OTHER WORK TRIP MILES: 7090552348.
    4:OTHER NONWORK TRIP MILES: 2223659064.

TOTAL VMT BY USE CATEGORIES
    1:SHORT-URBAN-WORK TRIP MILES: 44483210952.
    2:SHORT-URBAN-NONWORK TRIP MILES: 123187193510.
    3:OTHER WORK TRIP MILES: 41725462991.
    4:OTHER NONWORK TRIP MILES: 13099416459.

PERSONAL VMT
    CAR VMT: 184311119403.
    TRUCK VMT: 38184164509.
    TOTAL VMT: 222495283912.

FUEL USE BY PERSONAL VEHICLES:	CARS	TRUCKS	TOTAL
GASOLINE (GALS):	6089541420.	1663913810.	7753455230.
DIESEL (GALS):	159430808.	265189236.	424620044.
ELECTRICITY (KWH):	84165002.	0.	84165002.
METHANOL (GALS):	37078571.	0.	37078571.
LPG (GALS):	35810162.	0.	35810162.

```
PERSONAL VEHICLE DATA FOR 2000
              NO.                        FUEL USE
CLASS       VEHICLES        VMT        GALLONS OR KWH
  1         1571129.     19252700335.     332252455.
  2         1702095.     20262287691.     487305639.
  3         2531322.     29879817743.     824919919.
  4         7081851.     86495423826.    2502725722.
  5         3271525.     41342439862.     897468009.
  6          723012.      8792222571.     273329876.
  7           90813.      1100209616.      14828164.
  8           95504.      1137283901.      17908247.
  9          110688.      1315337342.      26080530.
 10          266807.      3347433124.      69189837.
 11           59307.       729972801.      11939025.
 12          129179.      1588443646.      37276510.
 13          126834.      1559314785.     331602008.
 14           48055.       548913634.      24640395.
 15           66197.       776703220.      39170494.
 16           42179.       487993798.      15325036.
 17           62962.       767357609.      25242176.
 18          771898.      9029649796.     310272166.
 19         1740149.     20115732266.     881167806.
 20           98055.      1113644708.      22937543.
 21           81566.       944541050.      30845362.
 22           12611.       156129268.       5563714.
 23          467287.      5951566798.     273603809.
 24           20100.       242270540.       5188299.
 25          508485.      6190899313.     199855426.

PERSONAL VEHICLES OWNED THIS YEAR
CARS:        17979460.
TRUCKS:       3700151.
TOTAL:       21679611.

CAR VMT BY USE CATEGORIES
    1:SHORT-URBAN-WORK TRIP MILES:        43406226554.
    2:SHORT-URBAN-NONWORK TRIP MILES:    134539313263.
    3:OTHER WORK TRIP MILES:              32287017491.
    4:OTHER NONWORK TRIP MILES:           9151298195.

TRUCK VMT BY USE CATEGORIES
    1:SHORT-URBAN-WORK TRIP MILES:        10486627479.
    2:SHORT-URBAN-NONWORK TRIP MILES:     25131103687.
    3:OTHER WORK TRIP MILES:               6351989865.
    4:OTHER NONWORK TRIP MILES:            1774712709.

TOTAL VMT BY USE CATEGORIES
    1:SHORT-URBAN-WORK TRIP MILES:        53892854033.
    2:SHORT-URBAN-NONWORK TRIP MILES:    159670416950.
    3:OTHER WORK TRIP MILES:              38639007355.
    4:OTHER NONWORK TRIP MILES:           10926010904.

PERSONAL VMT
CAR VMT:         219383855503.
TRUCK VMT:        43744433739.
TOTAL VMT:       263128289243.

FUEL USE BY PERSONAL VEHICLES:   CARS         TRUCKS          TOTAL
    GASOLINE (GALS):          5318001620.   1470607495.    6788609115.
    DIESEL (GALS):             177222313.    258826629.     436048942.
    ELECTRICITY (KWH):         331602008.            0.     331602008.
    METHANOL (GALS):            63810889.            0.      63810889.
    LPG (GALS):                 40567213.            0.      40567213.
```

Notes

Chapter 1

1. The possibility of ties (i.e., $U_{in} = U_{jn}$) is ignored in this discussion; in practice, ties never occur.

2. An alternative way of viewing the probabilities is to suppose that the researcher observes one decisionmaker facing the same choice repeatedly. In each repetition, the observed component of utility is the same, but the unobserved component changes (due, perhaps, to randomly varying tastes of the decisionmaker). P_{in} is then the proportion of times the decisionmaker chooses alternative i as the number of repetitions becomes large. With this interpretation, the probability still arises from the researcher's lack of knowledge. At each time, the decisionmaker's choice is deterministic, and if the researcher knew the varying component of utility with every repetition, then the researcher could perfectly predict each choice.

A third interpretation of the choice probabilities arises from the concept that probabilities are not necessarily limits of proportions for repeated events but rather reflect subjective views of an uncertain world. With this viewpoint, P_{in} is the subjective probability assigned by the researcher to the event that the unobserved utility components of person n are such that, given the observed components, the person will choose alternative i. Again, the probability reflects the researcher's uncertainty, not the decisionmaker's.

Chapter 2

1. Also called the Weibull distribution. See section 2.9 for the density function for this distribution.

2. Shoulder room is the width of the passenger cabin of a car measured at the height of a seated passenger's shoulders. Cars with greater shoulder room carry more passengers and, for a given number of passengers, allow more room per passenger than cars with less shoulder room.

3. Usually the planner's goal can be achieved consistently with the fact that derivatives of choice probabilities sum to zero by defining the choice set appropriately. For example, if an airport commission utilizes a qualitative choice model describing passengers' choice of airline (with the alternatives being the various airlines), increasing demand for one airline will necessarily imply reduced demand for other airlines. By expanding the choice set to include the alternative of traveling by nonair modes (auto, bus, rail), then one airline's demand can be increased without decreasing other airlines' demand as long as the additional demand is drawn from the nonair modes.

Unfortunately, standard logit models cannot be used for this purpose, since, as stated, increasing the representative utility of one alternative in a logit model decreases the probabilities for all other alternatives in proportion to their probabilities before the change. Consequently, drawing additional demand from nonair modes but not other airlines is not possible with logit; other qualitative choice models, such as GEV, handle this situation more appropriately.

4. The stratification cannot be on the basis of the individual's choice of alternative; if it is, more complex methods are required.

Chapter 3

1. A homebuyer's perception and concern about the risk of a variable rate is probably related to the maximum allowable increase in the interest rate for a loan. If this is the case, then we can write

$$R_{in} = \theta_n M_{in} + m_{in},$$

such that

$$e_{in} = -\theta_n M_{in} - m_{in} + \eta_{in},$$

which could be handled in a manner similar to that for taste variation. However, for the present example, we assume R_{in} is unrelated to M_{in}.

2. As in the taste variation example, a convenient normalization that reflects the fact that multiplicative transformations of utility do not affect choices is $\omega = 1$.

Chapter 4

1. The parameter λ_k is usually assumed to be between zero and one. If the parameter is within this range, then the resulting choice probabilities are consistent with utility maximization for all possible levels of observed data. If the parameter is above one (and hence $1 - \lambda_k$ is below zero), then the choice probabilities are consistent with utility maximization, if at all, only within a range of observed data. Values of λ_k below zero are inconsistent. See McFadden (1978).

2. That the product of these marginal and conditional probabilities equals the joint probability in (4.1) is verified as follows:

$$P_{in} = P_{in|B_n^k} \cdot P_{B_n^k} = \frac{e^{Y_{in}^k}}{\sum_{j \in B_n^k} e^{Y_{jn}^k}} \cdot \frac{e^{W_n^k + \lambda_k I_k}}{\sum_{l=1}^{K} e^{W_n^l + \lambda_l I_l}}$$

$$= \frac{e^{Y_{in}^k}}{\sum_{j \in B_n^k} e^{Y_{jn}^k}} \cdot \frac{e^{W_n^k}(\sum_{j \in B_n^k} e^{Y_{jn}^k})^{\lambda_k}}{\sum_{l=1}^{K} e^{W_n^l}(\sum_{j \in B_n^l} e^{Y_{jn}^l})^{\lambda_l}}$$

$$= \frac{e^{Y_{in}^k} e^{W_n^k}(\sum_{j \in B_n^k} e^{Y_{jn}^k})^{\lambda_k - 1}}{\sum_{l=1}^{K} e^{W_n^l}(\sum_{j \in B_n^l} e^{Y_{jn}^l})^{\lambda_l}}$$

$$= \frac{(e^{Y_{in}^k + W_n^k/\lambda_k})(\sum_{j \in B_n^k} e^{Y_{jn}^k + W_n^k/\lambda_k})^{\lambda_k - 1}}{\sum_{l=1}^{K} (\sum_{j \in B_n^l} e^{Y_{jn}^l + W_n^l/\lambda_l})^{\lambda_l}} \quad \text{since} \quad \begin{aligned} e^{W_n^k} &= (e^{W_n^k/\lambda_k})^{\lambda_k} \\ &= e^{W_n^k/\lambda_k} \cdot (e^{W_n^k/\lambda_k})^{\lambda_k - 1} \end{aligned}$$

$$= \frac{e^{V_{in}/\lambda_k}(\sum_{j \in B_n^k} e^{V_{jn}/\lambda_k})^{\lambda_k - 1}}{\sum_{l=1}^{K} (\sum_{j \in B_n^l} e^{V_{jn}/\lambda_l})^{\lambda_l}} \quad \text{since} \quad \begin{aligned} V_{in} &= W_n^k + \lambda_k Y_{in}^k, \\ V_{in}/\lambda_k &= W_n^k/\lambda_k + Y_{in}^k. \end{aligned}$$

3. The term "inclusive price" is also used occasionally. Actually, however, the **negative** of I_k more closely resembles a price.

4. Recall from section 2.3 that only differences in representative utility affect choice probabilities in logit models. Consequently, each of the two conditional submodels can be estimated with actual time and cost for each mode entering as explanatory variables rather than with deviations from the average. Since the average is constant over the two alternatives in each submodel, it drops out automatically.

5. Sequential estimation takes more steps than standard maximum likelihood estimation. When the labor involved in these steps is considered, sequential estimation is not necessarily less expensive.

Chapter 5

1. The indirect utility function must satisfy certain criteria, most of which are very intuitive, to be consistent with a direct utility function. For example, the indirect utility must be nonincreasing in price (i.e., if the price of a good rises, the utility that a consumer obtains after maximizing utility at the new price cannot rise). See Varian (1978) for a full discussion of these criteria.

2. This is simply a restatement of the fact that utility is maximized at a point of tangency between an indifference curve and the budget constraint. It can be demonstrated as follows:

$$(\partial U(x_1, (y - x_1 p_1)/p_2)/\partial x_1) = MU_1 - (p_1/p_2) MU_2 = 0,$$

or

$$MU_1/MU_2 = p_1/p_2.$$

3. If the choices are independent, a joint modeling approach is unnecessary. A precise meaning of the word "interrelated" in this context is given at the conclusion of this subsection.

4. Example: a person chooses a type of car and decides how many miles to drive. The price of driving (i.e., the cost per mile) that the person faces will be different for different types of cars.

5. For some situations, it might be useful to generalize the choice situation described in section 5.3 to allow for the possibility of some of the variables entering V_i being functions of the continuous good. Consider, for example, the choice of which long distance service to acquire (AT&T, Sprint, Allnet, etc.) and the choice of how much to use the long distance service. Given that volume discounts are given by some carriers, the marginal price of a long distance call depends on the number of calls made, such that p_i entering V_i is a function of x_i. A stepwise method for estimating choice probabilities in these types of situations is usually feasible. For the case of long distance service choice, (1) estimate the demand equation for the number of calls as a function only of variables that do not depend on the long distance service chosen; (2) use this equation to estimate the number of calls, and calculate a marginal price for alternative service given this number of calls; and then (3) estimate the choice model with this constructed price entering as an explanatory variable.

6. For choice situations with more than two alternatives, expression (5.10) is generalized as follows. For any alternative i in J, where J is the set of available alternatives,

$$E(e_i) = (\sqrt{6\sigma^2}/\pi)\left[\left(\sum_{j \in J} \rho_j P_j \ln P_j/(1 - P_j)\right) - (\rho_i \ln P_i/(1 - P_i))\right],$$

where σ^2 is the variance of e in the entire population, and ρ_j is the correlation of e with the unobserved utility associated with alternative j, for all j in J.

7. For choice situations with more than two alternatives, expression (5.11), and the correction mechanism are generalized as follows. Using the notation of the previous note, we know (for the same reasons that $\rho_c = -\rho_q$ in the binary case) that $\sum_{j \in J} \rho_j = 0$, or, stated equivalently,

$$\rho_i = -\sum_{\substack{j \in J \\ j \neq i}} \rho_j.$$

Substituting into the expression for $E(e_i)$ in the previous note, we have

$$E(e_i) = \sum_{\substack{j \in J \\ j \neq i}} (\sqrt{6\sigma^2}/\pi)\rho_j\left(\frac{P_j \ln P_j}{1 - P_j} + \ln P_i\right),$$

which is the generalized form of (5.11). Therefore, with N alternatives in the set J, there are $N - 1$ selectivity correction terms to be added to the regression equation, with coefficients of $(\sqrt{6\sigma^2}/\pi)\rho_j$ for each $j \neq i$.

8. That is, the coefficients in the structural equations (5.7) and (5.8) are not common. The coefficients of the selectivity correction terms that are added to these equations are equal in magnitude and opposite in sign.

Chapter 6

1. Often a researcher is unable to predict changes in the number of decisionmakers in each segment. Suppose instead that the researcher can predict the row totals and column totals in the segmentation (i.e., the marginals) but not the individual cell counts (i.e., the joint distribution). For example, for figure 6.2, the researcher might be able to predict changes in the proportion of males and females and changes in the proportion of decisionmakers at each education level, but is unable to predict changes in the proportion of each sex **and** education level. A method for estimating cell counts from predicted values of marginals, called iterative proportional fitting, can be used in these cases. See Bishop, Fienberg, and Holland (1975) for details.

2. The values of z_i in the forecast area will also differ from those in the estimation area. However, since z_i consists of input variables, no reestimation is required to accommodate these changes. The values of β, which reflect the behavioral importance, or weight, attached to each element of z_i, will be the same even if z_i changes, provided only that the process by which households make decisions is not area-specific.

Chapter 7

1. A note is needed regarding terminology. Throughout part II the word "automobile," or "auto" for short, designates both cars and trucks. "Truck" refers to pickups, vans, and utility vehicles such as jeeps, while "car" denotes any automobile that is not a truck. Even though "vehicle" encompasses, in common parlance, objects other than autos, the word is used herein interchangeably with "automobile," primarily to provide a possibility for textual variety when needed.

2. Hocherman, Prashker, and Ben-Akiva estimate the probability that a household will make a particular transaction (e.g., purchase a vehicle, or sell a currently held vehicle), rather than the probability that the household will hold a particular number of vehicles. Since the number of vehicles held at any time can be calculated by knowing the holdings in some base period and all transactions since the base period, this model is grouped with those of vehicle holdings per se.

3. The last four of these studies utilize a nested logit model, with number of autos (or the purchase decision, in the case of Hocherman, Prashker, and Ben-Akiva) as the "upper level" choice, and make and model of autos as the "lower level" choice of each of these models. Auto cost variables enter significantly in the lower level choice; they enter indirectly in the upper level choice through the inclusive value term, which itself enters significantly in each of these studies. Consequently, it is appropriate to say that auto cost enters these quantity models significantly.

4. Hensher and Le Plastrier do not enter price per se, but enter sales tax, which depends on purchase price.

5. The Cambridge Systematics, Inc., model includes age through the scrappage probability variable, which is a function of age.

6. Cambridge Systematics, Inc.; Booz, Allen, and Hamilton, Inc.; and Mannering and Winston reflected the effect of the number of autos owned by constructing separate models for one- and two-auto households.

7. Of the twenty studies using disaggregate compensatory models based on real choice situations, only four have examined both the number and type of vehicles owned: Hocherman, Prashker, and Ben-Akiva; Booz, Allen, and Hamilton, Inc.; Hensher and Le Plastrier; and Mannering and Winston.

8. Lave and Train; Booz, Allen, and Hamilton, Inc.; and Hensher and Le Plastrier enter current-year miles traveled. The number of miles traveled in the previous year enters the models of Mannering and Winston, and Winston and Mannering; these latter models are subject to the simultaneity bias (to be discussed) only if there is serial correlation in the number of miles traveled.

9. Lave and Bradley do not include vehicle characteristics in their model, but the concept of grouping into classes (in this case, foreign and domestic) and forecasting demand for each class, independent of variations of make/model characteristics within each class, still applies.

10. See section 2.2 for a full discussion of this property.

11. If a constant term were included in the representative utility of each make and model, then the logit model could possibly produce consistent estimates of the model parameters. However, none of the studies included constants for each make and model because the number of makes and models is so large.

12. The Cambridge Systematics, Inc., model forecasts quite large year-to-year fluctuations in demand for makes and models. The procedure of assigning vehicles can easily produce such a pattern. Consider, for example, a case of one household facing a choice between two vehicles that, in the eyes of the household, are exactly the same. The household is assigned in each year one of the two vehicles on the basis of a flip of the coin, reflecting the true probabilities of 50 : 50. For the first year, heads appears, and the first vehicle is assigned to the household. In the second year, tails appears, and the second vehicle is assigned. Since this household is the entire sample, the prediction of market share for the first vehicle is 100% in year 1 and 0% in year 2; for the second vehicle, predicted shares are 0% in year 1 and 100% in year 2. This phenomenon can occur whenever the sample size is sufficiently small with respect to the number of vehicles.

13. Weight is valued, at least partially, because of its real or perceived relation to crash worthiness.

14. It is worth noting that noncompensatory models can (depending on their exact form) be consistent with utility maximization by the consumer. Therefore, the distinction between the models discussed in this section and those in sections 7.2 and 7.3 is not whether utility maximization is assumed. Rather, the difference lies in the form of the utility function, with noncompensatory models having lexicographic preferences.

15. The researchers at Charles River Associates have called their technique "hedonic demand models." This is an unfortunate term since the word "hedonic" has already been established for a type of price analysis made popular by Griliches (1961). Charles River Associates's model is no more related to Griliches's method than other demand analyses are, and so it does not seem that their approach should be called "hedonic" to emphasize any inherent connection. The term can only cause confusion.

Chapter 8

1. The precise definitions of these categories will be given in the detailed discussion of the submodel.

2. Households that chose more than two vehicles were not included in the estimation sample. Given that the full choice set includes the alternatives of owning three vehicles, four vehicles, etc., eliminating households that own more than two vehicles is equivalent to estimating the vehicle quantity model on a subset of alternatives. With logit models, estimating on a subset of alternatives is consistent due to the independence of irrelevant alternatives property (see sections 2.2 and 2.6). Households were also eliminated if data were missing for any relevant variable.

3. This formula is based on the normalization $V_0 = 0$ such that $\exp(V_0) = 1$, which is the third term in the denominator. See the discussion "Differences in Representative Utility" in section 2.3 for an explanation of this normalization.

4. Note that the term representing the average utility in the class/vintage choice (i.e., I_n defined in equation (8.8)) depends on the parameters of the class/vintage submodels. Since these are estimated parameters rather than the true parameters, the term used in estimating the vehicle submodel is an estimate of I_n rather than of the true I_n. Amemiya (1978) has shown that using an estimate of I_n in logit estimation results in a downward bias in the standard errors (though the parameters themselves are estimated without bias). Consequently, the t-statistics given in the third column of table 8.1 should be viewed as upper limits on the true t-statistics.

5. To show this, let the indirect utility of a household be

$$V = \alpha P + \beta \text{OC},$$

where P is purchase price of the class/vintage, OC is operating cost, and α and β are parameters. To calculate the change in price required to keep a household at the same level of utility with a one-unit change in operating cost, totally differentiate V to obtain

$$\Delta V = \alpha \Delta P + \beta \Delta \text{OC}.$$

Constrain this total derivate to zero (that is, keep the household's utility unchanged), and solve for the change in price required to offset a change in operating cost:

$\Delta V = \alpha \Delta P + \beta \Delta OC = 0,$

$\Delta P = -\beta/\alpha \Delta OC.$

That is, the change in price that keeps utility constant with a one-cent change in operating cost (i.e., $\Delta OC = 1$) is the (negative of the) ratio of the operating cost and price coefficients.

6. The transaction cost variable introduces dynamic effects into the model such that a household's choice in one period affects its choice in the next period. Dynamics have only recently played a role in qualitative choice models of auto demand. Cambridge Systematics, Inc. (1980b), included a transaction cost variable in its model. However, since data on households' previous auto holdings were not available, the coefficient of this variable was not estimated within the model. Rather, a model excluding this variable was estimated, and the variable was added afterward, with its coefficient chosen so that the model produced the observed aggregate turnover rate of vehicles. The model presented in this chapter is the first to include a variable representing dynamics with its coefficient estimated statistically along with the other model parameters. More recently, Mannering and Winston (1983) have examined alternative variables for representing dynamics.

A transaction cost variable, and variables used by Mannering and Winston, are essentially lagged dependent variables, the inclusion of which raise econometric questions concerning the consistency and efficiency of the standard maximum likelihood estimation. Heckman (1981) has examined the situation in the context of probit models. However, the analysis is more complex for logit models since the convenient convolution properties of the normal distribution cannot be utilized.

7. Significance in this situation was defined as having a t-statistic exceeding 0.5.

8. Since W^2 in equation (8.13) necessarily increases with the variance of each characteristic, any variances that approximate W^2 must enter with a positive coefficient.

9. The author thanks D. McFadden for deriving this expression.

10. Since most 1976–1978 vintage vehicles are designated as prestigious, including this prestige dummy in the submodel reduces the coefficient of the vintage 1976–1978 variable below that of the vintage 1972–1975 variable. Perhaps the best way to interpret the coefficient of the vintage 1976–1978 variable is that it represents the extra utility that a household obtains from having two 1976–1978 vintage vehicles over that which it obtains with only one 1976–1978 vintage vehicle. This interpretation reflects the fact that the prestige dummy takes the value of one if either or both of the vehicles is prestigious, while the vintage 1976–1978 variable takes the value of one if one of the two vehicles is vintage 1976–1978 and two if both of the vehicles are vintage 1976–1978. This interpretation is not valid, however, for 1976–1978 vintage vehicles that are not classified as prestigious.

11. See section 5.4 for a full explanation of the potential bias and alternative methods for correcting it.

12. One further note is required concerning the estimation of the VMT submodel. Equation (8.10) includes the operating cost of the actual make and model of vehicle that a household owns. However, as stated the household's choice of make and model of vehicle is not predicted in our system of submodels. Consequently, the operating cost of the household's chosen class/vintage was used as a proxy for the operating cost of the particular make and model of vehicle chosen within the class/vintage.

13. A truly behavioral model of VMT by category would take as data for each household the cost and time of travel by each mode to work and nonwork destinations. Such data are unavailable for statewide or nationwide samples.

14. Gas price was entered rather than operating cost since operating cost is endogenous, and an instrumental variable approach to endogenous variables is not appropriate with logit.

Chapter 9

1. For cars, the Commission relied primarily on projections developed by Energy and Environmental Analysis, Inc.

2. The model is capable of handling a different income growth for each household in each forecast year, but this was not specified by the commission.

3. An elasticity is defined as the percent change in one variable resulting from a percent change in another variable. For example, the elasticity of VMT with respect to income is the percent change in VMT that results from a percent change in income (calculated in this case as $13.7\%/48\% = .29$.)

Appendix B

1. Provided by Energy and Environmental Analysis, Inc. (1982), and the California Energy Commission.

References

Amemiya, T. (1978), "On a Two-Step Estimation of Multivariate Logit Models," *Journal of Econometrics*, Vol. 8, No. 1 (August), pp. 13–21.

Ayres, R., R. M. Dogget, D. Dussec, C. Humpstone, and J. Lander (1976), "Automobile Forecasting Models," prepared by International Research and Technology Corporation for the Office of Technology Assessment, U.S. Congress, Working Paper IRT-446-R.

Beggs, S., and N. S. Cardell (1980), "Choice of Smallest Car by Multi-Vehicle Households and the Demand for Electric Vehicles," *Transportation Research*, Vol. 14, No. 5–6 (October–December), pp. 389–404.

Beggs, S., N. S. Cardell, and J. A. Hausman (1979), "Assessing the Potential Demand for Electric Cars," report prepared by Charles River Associates for the Electric Power Research Institute under project #1145-1.

Ben-Akiva, M., and S. Lerman (1985), *Discrete Choice Analysis: Theory and Application to Predict Travel Demand*, Cambridge, MA: MIT Press.

Berkovec, J., and J. Rust (1985), "A Nested Logit Model of Automobile Holdings for One Vehicle Households," forthcoming in *Transportation Research*.

Bishop Y., S. Fienberg, and P. Holland (1975), *Discrete Multivariate Analysis*, Cambridge, MA: MIT Press.

Booz, Allen, and Hamilton, Inc. (1983), "Forecasting Household Demand for Light Duty Motor Vehicles," report prepared for Oak Ridge National Laboratories under Contract No. 40X-40485C.

Bos, G. G. J. (1970), *A Logistic Approach to the Demand for Price Cars*, Netherlands: Tilburg University Press.

Boyd, J. Hayden, and Robert E. Mellman (1980), "The Effect of Fuel Economy Standards in the U.S. Auto Market: An Hedonic Demand Analysis," *Transportation Research*, Vol. 14A, No. 5–6 (October–December), pp. 367–378.

Burns, L., and T. Golob (1975), "An Investigation of the Role of Accessibility in Basic Transportation Choice Behavior," Research Publication GMR-1900, Research Laboratories, General Motors Corp., Warren, MI.

Calfee, Jack (1980), "The Econometric Estimation of Potential Demand for Electric Automobiles," unpublished paper, Department of Economics, University of California, Berkeley.

California Department of Transportation (Caltrans) (1981), *The 1976–1980 Statewide Travel Survey*, report by the Division of Transportation, Sacramento, CA.

Cambridge Systematics, Inc. (1980a), *Assessment of National Use, Choice and Future Preference toward the Automobile and Other Modes of Transportation*, Vols. 1, 2, 3, prepared for the National Science Foundation.

Cambridge Systematics, Inc. (1980b), *Consumer Behavior towards Fuel Efficient Vehicles*, Vols. I, II, III, Report No. DOT-H5-805-341, prepared for U.S. Department of Transportation, National Highway Traffic Safety Administration.

Cardell, N. S., and F. C. Dunbar (1980), "Measuring the Societal Impact of Automobile Downsizing," *Transportation Research*, Vol. 14A, No. 5–6 (October–December), pp. 423–434.

Chamberlain, C. (1974), "A Preliminary Model of Auto Choice by Class of Car: Aggregate State Data," Discussion Paper, Transportation Systems Center, U.S. Department of Transportation, Cambridge, MA.

Charles River Associates (1980), "The Demand for Electric Automobiles," report prepared for the Electric Power Research Institute under research project #1145-1.

Chase Econometrics Associates (1974), "The Effect of Tax and Regulatory Alternatives on Car Sales and Gasoline Consumption," NTIS Report No. PG-234622.

Chow, G. (1957), *Demand for Automobiles in the United States*, Amsterdam: North-Holland Publishing Company.

Chow, G. (1960), "Statistical Demand Functions for Automobiles and Their Use in Forecasting," in Arnold C. Harberger (ed.), *The Demand for Durable Goods*, Chicago: University of Chicago Press.

Clark, C. (1961), "The Greatest of a Finite Set of Random Variables," *Operations Research*, 9: 145–162.

Daganzo, C. (1979), *Multinomial Probit: The Theory and Its Application to Demand Forecasting*, New York: Academic Press.

Daganzo, C., F. Bouthelier, and Y. Sheffi (1977), "Multinomial Probit and Qualitative Choice: A Computationally Efficient Algorithm," *Transportation Science*, 11: 338–358.

Difiglio, C., and D. Kulash (1976), *Marketing and Mobility*, report of a Panel of the Interagency Task Force on Motor Vehicle Goals beyond 1980, available through the Office of the Secretary of Transportation, Publishing Section, TAD443.1, Washington, DC.

Dubin, J., and D. McFadden (1984), "An Econometric Analysis of Residential Electric Appliance Holdings and Consumption," *Econometrica*, 52.

Dyckman, T. (1966), "An Aggregate Demand Model for Automobiles," *Journal of Business*, Vol. 38 (July), pp. 252–265.

Energy and Environmental Analysis, Inc. (1975), "Gasoline Consumption Model," report for the Federal Energy Administration, Arlington, VA.

Energy and Environmental Analysis, Inc. (1982), "Automotive Technology Forecasting Model," prepared for the California Energy Commission, Sacramento.

Evans, M. (1969), *Macroeconomic Forecasting*, New York: Harper and Row.

Farrell, M. J. (1954), "Demand for Passenger Cars in the United States," *Royal Statistical Society Journal A*, Vol. 117.

Gensch, Dennis, and Joseph Svestka (1978), "An Exact Hierarchical Algorithm for Determining Aggregate Statistics from Individual Choice Data," unpublished paper, prepared for the U.S. Department of Transportation.

Griliches, Z. (1961), "Hedonic Price Indexes for Automobiles: An Econometric Analysis of Quality Changes," in *The Price Statistics of the Federal Government*, New York: National Bureau of Economic Research.

Hamburger, M. (1967), "Interest Rates and the Demand for Consumer Durable Goods," *American Economic Review*, Vol. 57, pp. 1131–1153.

Hausman, J. A. (1979), "Exact Consumer Surplus," Working Paper, Department of Economics, Massachusetts Institute of Technology, Cambridge, MA.

Hausman, J., and D. A. Wise (1978), "A Conditional Probit Model for Qualitative Choice: Discrete Decisions Recognizing Interdependence and Heterogeneous Preferences," *Econometrica*, Vol. 48, No. 2 (March), pp. 403–426.

Heckman, J. (1978), "Dummy Endogenous Variables in a Simultaneous Equation System," *Econometrica*, 46.

Heckman, J. (1979), "Sample Selection Bias as a Specification Error," *Econometrica*, 47.

Heckman, J. (1981), "Statistical Models for Discrete Panel Data," in C. Manski and D. McFadden (eds.), *Structural Analysis of Discrete Data with Econometric Applications*, Cambridge, MA: MIT Press.

Hensher, D., and V. Le Plastrier (1983), "A Dynamic Discrete Choice Model of Household Automobile Fleet Size and Composition," Working Paper No. 6, Dimensions of Automobile Demand Project, Macquarie University, North Ryde, Australia.

Hess, Alan (1977), "A Comparison of Automobile Demand Equations," *Econometrica*, Vol. 45, No. 3, pp. 683–701.

Hocherman, I., J. Prashker, and M. Ben-Akiva (1982), "Estimation and Use of Dynamic Transaction Models of Automobile Ownership," paper presented at Transportation Research Board annual meeting, Washington, DC.

Houthakker, H., and L. Taylor (1966), *Consumer Demand in the United States, 1929–1970*, Cambridge: Harvard University Press.

Huang, D. S. (1964), "A Microanalytic Model of Automobile Purchase," Research Monograph No. 29, Bureau of Business Research, Graduate School of Business, University of Texas at Austin (see Huang, 1966, for a later version of this paper).

Huang, D. S. (1966), "A Multi-Cross-Section Investigation of Demand for Automobiles," Research Monograph No. 31, Bureau of Business Research, Graduate School of Business, University of Texas at Austin.

Hymans, S. (1970a), "Consumption: New Data and Old Puzzles," Brookings Papers on Economic Activity, No. 1, Washington, DC.

Hymans, S. (1970b), "Consumer Durable Spending: Explanation and Prediction," Brookings Papers on Economic Activity, No. 2, Washington, DC.

Janosi, P. E. de (1959), "Factors Influencing the Demand for New Automobiles," *Journal of Marketing*, Vol. 23 (April).

Johnson, T. (1975), "The Structure of Markets for New and Used Automobiles," unpublished doctoral thesis, Department of Economics, University of Washington.

Johnson, T. (1978), "A Cross-Section Analysis of the Demand for New and Used Automobiles in the United States," *Economic Inquiry*, Vol. 16, pp. 531–548.

Juster, F., and P. Wachtel (1974), "Anticipatory and Objective Models of Durable Goods Demand," *Exploration and Economic Research*, Vol. I, No. 2 (Fall), National Bureau of Economic Research.

Kain, J., and M. Beesley (1965), "Forecasting Car Ownership and Use," *Urban Studies* (November).

Kain, J., and G. Fauth (1977), "Forecasting Auto Ownership and Mode Choice for U.S. Metropolitan Areas," Department of City and Regional Planning, Harvard University, Cambridge, MA.

Kreinin, M. D. (1959), "Analysis of Used Car Purchases," *Review of Economics and Statistics* (November).

Lave, C., and J. Bradley (1980), "Market Share of Imported Cars: A Model of Geographic and Demographic Determinants," *Transportation Research*, Vol. 14A, No. 5–6 (October–December), pp. 379–388.

Lave, C., and K. Train (1979), "A Disaggregate Model of Auto-Type Choice," *Transportation Research*, Vol. 13A, No. 1, pp. 1–9.

Lerman, S., and M. Ben-Akiva (1976), "A Behavioral Analysis of Automobile Ownership and Modes of Travel," Report No. DOT-05-3005603, prepared by Cambridge Systematics, Inc., for the U.S. Department of Transportation, Office of the Secretary, and the Federal Highway Administration.

Lerman, S., and C. Manski (1981), "On the Use of Simulated Frequencies to Approximate Choice Probabilities," in C. Manski and D. McFadden (eds.), *Structural Analysis of Discrete Data with Econometric Applications*, Cambridge, MA: MIT Press.

McFadden, D. (1973), "Conditional Logit Analysis of Qualitative Choice Behavior," in P. Zarembka (ed.), *Frontiers in Econometrics*, New York: Academic Press.

McFadden, D. (1974), "The Measurement of Urban Travel Demand," *Journal of Public Economics*, 3:303–328.

McFadden, D. (1975), "On Independence, Structure and Simultaneity in Transportation Demand Analysis," Working Paper No. 7511, Urban Travel Demand Forecasting Project, Institute of Transportation and Traffic Engineering, University of California, Berkeley.

McFadden, D. (1978), "Modelling the Choice of Residential Location," in A. Karquist, et al. (eds.), *Spatial Interaction Theory and Planning Models*, Amsterdam: North-Holland Publishing Company.

Mannering, F., and C. Winston (1983), "Dynamic Models of Household Vehicle Ownership and Utilization: An Empirical Analysis," Working Paper, Department of Economics, M.I.T.

Manski, C., and L. Sherman (1980), "An Empirical Analysis of Household Choice Among Motor Vehicles," *Transportation Research*, Vol. 14A, No. 5–6 (October–December), pp. 349–366.

Millar, M., J. Bunch, A. Vyas, M. Kaplan, R. Knorr, V. Mendiratta, and C. Saricks (1982), "Baseline Projections of Transportation Energy Consumption by Mode: 1981 Update," Argonne National Laboratory, Report ANL/CNSV-28.

Mogridge, M. (1978), "The Effect of the Oil Crisis on the Growth in the Ownership and Use of Cars," *Transportation*, Vol. 7, pp. 45–68.

Murtaugh, Michael, and Hugh Gladwin (1980), "A Hierarchical Decision-Process Model for Forecasting Automobile Type-Choice," *Transportation Research*, Vol. 14A, No. 5–6 (October–December), pp. 337–348.

Nerlove, M. (1957), "A Note on Long-Run Automobile Demand," *Journal of Marketing*, Vol. 22 (July), pp. 57–64.

Nerlove, M. (1958), "On Automobile Demand: A Reply," *Journal of Marketing*, Vol. 22 (April).

Pindyck, R., and D. Rubinfeld (1981), *Econometric Models and Econometric Forecasts*, 2nd ed., New York: McGraw-Hill Book Company.

Recker, Wilfred, and Thomas Golob (1978), "A Non-Compensatory Model of Transportation Behavior Based on Sequential Consideration of Attributes," General Motors Research Publication GMR-2621.

Roos, C. F., and V. von Szelski (1939), "Factor Governing Changes in Domestic Automobile Demand," in *The Dynamics of Automobile Demand*, a collection of papers presented at a joint meeting of the American Statistical Associate and the Econometric Society in Detroit.

Suits, D. (1958), "The Demand for New Automobiles in the United States, 1929–1956," *Review of Economics and Statistics*, Vol. 40 (August), pp. 273–280.

Suits, D. (1961), "Exploring Alternative Formulations of Automobile Demand," *Review of Economics and Statistics*, Vol. 43 (February), pp. 66–69.

Talvitie, A. (1976), "Disaggregate Travel Demand Models with Disaggregate Data, Not with Aggregate Data, and for What," Working Paper 7615, Institute of Transportation Studies, Urban Travel Demand Forecasting Project, University of California, Berkeley.

Train, K. (1980a), "A Structured Logit Model of Auto Ownership and Mode Choice," *Review of Economic Studies*, Vol. XLVII, pp. 357–370.

Train, K. (1980b), "The Potential Demand for Electric Vehicles," *Transportation Research*, Vol. 14A, No. 5–6 (October–December), pp. 405–414.

Train, K., and D. McFadden (1978), "The Goods/Leisure Tradeoff and Disaggregate Work Trip Mode Choice Models," *Transportation Research*, 12:349–353.

Varian, H. (1978), *Microeconomic Analysis*, New York: Norton and Co.

Wharton Econometric Forecasting Associates, Inc. (1977), "An Analysis of the Automobile Market: Modeling the Long-Run Determinants of the Demand for Automobiles," Vols. 1, 2, 3, prepared for the U.S. Department of Transportation, Transportation Systems Center, Cambridge, MA.

Wildhorn, S., B. Burright, J. Enns, and T. Kirkwood (1974), "How to Save Gasoline: Public Policy Alternatives for the Automobile," prepared for the National Science Foundation by the RAND Corporation.

Winston, C., and F. Mannering (1984), "Consumer Demand for Automobile Safety," *American Economic Review*, 74(2):316–319.

Wolff, P. de (1938), "The Demand for Passenger Cars in the United States," *Econometrica*, Vol. 6 (April).

Wyckoff, Frank C. (1973), "A User Cost Approach to New Automobile Purchases," *Review of Economic Studies*, Vol. 40, No. 3 (July).

Index